Mr. Abrams is Assistant Professor of History at the University of California at Berkeley. He is currently on leave with a fellowship from the Social Science Research Council (1964-1965) for research in government-business relations in the United States.

CONSERVATISM IN
A PROGRESSIVE ERA

MASSACHUSETTS POLITICS
1900–1912

CONSERVATISM IN
A PROGRESSIVE ERA

MASSACHUSETTS POLITICS
1900–1912

Richard M. Abrams

HARVARD UNIVERSITY PRESS

Cambridge, Massachusetts

1964

Distributed in Great Britain by Oxford University Press, London

Publication of this book has been aided
by a grant from the Ford Foundation

Library of Congress Catalog Card Number 64-21236

Printed in the United States of America

FOR
MY MOTHER AND FATHER

PREFACE

With some exceptions, the American progressive movement derived its outstanding leaders from the western and southern states. On the national level those leaders often had to contend with the resistance of the chief spokesmen for the eastern states. Men like Wisconsin's Robert LaFollette, Iowa's Albert Cummins, and Nebraska's George Norris stand out in the fight for reform; while Rhode Island's Nelson Aldrich, Pennsylvania's Boise Penrose, and Massachusetts' Murray Crane and Henry Cabot Lodge count among the chief villains of the story. Historians who tell the story have, in fact, tended to describe those who opposed the progressive movement as laissez-faire idealogues, narrow-minded obstructionists, or callous representatives of "the vested interests," who abounded especially in the East.

There is unquestionably a great deal of truth in this presentation. But it occurred to me when I began my study of Massachusetts politics that there might also be a more "generous" explanation for the eastern states' evident opposition to reform on the national level. It seemed hard to accept the view implicit in the orthodox treatment that the eastern states produced chiefly callous and obstructionist leaders. Yet, there was little in the literature on the period to suggest otherwise. I have come to believe that one reason for this is that, in undertaking to tell the story of reform, historians have confined their attention to the conditions which justified the reformers' rationale. Moreover, the leading historians of the period have focused on national politics, where the campaign for progressive reform was indeed the most significant story of the day, so that few historians have found something other than reform to write about. This seems quite as true of the few state

studies we have had: historians either have chosen the states
where progressivism was as outstanding a feature of politics
as it was on the national level — Wisconsin and California,
for example — or have chosen to focus on what little reform
activity there was in states where progressivism was of only
tangential significance. With the exception of Albert Kirwan's
Revolt of the Rednecks, which appropriately covers the politics of Mississippi for a much longer period than the Progressive Era, no one to my knowledge has studied the politics of
a state where the big story of the day was something other
than the campaigns of reformers. In this respect, we have had
considerable reform history but very little political history.

I have chosen to write a book about a state noted for its
evident conservatism in the Progressive Era. As I have conceived it, it is of necessity not a book about champions of
social justice who did battle with the knaves of financial and
civic corruption. Massachusetts *did have* such champions, just
as it clearly had such knaves. The point is, however, that they
did not "make the story" of the state's politics in the period,
as the reformers and their antagonists evidently did in California, New Jersey, and Wisconsin. Throughout the Era, the
dominant theme of Massachusetts politics was *conservatism*
— that is, the inclination to preserve rather than to change.

Let me make it clear at the start, however, that I do *not*
mean to suggest that the state preferred to live without the
things which the nation's progressives sought. On the contrary,
the fact is — and it is a major point — that when the Progressive Era began, Massachusetts already enjoyed most of
the institutions and laws for which progressives elsewhere were
just beginning to wage strenuous campaigns. Throughout the
course of the Era, moreover, Massachusetts continued to enjoy reform legislation — "without blare of trumpets," as one
of the state's reformers put it — which compared favorably
with that passed anywhere else in the country.

These facts may suggest that I should have written a "revisionist" book which showed that Massachusetts was not con-

servative at all but was instead "a progressive state." The phrase is a mischievous one. If we were to apply a dictionary meaning to "progressive," perhaps it would be accurate to call Massachusetts "a progressive state." But "progressive" also has an historical meaning. In this context, it is closely tied to the cause, or causes, of the LaFollettes, the Cumminses, and the Hiram Johnsons. It implies, moreover, that a movement for progressive reform dominated, or at least figured in a major part of, the history of the state during the period. In such a context it would be at best *misleading* and at worst literally *nonsense* to describe Massachusetts as "a progressive state." In the first place, on national progressive measures the state functioned undeniably in a conservative role. Its national representatives opposed much more often than they supported the reform proposals offered by the nation's acknowledged leading progressives. A major part of the national progressive movement, indeed, aimed at the redistribution of economic and political advantages for the benefit of the less favored states of the West and South, distinctly at Massachusetts' expense. In addition, the state rebuffed the efforts of Republican insurgents to rehabilitate the state and national G.O.P. And on many issues which vitally concerned the progressives, such as regulation of corporations, Massachusetts' own legislation actually moved the state directly contrary to the currents of the day. These facts, and others less easily summarized for prefatory purposes, confirm the view of Massachusetts as a *conservative* state.

In addition, it can be said without the slightest semantic flippancy that in Massachusetts even the progressives — or perhaps "progressive-equivalents" is the expression I should use — functioned in a conservative role. I do not mean this merely in the sense that they had only limited reform objectives. I mean that the progressive-equivalents in Massachusetts functioned primarily as conservators or defenders of the tradition and laws which had already given Massachusetts so many of the things which progressives elsewhere had to cam-

paign for in the twentieth century. While the LaFollettes and
Johnsons were fighting to achieve for their states what in large
measure Massachusetts already had, their counterparts in the
Bay State typically were engaged in fights to keep the state
from withdrawing from its advanced position.

It should be clear that one must make a critical distinction
between conservatism as it appeared in Massachusetts and
conservatism in the context of other states' traditions. The advanced conditions which Massachusetts enjoyed at the turn of
the century did not derive primarily from an insurgent, cus-
tom-breaking impulse. Rather, it seems, they derived from a
tradition of government leadership and social responsibility
that was rooted far back in the Commonwealth's history. In
other words, they derived largely from a conservative impulse,
which worked continually to readjust the state's laws and institutions so as to preserve the state's traditional standards of
social behavior in the face of the challenges of industrialism,
high-speed transportation, and continental expansion.

By 1900, massive immigration and the advent of large-scale
corporate finance had begun to place severe strains upon the
power of the Commonwealth's traditions. The survival of
those traditions had always depended in part on human will
and intelligence, and, perhaps in larger part, on favorable
economic circumstances. It was the incipient breakdown of
those circumstances and the state's eschewal of its own Commonwealth heritage that constituted the most significant
changes in Massachusetts during the Progressive Era. That is
the story I shall attempt to tell.

A note about my use of the words "insurgent," "progressive," and "reformer." Since much American political history
has been written as the history of American reform, it is not
astonishing that the words may seem interchangeable. But for
the small slice of history which I have focused upon, I believe the proper distinctions are sometimes vital. Readers who

fail to make such distinctions may misinterpret some parts of the chapters that follow.

If one reflects that men like John D. Rockefeller and Samuel Insull were reformers in their fields but are not often called progressives, it should be clear that the word "reformer" needs a modifier. For the sake of clarity, therefore, I believe it is essential that we distinguish among business reformers like Rockefeller, socialist reformers like Debs, unionists like Gompers, and progressive reformers like Theodore Roosevelt, Woodrow Wilson, and Louis Brandeis.

As I see it, the picture of the progressive reformer which emerges from the works of the leading students of the Progressive Era is that of someone who strove to establish (or, in some places, to maintain) conditions favorable to a generalized but somehow generally agreed-upon set of cultural standards. Those standards included the ideal of devoted and disinterested public service, the sanctity of individual property rights restrained primarily by a keen sense of social responsibility, and a constant sensitivity to the general welfare. Though perhaps best known in reform history for their assault upon monopolies and corporate finance, the progressives as a rule also opposed (or were at least unfriendly to) three other contemporary developments: (1) the demands of union leaders for the closed shop, the right to strike, and, generally speaking, a place in the policy-making councils of government and industry; (2) the drive for a better share of political recognition and social rewards by various ethnic minority groups; and (3) the efforts of socialists to subordinate the rights of private property to a program of drastic social reorganization. The unionists, the ethnic-minority leaders, and the socialists were all reformers of a sort, but they were not typically progressive reformers — even though at different times they worked with the progressives for some specific measures.

Finally, I would reserve the word "insurgents" for men who sought a major change of long-standing social policy (for example, the subordination of previously favored financial and railroad interests to agricultural or mercantile interests), or sought to overturn the existing leadership of a political party (for example, the insurgent Republicans during the Taft administration). In some places, like New Jersey or Wisconsin, the progressives clearly were also insurgents. But, as I have already indicated, Massachusetts was out of phase with much of the country; thus, while the Wisconsin progressives functioned as insurgents, Massachusetts' progressives (or progressive-equivalents) performed primarily a holding action against different kinds of insurgents. In the interest of clarity, therefore, it is important not to confuse the insurgent groups in Massachusetts with the progressives.

In the course of preparing this book, I have had the pleasure and good fortune to receive aid and encouragement from many generous individuals. In particular, I am indebted to Professor William E. Leuchtenburg of Columbia University, who guided my work from the very beginning; indeed, my debt to him goes far beyond this small project. My special thanks also to Professors Robert D. Cross and John A. Garraty, who read through the entire manuscript and offered many vital suggestions for its improvement; to Professors Richard Hofstadter, Henry F. Graff, Bernard Wishy, and James P. Shenton of Columbia University, each of whom read one or more of the chapters in early drafts and helped me to locate major weaknesses; to Professors Henry F. May, Charles G. Sellers, Jr., and Lawrence W. Levine of the University of California, Berkeley, who offered suggestions on the completed manuscript; to my friends, Professors Stanley Coben of Princeton University, Alan Holder of Williams College, Clyde Griffen of Vassar College, and Albert U. Romasco of New York University; to Mr. George C. Keller of New York City, and Dr. Gerald Ehrenstein of Washington, D.C., whom I frequently trapped into long discussions about Massachusetts and its politics and whose conversation and criticisms were indispensable to me throughout the shaping of my thesis; and to Miss Rebecca Young, who gave freely of her time to aid me with the tabulation of legislative roll calls.

In addition, there are many individuals who helped in various ways to facilitate my research: Mr. Frank Buxton of Brookline, Massachusetts, who introduced me to a number of persons active in Massachusetts affairs during the Progressive Era, and whose own recollections of his work on the editorial board of the *Boston Herald* proved valuable; Mr. Claude M. Fuess of Chestnut Hill, Massachusetts, who also provided introductions, and who gave me access to the Frank P. Stearns and Calvin Coolidge papers in his possession, shared his knowledge of Joseph B. Eastman, Henry Cabot Lodge, Murray Crane, and Calvin Coolidge with me, and obtained permission for me to use facilities at the Boston Athenaeum; the late President John F. Kennedy, then Senator, who took the time to talk with me about his grandfather, the late John F. Fitzgerald; Mr. Richard Hooker of Longmeadow, Massachusetts, who reminisced of his work on the board of editors of the *Springfield Republican;* Mr. George C. Lodge, who gave me permission to use his great-grandfather's papers at the Massachusetts Historical Society; Miss Ruth Hedden, Head Librarian, as well as her staff at the Massachusetts State Library, without whose interest and assistance much of my work would have been impossible; the Rev. Father William L. Lucey of the College of the Holy Cross, who helped me to make the fullest use of the College's collection, including the David I. Walsh manuscripts; Mr. Winthrop M. Crane of Dalton, Massachusetts, who gave me access to his father's papers in his possession; Mr. George Walker of Concord, Massachusetts, who let me use his father's papers in his possession; Professor Arthur Mann of Smith College, who offered me his vast bibliography and gave me valuable insights into New England reform movements; Professor Thomas Ryder of Northeastern University, who gave me his notes on Martin Lomasney; Professor John M. Blum of Yale University, who on two occasions shared his knowledge of Massachusetts politics, Joseph Tumulty, and Theodore Roosevelt with me; and the library staffs at the Massachusetts Historical Society, the Boston Public Library, Harvard University, Columbia University, the New Hampshire Historical Society, the American Antiquarian Society, Yale University, the University of Louisville (special thanks to Mrs. Pearl von Allmen of the Law Library), the University of Michigan, Amherst College, the New York Public Library, and the Library of Congress.

Two chapters in this study make use of previously published articles of mine. Chapter One appeared in substantially the same form under the title "A Paradox of Progressivism" in the *Political Science Quarterly*, September 1960, and much of Chapter Eight is drawn from "Brandeis and the New Haven–Boston & Maine Merger Battle," *Business History Review*, Winter, 1962. Permission to reproduce this material is gratefully acknowledged.

Finally, let me express my affectionate gratitude to my wife, Marcia, who managed to tolerate me during varying moods and who undertook many onerous tasks for which I did not have the patience myself; and to my mother and father, Mr. and Mrs. Nathan Abrams of Belle Harbor, New York, who not only endured with me the inevitable anxieties ("will it *ever* be done?"), but assisted me in the tedious work of preparing scores of pages of statistics from which some minor, but necessary, bits of information could be gleaned.

From August 1960 to August 1961, during which time the major part of this book was completed, I enjoyed generous financial assistance from the Social Science Research Council.

R. M. A.

Berkeley, California
March 1964

CONTENTS

CONSERVATISM IN
A PROGRESSIVE ERA

MASSACHUSETTS POLITICS
1900–1912

ABBREVIATIONS

Hearings, 1905   Senate Committee on Interstate Commerce, *Hearings on Proposed Amendment of the Interstate Commerce Act,* Senate Document 243, 58 Congress, 3 Session, 1905.

I.C.C. Hearings   "Evidence taken before the Interstate Commerce Commission relative to the financial transactions of the New York, New Haven & Hartford Railroad Company, together with a report of the Commission thereon," Senate Document 543, 63 Congress, 2 Session, 1914.

MBSL   Massachusetts Bureau of the Statistics of Labor.

MHRJ   Massachusetts, General Court, *Journal of the House of Representatives.*

MSJ   Massachusetts, General Court, *Journal of the Senate.*

RMA   Roosevelt Memorial Association.

CHAPTER ONE

ON THE EVE OF PROGRESSIVISM

The New England Puritans created a distinct culture because they were peculiar from the start. However narrow in some matters, theirs was a very able migration, with high intellectual standards, the strongest sense of duty, and a passion for work. They were also filled with an extraordinary moral devotion and faith and showed themselves preeminent for resolution and fortitude . . . On top of that, the Puritans developed an unusual talent for association, for organization, for concerted effort. Consider the three social instruments which they developed — the congregation, the town meeting, and the public school system — and you realize that here were so many power plants, just town-size . . . They were almost un-American. For what were good Americans to make of a people who chose to be pessimists rather than optimists, frugal not wasteful, introvert not extrovert? When we consider that they were also afraid of the arts and graces of life, yet so often ahead in books, tools, organizations, and social reforms, then it becomes clear why they drove the Southerners to scorn or to fury, and gave the Westerners an inferiority complex.

George Wilson Pierson*

WHAT characterizes an era and often gives it its popular historical name is the effort which the contemporary society makes to solve the dominant problem of the era. Not all elements of the society, of course, may participate in the effort. In the years after the turn of the twentieth century, American society strove for a way to enjoy the fruits of industrial progress without continuing the brutal sacrifice of human dignity which so far seemed to have characterized industrial advance. Americans took long strides toward strengthening republican institutions, creating safeguards against waste and corruption,

---

* "The Obstinate Concept of New England: A Study in Denudation," *New England Quarterly,* March 1955.

establishing greater control over corporations and public utilities, and promoting the general welfare through social legislation. Contemporaries and historians named the movement to achieve these objectives "progressive." Because Massachusetts did not participate significantly in the progressive movement, contemporaries tended to view the state as stolid and backward, and historians have looked elsewhere for progressive achievements.

In an early account of the period, for example, Harold U. Faulkner chose Wisconsin as "the most conspicuous example" of the states which established controls over public utilities and promoted the general welfare through social legislation. Matthew Josephson agreed that "for other states, Wisconsin became a sort of experimental social laboratory where new legislation was carefully tested and perfected," adding that "the 'Wisconsin Idea' . . . was a product of the intensely democratic Middle West farmers." [1] In *The Era of Theodore Roosevelt*, the most recent scholarly survey of the era, George E. Mowry also attributed the pioneering role to Wisconsin. Under the leadership of Robert M. LaFollette, he asserted, "Wisconsin had gone further than any other state along the path toward a social democracy." For Massachusetts, on the other hand, Professor Mowry, like other historians, reserved only casual citation. "*Even* in traditionalist New England" he observed "faint" marks of enlightenment late in the era.[2]

Yet before 1900, with a few exceptions,[3] Massachusetts had enjoyed in practice if not in form all the democratic innovations which progressives emphasized after 1900. It had, in addition, the most effective corporation laws in the nation,

[1] Harold U. Faulkner, *The Quest for Social Justice, 1898–1914* (New York, 1931), p. 124; Matthew Josephson, *The President Makers* (New York, 1940), pp. 217–218. See also Robert S. Maxwell, *La Follette and the Rise of the Progressives in Wisconsin* (Madison, 1956), esp. p. 195.

[2] George E. Mowry, *The Era of Theodore Roosevelt* (New York, 1958), pp. 294, 79 (my emphasis).

[3] Three outstanding progressive innovations which Massachusetts still lacked were direct election of United States senators, woman suffrage, and the direct primary. It initiated a primary system in 1903.

and it led the country in labor legislation. It owed most of these achievements, however, not to any reform *movement*, but rather to the character of its tradition, rooted in the Puritan-colonial experience. For that reason it would be confusing to call Massachusetts a "progressive" state, as the word is conventionally used. Nevertheless, in most matters identified with progressivism after 1900, Massachusetts had earlier taken an advanced position.

I

As a model of republican government, Massachusetts had long attracted the attention of civic reformers and students of politics. Even in the "Gilded Age" that incisive critic of American institutions, Lord Bryce, could write:

The best [state legislatures] seem to be those of the New England states, particularly Massachusetts, where the venerable traditions surrounding an ancient commonwealth do something to sustain the dignity of the body and induce good men to enter it. The legislature, called the General Court, is, according to the best authorities, substantially pure and does its work well.[4]

A generation later, when Wisconsin was capturing the attention of the nation's reformers with its program of political democracy, social justice, and regulation, Professor Paul S. Reinsch of the University of Wisconsin observed that "the General Court of Massachusetts is in all respects nearest the people, and most responsive of any American legislature to intelligent public opinion." [5]

While reformers in other states during the Populist and Progressive Eras fought for closer electoral checks on representatives, state officials in Massachusetts had had to face the electorate annually since colonial times. To safeguard that electorate, Massachusetts became in 1888 the first state to

[4] James Bryce, *American Commonwealth* (London and New York, 1888), I, 515.
[5] Paul S. Reinsch, *American Legislatures and Legislative Methods* (New York, 1907), p. 175. Cf. Walter F. Dodd, *State Government* (New York, 1928), p. 188.

require the Australian ballot. Reformers elsewhere had to fight for the initiative and referendum in order to secure greater legislative response to the popular will. But in the Bay State the legislature could always attach a referendum provision to any bill applying to local affairs, and failure to do so with highly controversial bills often led to a veto. All legislative measures were introduced as "petitions," and it was not unusual for a private citizen to draft such a petition, or for the ultimate bill to bear the name of that citizen.[6] Even beyond the right of personal petition in the General Court, the traditional town meeting provided a highly effective form of initiative; although the law did not compel legislators to introduce or vote for measures petitioned at such meetings, they ran the risk of defeat at the annual election if they did not.

In the legislature, bills were subject to open and formal hearings which members of the public not only could attend but in which they also could actively participate.[7] Although in most states public hearings did not usually influence legislation (perhaps because in most states, unlike Massachusetts, the legislature was located away from the business and population centers), Paul Reinsch noted in 1907 that, in Massachusetts alone, committee hearings were "a very important part of legislative action." [8] Reformers elsewhere had to contend with small minorities, often entrenched in key committee positions, who bottled up reform measures. But the standing rules of the General Court required committees to report all measures referred to them, and they usually did report well in advance of the close of the legislative session. The constitutions of many states restricted the legislatures to a certain number of months during the year, for economy reasons, and because

<hr>

[6] Thomas J. Wood, "Distinctive Legislative Practices of the Massachusetts General Court," unpublished doctoral dissertation, Harvard University, 1947. See also John W. Plaisted, *Legislative Procedure in the General Court of Massachusetts* (Boston, 1948), pp. 13–15, and Reinsch, p. 184.

[7] Such men as Louis D. Brandeis and Joseph B. Eastman began their long public careers early in the Progressive Era by appearing as representatives of the public at such hearings.

[8] Reinsch, p. 174.

conservative interests feared "too much" legislation. The Massachusetts legislature, however, was authorized to remain in session throughout the year.

In sum, Massachusetts possessed almost all the institutional "guarantees" for legislative responsibility in advance of the movements launched to achieve them elsewhere.

II

Massachusetts enjoyed benefits still more important than the political practices which progressives elsewhere in the country began to demand at the turn of the century. In an important sense, one may view progressivism as a response to the collectivization of American life, and in particular to the disproportionate and insidious influence which public utilities and business corporations exerted upon public policy. In this respect, perhaps the most striking of Massachusetts' achievements was its effective regulation of corporations, particularly of railroads and other public services.

Though other states had anticipated Massachusetts in establishing temporary and *ad hoc* commissions, the Massachusetts Railroad Commission, created in 1869, was the first to function as a permanent mediator of conflicts between the railroads and the public.[9] Under the able and conscientious leadership of Charles Francis Adams, Jr., and fortified by annual salaries of $4000 (which awed commissioners elsewhere), the three-man commission won the respect and envy of similar bodies. The duties of the board included investigation of the physical and financial status of all the railroads operating within the state, with the right to inquire into the records of the companies. On the basis of its investigations, the Commission could make recommendations concerning repairs, safety,

[9] Each of the other New England states had previously provided for commissions to handle particular problems; e.g., New Hampshire created a commission to enable private railroad companies to assume the form of a public corporation so that they might preempt land for railroad construction by right of eminent domain. See Edward C. Kirkland, *Men, Cities, and Transportation* (Cambridge, 1948), II, 231–237.

junctions, stock issues, and all other matters which might concern the public, including freight and passenger rate levels. These recommendations were to be made to the company, as well as to the public in annual reports. As Adams later observed, "The board of commissioners was set up as a sort of lens by means of which the otherwise scattered rays of public opinion could be concentrated to a focus and brought to bear upon a given point." [10]

By acts of 1885 and 1887, the General Court established a Board of Gas and Electric Light Commissioners to regulate companies which supplied power and light to the fast-growing municipalities in the state. Essentially the Board had the same duties as the Railroad Commission. But, in addition, the legislature armed this Board with "summary powers as to rates and service." [11] These included the power to investigate complaints, and upon investigation to order a reduction in price or an improvement in service; the power to fix rates upon the application of a service company; the right to prohibit companies from invading cities and towns serviced already by at least one gas and electric company; and the power to demand annual reports from the companies.[12]

On the face of it, the purpose of both public service commissions in their original forms appeared to be to act primarily as coordinating agencies for public utilities, to protect them and the public from the effects of wasteful competition and recurrent disputes over service. Especially in the case of the Railroad Commission, the General Court fortified the restrictive functions with little more than the power to make recommendations and to give publicity to company affairs. Since, by the 1890's, insurgents in many western and southern states sought, not conciliatory and advisory instruments to eliminate the causes of disruptive conflicts, but rather weapons against

[10] Quoted by Kirkland, II, 239.

[11] Irston R. Barnes, *Public Utility Control in Massachusetts* (New Haven, 1930), p. 15.

[12] *Ibid.*, pp. 15–16.

the power of overbearing corporations, they regarded the Massachusetts body as the model illustration of a "weak commission."

It would be a mistake, however, to underestimate the effectiveness of investigatory and publicity functions in a state which was "an abode of restless reformers," [13] and which had a long tradition of government intervention in the economic affairs of its citizens.[14] Even more important, the General Court frequently appended additional powers to the commissions. In the case of the railroad board, these included requiring its approval for various technical innovations, and giving it authority to review — and sometimes to set — commuter rates, and power to determine the public need for new roads and how much the roads and the localities were to pay toward the elimination of grade crossings. Statutes of 1887 and 1889 required the Railroad Commission to ascertain property valuation before a railroad could increase its capital stock and before the board authorized a bond issue. After 1894, moreover, railroads and gas and electric utilities had to secure the approval of the commissions for all issues of stocks and bonds, and for the terms of every lease, purchase, and sale.[15]

In fact, the powers which the acts of 1893 and 1894, especially, gave to the commissions make it fallacious to call those bodies "weak." This legislation included the then unprecedented requirement that all stock issues of more than 4 per cent of the total stock of a railroad, gas, or electric company be sold at auction, or be sold proportionately to stockholders at a price estimated to be market value by the appropriate com-

[13] Kirkland, II, 244.

[14] See Oscar and Mary Handlin, *Commonwealth: A Study of the Role of Government in the American Economy, 1774–1861* (New York, 1947), *passim.*

[15] Massachusetts Board of Railroad Commissioners, *26th Annual Report* (Boston, 1895), pp. 13–14, 127–134, 147, 149; *27th Annual Report* (1896), pp. 141–153, 168, 181; also William A. Crafts (secretary, Mass. Board R. R. Commissioners), "The Second Decade of the Massachusetts Railroad Commission," *Railroad Gazette*, 25:551 (July 21, 1893); Kirkland, II, 248.

mission.[16] The purpose of such legislation was to keep the out-standing securities at a minimum by requiring issues to be sold at the highest possible prices. To the same end, the legislature prohibited stock dividends and capitalization of earnings.[17]

During the Progressive Era, some of the sharper critics of the practices of railroad corporations believed that Massachu-setts overemphasized regulation of capitalization as compared with regulation of price and service.[18] Yet, as long as it was assumed that a stockholder had a right to earn a "fair return" on his capital, excessive rates followed perforce from exces-sive dividend demands which were created by the multiplica-tion of stock disproportionate to physical value. Unless the state had effectively prevented excessive capitalization, rate control would have been a meaningless gesture. In opposing an order to reduce rates, a utility company could always argue that reduced revenues would not permit stockholders to earn a "fair return" and would therefore amount to confiscation. Eventually, most progressives at least tacitly accepted the prin-ciples of the Massachusetts laws.[19] As late as 1908, the *Chi-*

[16] Mass. Board R.R. Commissioners, *26th Annual Report,* pp. 13–14. Also Barnes, pp. 37, 58–59; *Report of the Massachusetts Commission on Com-merce and Industry* (Boston, 1908), p. 60.

[17] "This supervision," wrote Irston Barnes, "has included all types of securities and has been applied virtually from the beginning of public utility development in Massachusetts." Barnes, p. 3; see also pp. 77–78. "The entire course of legislation," the Gas and Electric Light Commission observed in 1913, "clearly indicates the well-founded conviction that the volume of securities outstanding against any public utility has a potent effect upon rates and quality of service, since prices are made and maintained to meet the expectations of stockholders as to dividends, and service may be seriously impaired by a continued endeavor to meet those expectations." Massachu-setts Board of Gas and Electric Light Commissioners, *29th Annual Report* (1915), p. 12.

[18] See, e.g., Edward Bemis, "Control of the Capitalization of Public Serv-ice Corporations in Massachusetts," *American Economic Association Quar-terly,* 10:426 (1909).

[19] The contemporary economist-reformer, William Z. Ripley, pointed out: "While of course there is no direct relation between capitalization and prices, an excess of securities craving dividends is in itself an indirect incentive to unreasonable charges . . . This was the underlying motive in the enactment of the Massachusetts Anti-Stock Watering Laws of 1894. For a divergence

cago Tribune, then moving toward an insurgent position, cited Massachusetts corporation law as a "model which the nation might well follow in regulating the great corporations . . . the control of which . . . has become such a problem for Congress." [20]

Massachusetts law restricted private corporations nearly as much as it did the utilities. When corporate organization came to be widely adopted as a business form in the 1890's, many states competed for the business of issuing charters; Massachusetts was slow to meet the competition.[21] In fact, businesses which chose to incorporate in Massachusetts had a rugged time of it. Since the Bay State taxed not only the value of the tangible property of a corporation, but also the "corporate excess," that is, the market value of the securities in excess of property value, the more successful corporations fled from Massachusetts to states with more lenient taxation laws. Massachusetts laws, moreover, discouraged holding companies not only because the principal assets of holding companies were securities which were taxable even though representing other taxable securities,[22] but because the law required all corporations to secure special permission from the General Court in order to

---

between the actual property value and capitalization may lead to exorbitant prices and dividends at the expense of the public." *Trusts, Pools and Corporations* (Boston, 1905), p. xxiii. Without ever referring to Massachusetts, Wisconsin insurgent Robert M. LaFollette acknowledged those principles in his repeated efforts after 1906 to have the Interstate Commerce Commission authorized to determine the physical valuation of interstate railroads preliminary to setting rates. But as early as 1901, Henry C. Adams, statistician for the I.C.C., argued for federal adoption of the Massachusetts techniques because they amounted to physical valuation for purposes of ascertaining just rates and just taxes. See testimony before the United States Industrial Commission, *Report on Transportation,* vol. IX (1901), House Document 178, 57 Cong., 1 Sess., p. 373ff. See also testimony of W. Z. Ripley, *ibid.,* pp. 291ff.

[20] Quoted in the *Brockton Enterprise,* December 17, 1908.

[21] Henry R. Seager and Charles A. Gulick, Jr., *Trust and Corporation Problems* (New York and London, 1929), pp. 35ff.

[22] Harry G. Friedman, *The Taxation of Corporations in Massachusetts* (New York, 1907), pp. 78, 83.

hold the securities of other corporations.[23] When the depression of the 1890's lifted and incorporations multiplied throughout the country, Massachusetts did not share in the movement. Annual incorporations in the state barely increased between 1897 and 1901. In the latter year, nearly two thirds of the newly chartered corporations doing business in Massachusetts obtained their charters from other states.[24]

In general, those who aimed their fire at the misdeeds of the "trusts" considered Massachusetts' techniques worth copying. President Roosevelt declared before a Boston audience in 1902: "Most of our difficulties [with trusts] would be in a fair way of solution if we had the power to put in the national statute books, and did put upon them laws for the nation such as those you have here on the subject of corporations in Massachusetts." [25] Charles E. Littlefield, chairman of a congressional subcommittee on trusts, urged copying at least the publicity features of Massachusetts laws, arguing that "none of the great combinations of which complaint is made . . . could have been financed" if the public had known about overcapitalization.[26]

[23] Seager and Gulick, p. 40.

[24] Grosvenor Calkins, "The Massachusetts Business Corporation Law," *Quarterly Journal of Economics,* 18:269–280 (1904), reprinted in Ripley, *Trusts,* pp. 382–392. In 1897, 280 Massachusetts businesses incorporated under Massachusetts law, while 263 took foreign charters; in 1898, the numbers were 251 and 298, respectively; in 1899, 281 and 466; in 1900, 264 and 423; and in 1901, 211 and 524. Frederick J. Stimson and Charles G. Washburn, *Report of the Committee on Corporation Laws,* 1903 (Printed as a Massachusetts Senate Document), p. 19.

[25] *Boston Herald,* August 27, 1902. Roosevelt cited in particular the provisions in the Massachusetts law (1) requiring that all stock be paid in before any corporate charter could be granted, (2) requiring auction sale or price fixing by commissions of stock issues by public service corporations, (3) holding corporate directors personally responsible for debts exceeding capitalization and for dividends which rendered the corporation insolvent, and (4) requiring publicity for a corporation's financial condition to the extent of ordering dissolution if such reports were not filed for two successive years.

[26] House Subcommittee on Trusts, *Majority Report on a Bill to Amend the Sherman Anti-Trust Act,* House Report 3375, to accompany H.R. 17, 57 Cong., 2 Sess., 1903, p. 18. Cf. L. S. Rowe, "Relation of Cities and Towns to Street Railway Companies." *Annals of the American Academy of Political and Social Science,* XII (July–December 1898), 103–108.

III

Massachusetts' contributions to "social justice" at the turn of the century were not confined to democratic political institutions and restraint of business practices. Contemporaries generally recognized its leadership in labor legislation. In a volume published in 1907, historian John H. Latané wrote: "In the effort to improve the condition of the laboring classes through direct legislation, Massachusetts has led the way, and her child-labor and factory laws have been followed by many of the other states." [27] Massachusetts pioneered in child labor legislation (1836), instituted the first state factory inspection system (1866), and first limited the day's work for women and minors to ten hours (1874). The Bay State was the first to establish a bureau of labor statistics, the first to compel corporations to pay employees weekly, and the first to forbid corporations to pay wages in store truck.

But Massachusetts' claim to fame does not rest on priority alone. As two careful students of the subject wrote in 1910,

Massachusetts has been generally regarded as the center of advanced labor legislation in America. Part of that well-earned reputation is due to the priority of important laws passed in this Commonwealth which have been copied, often verbatim, by many other states; but it cannot be explained on that basis alone. Although several of the states which have followed Massachusetts as a leader have at some points distinctly bettered her instruction, it is still true that not many other states in America have laws which go so far toward complete protection of employees as do those of Massachusetts.[28]

[27] John H. Latané, *America as a World Power* (New York, 1907), p. 308.
[28] Edith Reeves and Caroline Manning, "The Standing of Massachusetts in the Administration of Labor Legislation," in Susan M. Kingsley, ed., *Labor Laws and Their Enforcement* (New York, 1911), p. 223. It is important to understand that Miss Reeves and Miss Manning directed their study toward finding weaknesses in the Massachusetts legislation and administration. The quoted passage is an introductory one; the bent of the article is that, as progressive as Massachusetts was, it did not go far enough. See also Robert H. Whitten, "Trend of Legislation in the United States," [*New York*] *State Library Bulletin*, No. 12 (Albany, 1902), p. 411.

The same investigators also found that, "without a doubt," Massachusetts had a larger proportion of employers who made a serious effort to provide good working conditions for their employees than did other states. They attributed this to the fact that Massachusetts factories on the average were older than factories in other states, and many such establishments had been run by families for generations. Labor laws, in fact, were often sponsored by precisely these familial factory owners in order to bring into line newer factory owners who might otherwise compete too successfully with the more paternalistic ones.[29] Moreover, labor legislation early became a "habit" with Massachusetts employers; they learned to live with regulations and assumed that they embodied an indigenous social standard.

Massachusetts also led in the enforcement and administration of labor laws. During the enthusiastic progressive years, New York and Wisconsin surpassed Massachusetts in providing certain advanced machinery for the enforcement of laws. But even in this respect, the deficiencies in Massachusetts were limited to milder penal provisions than other states had, some uncertainty in the relation between local and state inspection procedures, insufficiently comprehensive civil service examinations, and the failure to make factory inspection the sole occupation of inspectors. The same investigators who noted these deficiencies, however, also maintained: "It is not to other states of the Union that . . . [Massachusetts] must look for a model toward which to reconstruct existing methods . . . Not only in her laws regulating conditions of labor, but in laws requiring their enforcement, does Massachusetts seem to stand toward the top in the United States." [30]

It is not difficult to list additional achievements, identified after 1900 with progressivism, in which Massachusetts led the country. Massachusetts Congressman Augustus P. Gardner, for example, was able to quote in 1902 from a compendium

[29] Cf. Handlin, *Commonwealth,* pp. 204–205, 241.
[30] Reeves and Manning, pp. 263–264.

of pure-food legislation prepared for the state legislature of Georgia: "Massachusetts may be said to have nearer a perfect code of pure-food laws than any other State or country which has given thought to the subject of preventing food adulteration under its myriad forms and disguises." [31] The New York State legislative reference service reported in 1902 that "the movement to encourage the establishment of free public libraries . . . [which] started in 1890 with the establishment of a free public library commission in Massachusetts" had equipped more than 1,800 Bay State towns with free libraries, leaving by 1901 less than .05 per cent of the state population without such service. "Following the example of Massachusetts," the report continued, "special library commissions . . . have now been provided in fourteen states." [32] In sum, as the reform-conscious *Independent* declared on the morn of the new century: "It is Massachusetts that leads all her sister commonwealths in progressive legislation, and in wisely directed reform movements." [33]

IV

One might expect, therefore, that the nation's insurgents during the Progressive Era would have used Massachusetts as the model for advanced legislative techniques, for the responsiveness of its political institutions, for its quality of political behavior, for its techniques of regulating corporate practices, and for its methods of securing "social justice." One might expect, moreover, that the Bay State would have welcomed insurgency and the adoption of its laws, even without acknowledgment, by other states. But complex political and economic circumstances denied those possibilities. To put it (for present purposes) in abstract form, Massachusetts never caught the

[31] *Congressional Record,* 57 Cong., 2 Sess., December 18, 1902, p. 440. See also Senate Committee on Manufacturers, *Digest of the Pure Food and Drug Laws of the United States and Foreign Countries,* Senate Report 3 (1901), *passim.*

[32] Whitten, pp. 429–430.

[33] "Contrasting Records of Pennsylvania and Massachusetts," *Independent,* 53:1568–1570 (July 4, 1901).

spirit of *change* which dominated the era, and consequently it appeared, at best, merely conservative. It was rather the "Wisconsin Idea," the "Iowa Idea," and (in New Jersey) simply the "New Idea" which quickened the hearts of men of good will and good hope during the Progressive Era. Historians have followed this lead by neglecting Massachusetts' achievements and emphasizing its undeniable conservatism.

If Massachusetts did not share conspicuously in the "quest for social justice" characteristic of the American states during the earlier years of the twentieth century, it may well be because it had less to search for. What was "new" to reformers elsewhere in the country was often "old" to Massachusetts. For example, its political leaders resisted formal democratic innovations in the state's political system, and therefore they deserved the epithet "conservative" which contemporary insurgents and subsequent historians applied to them. Yet it is important to keep in mind that if Massachusetts did not have in name the kind of laws which progressives demanded elsewhere in the country, it did have to a substantial degree the benefit of the practices which the reformers advocated. "There are many States," Theodore Roosevelt wrote to his friend Henry Cabot Lodge, "in which Legislatures have functioned badly, and in which the people are groping for a remedy"; for such states, the initiative and compulsory referendum appeared "the only remedy in sight." He agreed with Lodge that "I & R" were unnecessary in Massachusetts.[34] Roosevelt felt similarly about the recall of judges and judicial decisions: "You are absolutely right," he confided to his biographer, Charles G. Washburn, ". . . I have always said that in Massachusetts recall by the Legislature was enough . . . In Missouri and California, more was needed."[35] He added ironically to another acquaintance, "It is rather funny to think that if the Massachusetts and Vermont methods of electing and removing

[34] Roosevelt to Lodge, December 13, 1911, in Henry Cabot Lodge, ed., *Correspondence of Theodore Roosevelt and Henry Cabot Lodge* (New York, 1925), II, 416–417.
[35] Roosevelt to Washburn, March 31, 1915 (RMA MSS).

judges were advanced by me, I should be denounced as almost a Communist." [36] Massachusetts had enjoyed the practices to which Roosevelt alluded from the time it had become a state.

Similarly, Massachusetts derived its advanced position on corporation regulation from a long tradition of conservative business practices under government supervision. Incorporation originated in Massachusetts as a device by which groups of private entrepreneurs served as agencies of the state toward a public purpose. The services which the corporate body was to provide for the commonweal justified the privileges which the state granted in the charter.[37] Massachusetts business at the beginning of the twentieth century had not entirely outgrown the discipline imposed by that early tradition. Whatever their social or political views, many in the Massachusetts business community — especially, but not exclusively, the dominant older families — tended to suspect the radical tendencies of American finance capitalism.[38]

"Overcapitalization is a fraud" — it was as plain as that to Massachusetts Congressman George P. Lawrence. In arguing for a national incorporation law and a stronger Interstate Commerce Commission, Lawrence announced his determination "to make these creatures of the State render honest service to the State." [39] Similarly, Senator Lodge wrote to Lucius Tuttle, president of the Boston & Maine Railroad, who was resisting expanded federal regulation of corporations in interstate commerce:

[36] Roosevelt to Louis A. Frothingham, December 17, 1914 (RMA MSS).

[37] Oscar and Mary Handlin, "Origins of the American Business Corporation," *Journal of Economic History,* 5:1–23 (May 1945).

[38] For example, George von L. Meyer, a State Street stockholder who served as Postmaster General under Roosevelt and Secretary of the Navy under Taft, asserted: "The laws of New Jersey and Delaware and even Maine which permit these corporations of enormous capital to be formed, often with very limited amounts of cash paid in, are really a curse . . ." Meyer continued, "If the corporation laws of Massachusetts or those similar to them" were adopted by the federal government, the country would be spared the panics which periodically threatened the economy. Meyer to H. C. Lodge, August 12, 1903 (Meyer MSS).

[39] *Congressional Record,* 57 Cong., 2 Sess., February 6, 1903, p. 1793.

I don't quite accept your proposition that these questions can be left to natural law because the railroads don't exist by natural laws . . . They are founded on the grant of the highways of commerce and they are given by the government what amounts to a general power to tax all persons who use it . . . The taxing power cannot exist without any appeal of its abuse . . . You substantially admit this by your approval of the principle of supervision adopted in Massachusetts.[40]

The events which motivated the passage of the "anti-stock watering" laws of 1894 further illustrate the distrust of financial practices then acceptable in most parts of the country. In 1892, the Connecticut River Railroad persuaded the General Court to permit it to issue to its stockholders at par 24,200 shares of stock, then selling on the market at $235. To many it appeared a gratuity to stockholders of more than $100 per share. The issue, moreover, would have doubled the total capitalization of the company upon which dividends had to be paid. A public uproar followed, and Governor William E. Russell vetoed the enabling legislation, declaring that it would place "an unnecessary burden . . . each year upon the business of the railroad, that is, upon the public." [41] The next year a new legislature passed the restrictive acts. As one economist complained some years later, "In most other states the matter would probably have attracted little attention at that time . . . After all, the new stock was to be paid for in cash at the par value, and the proceeds were to be devoted to necessary improvements . . . But in Massachusetts the project was assailed as 'indirect stock watering'." [42]

[40] Lodge to Tuttle, c. January 1905 (Lodge MSS). Cf. Kirkland, II, 232: "Although individual railroad managers and investors sometimes asserted that the railroad was in the same business and legal category as a factory, that the state ought to refrain from interfering with railroad management . . . their chatter was wishful and instinctive; it was neither representative of dominant thinking nor in accord with New England practice."
[41] Quoted in Barnes, p. 35n.
[42] Charles J. Bullock, "Control of the Capitalization of Public Service Corporations in Massachusetts," *American Economic Association Quarterly*, 10:401 (1909). The Railroad Commission, in its report of 1894, commented favorably on the legislation: "It was the evident purpose of the Legislature . . . to guard against the dangers and temptations of . . . gratuitous capitalization, and to eliminate as far as possible the speculative ele-

Probably one reason for this kind of conservatism was that many in Massachusetts found the laws and the economic attitudes they expressed conducive to good business.[43] At a Senate hearing on railroad legislation, Senator Francis Newlands of Nevada asked Lucius Tuttle whether he considered Massachusetts' restrictive laws wise. Tuttle replied: "I think they are . . . The conservative character of . . . our laws very greatly strengthens the market value in the minds of the investors in our securities." [44] Certainly the experience of Massachusetts railroads bore out Tuttle's observation. At the depth of the depression following the Panic of 1893, the Railroad Commission was able to report: "There has been no dearth of capital seeking investment; . . . [Massachusetts railroad stocks] are sought by conservative investors at higher prices today than twelve months ago; and the same is true of some of the street railway stocks." [45]

Massachusetts had had no need of a reform movement to alert its community to the excesses of modern corporate enterprise. On the other hand, most of the states conspicuous for reform movements after 1900 entered the Union just at the time when corporate enterprise was gaining independence from the original principles of incorporation. Populated by individuals "on the make," who had left established com-

---

ment from the financial economy of the railroad and other corporations created for public use." Mass. Board R.R. Commissioners, *26th Annual Report* (1895), pp. 13–14. The Commission reaffirmed these sentiments in 1900: see *32nd Annual Report* (1900), pp. 93–94.

[43] The same conservative attitude sometimes extended to corporate enterprise conducted by Massachusetts businessmen outside the state. William B. Gates, Jr., historian of the Michigan copper mining industry, has written: "Conservative Boston financing and management also explains why rapid exploitation of properties for stock manipulative purposes played an insignificant part in the Michigan history, in marked contrast with certain periods of the Montana and Arizona story." *Michigan Copper and Boston Dollars* (Cambridge, 1951), p. 69; see also p. 189.

[44] Senate Committee on Interstate Commerce, *Hearings on Proposed Amendment of the Interstate Commerce Act,* Senate Document 243, 58 Cong., 3 Sess., 1905, pp. 947–948.

[45] Mass. Board R.R. Commissioners, *26th Annual Report* (1895), p. 97. See also succeeding reports. Cf. W. Z. Ripley, *Trusts,* pp. 126–128.

munities to break away from the traditions and institutions
and anything else they held responsible for their past discontents, these states — it seems reasonable to argue — lacked
the sources of a rooted tradition which might have enabled
their citizens to look to the government as a legitimate agent
of a unified and purposive community. By the end of the nineteenth century they began to learn, in the words of Frederick
Jackson Turner, "that unrestrained competition and combination meant the triumph of the strongest, [and] the seizure in the
interest of a dominant class of the strategic points of the nation's
life"; that "between the ideal of individualism, unrestrained by
society, and the ideal of democracy, was an innate conflict";
and "that their very ambitions and forcefulness had endan-
gered their democracy." [46] By then, it was necessary to inaugu-
rate sensational "exposés" to carry reform measures against the
opposition of entrenched political interests, to wage dramatic
campaigns on behalf of ordinary democratic principles, and
to acclaim the "new" so that old virtues and social values could
be restored. These were genuine causes. But Massachusetts did
not have the same battle to fight.

In addition to legal and social traditions which made melio-
rative action "normal" in Massachusetts, its business community did not suffer from many of the specific grievances
which motivated so many of the radical demands in the insurgent states. Massachusetts corporations did not have to
depend upon great outside financial centers for funds.[47] Local
stock ownership was widespread, and major owners were
rarely more distant than Boston. Railroad directors and the

[46] F. J. Turner, *The Frontier in American History* (New York, 1920),
p. 203.
[47] See testimony of Stuyvesant Fish before the Senate Committee on Interstate Commerce in 1905, in *Hearings*, 1905, p. 296. During the same hearing, Senator Newlands asked Lucius Tuttle, "Is it not a fact that all these
conditions are of the very best in Massachusetts, as contrasted with other
parts of the country, and is it not a fact that so far as the southern . . .
and . . . western railroads are concerned most of them are financed
through a few great financiers in New York?" Tuttle replied that it was so,
and that the reason was that the western and southern railroads could not
easily raise the capital any other way. *Ibid.*, p. 1002.

merchants who depended upon them, as well as financiers and the manufacturers who required their services, tended to mingle in the same social milieu. These conditions reduced the opportunities for misunderstandings as well as the temptations for underhanded or suspicious business practices.[48]

A clash of temperaments and of interests sharpened the alienation of Massachusetts from the progressive movement. Although Theodore Roosevelt, on the eve of his bolt from the Republican party, credited Massachusetts with an advanced position in many things identified with progressivism, no one in 1911 would seriously have expected Massachusetts to contribute significantly to the insurgents' cause. "I have always insisted that a good many of you were progressives," Roosevelt wrote to Lodge, "only unfortunately without knowing it and therefore without being able to impress the fact upon the rest of the country." [49] He also noted that men like Lodge shared certain important values with the progressives, in particular the premium they placed on social responsibility over individual liberty in the management of private property.[50] But Lodge could not "know" he was a progressive — he was not — not only because of his profoundly conservative temperament, but also because he was by circumstances unsuited for an insurgent role.

The progressives directed their assault not merely against abuses in American society, but also against vested political and economic interests which they held responsible for those abuses. Even if their temperament had allowed them to sympathize with the insurgents, Lodge and his colleagues were vulnerable as leaders of an incumbent political party. In addition,

---

[48] See Kirkland, II, 249, 252, 255.

[49] Roosevelt to Lodge, May 31, 1911 (RMA MSS).

[50] Lodge and many of the Massachusetts congressmen and state officials also shared with a great many of the progressives a nationalistic fervor, with racist overtones, which led them to promote America's imperialist ventures in the 1890's as well as the drive to restrict immigration and to build a large navy. See William E. Leuchtenburg, "Progressivism and Imperialism: The Progressive Movement and American Foreign Policy, 1898–1916," *Mississippi Valley Historical Review*, 39:483–504 (1953).

as representatives of established economic interests in their state, they had a responsibility which placed them even more certainly on the defensive than did political incumbency or conservative temperament; for, newly insurgent interests — sectional, political, and economic — provided much of the power behind the impulse for progressive reform.[51] And, although insurgent leaders usually assumed a moral rhetoric, the "evil" they condemned in many cases was merely the greater power or advantage of their competitors.

For many reasons, Massachusetts at the turn of the century held an advantageous competitive position in such enterprises as woolens, cottons, and shoe manufacturing. Though it produced no wool, it made most of the woolen fabrics in the country and sold them back to the wool-growing regions. It produced no cotton but sold cottons in the South and fine cotton goods in the southern mill towns themselves. It produced no hides, but sold leather, boots, and shoes throughout the Southwest and West. It was also an important producer of paper and paper products, machinery, wire, watches, and tools — and similarly dependent upon the outside for its raw materials.

One reason Massachusetts could do all this was that it had the advantage of skilled labor, and well-trained direction of that labor. Its financial facilities, moreover, were nearby and it could obtain credit at low cost. Its industry had the advantage of proximity to the great export markets in New York City and its own capital, Boston. Certainly not least important, however, was the simple fact that Massachusetts industry was established *early,* and therefore enjoyed the economic advantages of priority in important markets, and the political advantages of a vested interest.

The accessibility of Massachusetts industry to water transportation somewhat offset the great rail distances of the sources of its raw materials, but the state's economy was nevertheless

---

[51] Cf. Arthur S. Link, "What Happened to the Progressive Movement in the 1920's," *American Historical Review,* 64:833–851, esp. 834 (July 1959).

extraordinarily dependent on long-haul rail transportation. Fortunately, as long as the chief terminals were in Boston, and as long as railroads servicing New England remained competitors of railroads servicing other regions, New England roads had a substantial interest in maintaining the region's prosperity. The country's railroads generally favored Massachusetts industry with advantageous rates — privileged rates, if you will — against the rates which newly developing competitors nearer chief domestic markets and raw materials managed to obtain. For example, the Boston & Albany Railroad and trunk lines connecting with it at the Hudson River gave wire manufacturers in Worcester, Massachusetts, special rates so that the total cost of shipping wire to points west of Pittsburgh would not exceed the shipping cost from Pittsburgh manufacturers. Without such differentials, the Worcester manufacturers would have gone out of business.[52] Similarly, railroads from cotton-producing regions in the South charged lower through rates to Massachusetts than to nearer points in the Midwest, Georgia, or North Carolina. Partly this was because of water competition from New Orleans and Galveston to Boston. But railroad men willingly admitted their desire to support the New England mills.

As Lucius Tuttle explained to Democratic Senator Edward W. Carmack of Tennessee during the hearings on the Esch-Townshend bill in 1905,

Suppose a city has a population of 30,000 . . . engaged in the manufacture of shoes and the product of their manufacture is distributed to the world at a loss to the railroads; yet the carrying of the other things for those 30,000 people at . . . profitable rates compensates for the loss occasioned by the low rates. So it is all through the administration of railways . . . Perhaps in the city of Lowell 40,000 out of the population of 80,000 are dependent upon textile industries for their living. If these mills for any reason are closed that [sic] 40,000 people cease to live in Lowell, for they have nothing else to do; the traffic of that [sic] 40,000 people over the railroads going into Lowell would cease.[53]

[52] *Hearings,* 1905, p. 923.
[53] *Ibid.,* pp. 919, 975–976.

Carmack protested: "That is a case, then, where the railroads have practically created an industry and built up a great community by giving a very low rate for a very long haul . . . And yet at the same time other communities have languished because they could not get equal rates for a short haul." Tuttle agreed this was so. As Carmack and insurgents elsewhere in the country viewed it, "These artificial conditions created by the railroads . . . counter-acted the natural economical disadvantage" of a particular industrial site. The insurgents would have corrected these artificial conditions with a rate-setting commission. New Englanders, on the other hand, viewed exactly *that* kind of action as artificial;[54] it is small wonder that they tended to suspect innovations in federal law which would remove or weaken their influence with railroad rate policy.

The tariff issue further illustrates the point. Probably no issue was more important in provoking revolt within and against the Republican party across the nation. As the twentieth century opened, the Dingley Tariff of 1897 governed American foreign trade. Although it is not clear that Massachusetts industries benefited inordinately from the Dingley provisions,[55] protectionism had become for many a tenet of the Republican creed and a test of party fealty. Progressive leaders in Congress never disputed the protectionist principle; they challenged rather the existing distribution of the benefits of protectionism under the Dingley Act. Curiously, important Massachusetts interests early took the lead in urging downward revision of the tariff rates: as new competitors entered the domestic markets, and transportation costs proved increasingly disadvantageous to Massachusetts industry, the state's business turned to foreign markets and sources of raw materials. Nevertheless, most Republican leaders in the state were

[54] *Ibid.,* pp. 973–976. For some contemporary discussion of this issue, see William Z. Ripley, *Railroads: Rates and Regulation* (New York, 1912), pp. 159–162.

[55] In exchange for a duty on raw wool, Massachusetts wool manufacturers received a more-than-compensatory "protective" duty. Other manufacturers also received protection. But the increase in the rates on hides, ores, coal, sugar, and such could in no way have benefited Massachusetts.

reluctant to urge revision because it might tend to undermine the protectionist principle on which the party based its appeal to the labor element as well as to the sizable woolen, watch-making, and other industries. They pointed out, moreover, that the rest of the country would not accept a revision which placed raw materials on the free list while maintaining the protective duties on manufactured products. Massachusetts representatives in Washington therefore usually opposed insurgent leaders on a major issue.

In other words, one reason that Massachusetts was to remain estranged from the progressive movement, as a movement, was that the state became a principal object for attack by insurgent leaders elsewhere in the country. Both in their capacity as representatives of particular interests which competed with Massachusetts interests, and in their genuine conviction that Massachusetts interests had appropriated an undue share of the rewards of American society, insurgents tended to place the Bay State on the defensive. Massachusetts' achievement, by the eve of the Progressive Era, of an advanced position on the issues called "progressive" during the Era counted for little when its spokesmen were often impelled to oppose the courageous efforts of reformers elsewhere to redress the balance of social justice in America.

Perhaps it is unnecessary to elaborate on the specific predicaments faced by Massachusetts and the progressives. To explain the penumbral status of Massachusetts among progressive insurgents it may be sufficient to note again that its achievements were often inspired by a tradition of conservatism. To a maturing nation hurrying to catch up with its age in a brand-new century, the insurgent spirit of LaFollette's Wisconsin as well as its program appeared more appropriate. The Wisconsin program of responsible government, corporation control, and social justice, then and subsequently advertised as "more comprehensive and far-reaching" than that of other states, and conspicuous for the struggle waged on its behalf perhaps even more than for its success, "became an article for export both to other states and to other countries." [56] "But in 1900," observes the historian of Wisconsin progressivism, "all this lay in the future." [57]

For Massachusetts in 1900, the achievement of most of this program lay in the past. In years ahead, while it continued to seek solutions to the problems which occupied the progressives, Massachusetts waged its principal battle against the erosion of its economic power in the nation and of its venerated traditions at home.

[56] Maxwell, p. 8.
[57] *Ibid.*, p. 9.

CHAPTER TWO

THE CONDITION OF POLITICS

So Laura Jean Libby is dead. What recollections her name
calls up! School days, strawride days, days when the bees
bumbled outside and the smell of flowers floated in, days when
boys, as though by psychic agreement, stoutly refused to work
and hid "Nick Carter" and "Dick Merriwell" behind their
geometries . . . Laura Jean Libby. Laura the incomparable,
the delightful . . . Laura who never failed to deliver the lov-
ing couple into each other's arms, while bells banged the nup-
tials and friends wept into their handkerchiefs . . . She once
said she never had any trouble writing; no halting or doubt,
no tramping the floor at midnight to capture an elusive concept, no temperamental fits, starts, or sulks, no waiting for inspiration. She always knew where she was going; right always
conquered might, wrong, or what-not, and right was always
perfectly easy to perceive. Well, all honor to her. Her works
may not be great literature, but they were in key with youth.
Editorial obituary of nineteenth-century
America's most prolific novelist*

THE new century opened on a theme of optimism. The country had emerged from one of the most severe depressions of its
history, a calamity which had put fight into the hearts of the
nation's industrial and farm operatives, and frightened the
devil out of many of the comfortable classes. The country now
appeared reunited. It had stood on its hind legs, peered out
beyond its coastal borders, flexed its muscles and won a
"splendid little war" with a grand old power of the Old World.
The imperialist fervor had helped to weld "the North" to
"the South" once more: as compared with the cruel Spaniard,
the hapless Cuban, and the petulant Filipino, we were all
Americans. Most respectable Americans had pretty well agreed
by this time that the Negro *was* inferior — "Of course I recog-

* Quoted in Mark Sullivan, *Our Times: The Turn of the Century, 1900–
1904,* I (New York, 1926), 213.

nize the supremacy of the Caucasian race," declared Massachusetts Congressman Fred Gillett, "I suppose everybody does" [1] — there was no point in restoring the mistakes of the Reconstruction era. Anyway, prices were rising,[2] American goods had invaded foreign markets on a large scale, and investment opportunities were bullish. "Material prosperity," intoned Bishop William Lawrence of Massachusetts, "is helping to make the national character sweeter, more joyous, more unselfish, more Christlike." [3]

However exuberant, few Americans could escape the profound changes that the new America had undergone during the previous twenty years or so. Small town, private shop, white Protestant America was on the way out. Between 1890 and 1910, urban population increased nearly 20,000,000, or almost 100 per cent. The number of cities with 100,000 or more people jumped from 28 to 50; the number with 25,000 to 50,000 doubled; and 265 communities qualified for the first time as "urban" in the 5,000 to 10,000 group.[4] The depression had cut in half the rate of foreign immigration during the nineties, reaching a low of 230,000 during 1898; but from that point it rose steadily until 1907 when it hit the all-time peak of 1,285,000. After 1890, moreover, for the first time none of the three leading sources of immigration was an English-speaking country.

The full development of the nation's industrial system had by this time made the United States one great market area. Modern transportation and communications challenged provincial monopolies by bringing rugged price competition to local businesses. Old shibboleths about "private enterprise" and "free competition" became irrelevant, as businessmen joined together to thwart "destructive competition" and invest-

[1] *Congressional Record*, 58 Cong., 2 Sess., March 30, 1904, p. 3995.

[2] The general price index rose 42 per cent in fifteen years of economic recovery.

[3] Bishop William Lawrence, "The Relation of Wealth to Morals," *World's Work*, 1:287 (January 1901).

[4] United States Department of Commerce, *Historical Statistics of the United States, 1789–1945* (Washington, 1949), p. 29.

ment bankers wove a web of control over the major enterprises of the nation. As the consolidation movement crept in upon local vested interests — retailers, teamsters, bankers, merchants — and absorbed the local financial institutions, traction companies, and gas and electric utilities, more and more conservative businessmen came to discern the behemoth they had previously considered the hallucination of radicals.

Economic recovery ended the sensational and potentially dangerous marching armies of unemployed. But bitter conflicts recalling Homestead, Coeur d'Alene, and Cripple Creek continued, alerting American society to deep-lying class antagonisms. The class-conscious civic leaders, moreover, would have to find a way to deal with labor groups without calling in the Pinkertons; for in the half dozen years following recovery, strikes for the purpose of obtaining union recognition rose 600 per cent. By 1903, 89 per cent more workers than in 1897 (788,000 all told) participated in such strikes; and by 1911, American union membership had increased five times over membership in 1897.[5] American socialists, moreover, had begun to untangle themselves from their internecine feuds, most of them uniting behind Eugene V. Debs. Though no threat to the major parties, the Socialist Democratic party in 1900 more than doubled the total socialist vote for 1896.

Few sections and only a minority of the population remained remote from America's social problems. The crowding cities and towns, often jammed with the New Immigrants, touched sensitive spots in the morally alert. The evils they faced and could not escape perhaps were not new, but the discovery that they were evils perhaps was. Publicists and reformers enjoyed a public more responsive to exposé and to proposals for directed change than at any time in more than a generation. As one contemporary observed, they "spoke to a public willing to recognize as corrupt an incredibly varied assortment of conventional acts."[6]

[5] *Ibid.*, pp. 72–73.
[6] Walter Lippmann, *Drift and Mastery: An Attempt to Diagnose the Current Unrest* (New York, 1914), p. 5.

For the local descendants of the *Mayflower* landing party, meanwhile, the facts of modern life showed up more starkly than for the rest of the country. As early as 1880, the foreign-born and native-born of foreign parents together had constituted half the Massachusetts population. By 1890, they had amounted to 56.3 per cent, or 1,260,000 of a total population of 2,240,000, and the proportion rose to 61.9 per cent, or 1,740,000, of a population of 2,800,000 at the close of the century. At that time, more than 840,000 or 30 per cent were foreign-born, of whom more than one third did not speak English. The ratio continued to rise during the next decade.[7]

Most of this population crowded into thirty-three incorporated cities, twenty-five of which had 25,000 people or more. The Bay State had been predominantly urban since before the Civil War. In the last two decades of the old century, the industrial centers absorbed newcomers at a rate more than double the national rate. Despite the depression of the nineties, the population of Haverhill (for example) increased 35.6 per cent in the decade; that of Worcester, Lawrence, Springfield, and Fall River grew about 40 per cent; that of Fitchburg, 43 per cent; of Brockton, 47 per cent; and of New Bedford, 53.3 per cent. In almost all these cities, the major increase was in non-English-speaking, non-Protestant foreign-born.[8]

Massachusetts had never had a real labor movement, but nearly every city, town, and industry had its independent trade unions, often loosely federated in city or town central labor unions. The Knights of Labor still had some influence, especially in Essex County, but most of the formal unions followed

[7] Thirteenth Census of the United States, 1910, Volume II, Population, Reports by States (Washington: Government Printing Office, 1913), pp. 876 and 877. Twelfth U.S. Census, 1900, Population, I (Washington: United States Census Office, 1901), pp. xcix, ciii, clxxxii, and clxxxvi. By 1910, the non-English-speaking foreign-born, who by that time had passed the million mark, outnumbered the English-speaking foreign-born. The foreign-born and the children of the foreign-born by that time amounted to 66 per cent of Massachusetts' population.

[8] U. S. Bureau of the Census, *Thirteenth Census of the United States; 1910 Statistics on the States, Massachusetts* (Washington, 1910), pp. 595–599.

the traditional craft lines. Immigrants generally remained out-side the union organizations, but they formed associations along ethnic lines which performed the same essential func-tions during labor crises. From 1880 to 1900 the state suffered an annual average of ninety-seven such crises, which involved about 38,800 workers per year. It ranked third in the country in that respect, behind only the more populous New York and Pennsylvania.[9]

Meanwhile, the Bay State gave the new Socialist Demo-cratic party its most outstanding successes in the nation. In 1898, James F. Carey of Haverhill became the first Socialist to serve in a state legislature. He was elected three times and was soon joined in the legislature by two Socialist colleagues. The Socialists also won and held mayoralties, even against coalition candidates, in both Haverhill and Brockton, and they took several city council seats in Lynn and Newburyport. On the surface these developments appeared to hold portentous significance for the stability of the Old Yankee Common-wealth.

But beneath the surface the country's industrial transforma-tion constituted the more serious challenge to the traditional Massachusetts polity during the Progressive Era. That trans-formation underlay the labor agitation and the Socialist suc-cesses. It also helped inspire the mass immigration which so severely tested Yankee culture. Still more important, at least for the early years of the new century, it placed in jeopardy the continued prosperity of the Bay State's principal industries, and forced upon the Commonwealth a reappraisal of the con-trols it had placed upon its own business community.

Despite these developments, Massachusetts politics in 1900 presented a placid picture. The Republican party remained confidently in power. Massive European immigration had not stopped the Bay State from sending a Cabot Lodge and a

[9] MBSL, "Strikes and Lockouts in Massachusetts for Twenty Years," *Labor Bulletin*, No. 25 (Boston, February 1903), pp. 40–49.

Frisbie Hoar to the United States Senate, even as it had sent Yankee stalwarts like Daniel Webster and Charles Sumner in the past. "It is doubtful," exulted the Republican-appointed chief of the Bureau of Statistics, "whether any country or State in the world could absorb so many diverse nationalities and yet retain so fully old-time ideas and customs." [10] Through two decades of industrial, social, and ethnographic change, the Republicans had yielded the governorship only four times and had not once lost secure control of the General Court. As the new century opened, there seemed little prospect that the party would face a severe political test in the immediate future.

I

Except for a small and dwindling faction of anti-imperialists, led by aging Senator George Frisbie Hoar of Worcester and Congressman Samuel W. McCall of Cambridge, the Republican party was a well-integrated organization accustomed to power and generally in agreement upon basic principles. Specifically it represented protectionism and "sound" money based on gold. Beyond that, in Massachusetts at least, it represented a long tradition of conservatism of a type not to be identified specifically with industry or commerce.

The Grand Old Party in Massachusetts drew its leadership largely from the so-called Brahmin set, a self-conscious class of colonial descent which possessed "a carefully nurtured sense of superiority and responsibility." [11] It traced its political philosophy to the Presidents John and John Quincy Adams and to Alexander Hamilton, and before them to Thomas Hutchinson and John Winthrop. Thus, Republicans tended to distrust basic human instincts, to deny the theory of a natural social harmony, to regard the state as a necessary (even divinely ordained) instrument for the ordering of society, and to favor government of the majority by a specialized, responsible mi-

---

[10] MBSL, "Race in Industry," *34th Annual Report* (Boston, 1904), p. 130.
[11] Duane Lockard, *New England State Politics* (Princeton, 1959), p. 119.

nority. For Republicans, the function of government was to govern, that is, to control; though government was a necessity it was not also perforce an evil, nor was its aggrandizement fearsome. Although many of the founders of the G.O.P. had expounded the theory of the "Higher Law," Republicans more usually gave emphasis to the supremacy of man's law, upon which society, albeit not the Universe, was founded. They valued personal liberty but emphasized its dependence upon law, regarded private property as its cornerstone, and the preservation of private property as a principal objective of law. Finally, they were nationalists, in the fashion of Hamilton, Quincy Adams, and the Grand Army of the Republic: they tended to think primarily as citizens of continental America, believed in the nation's manifest destiny, and asserted with more conviction than rhetoric that if one were not a Republican his patriotism and general good faith were, at the least, open to inquiry.

The character of Massachusetts Republicanism is perhaps best illustrated by the party's outstanding figure, Henry Cabot Lodge of Nahant. Descended from what he liked to regard as old gentility, like many of the class he identified with, Lodge chose public service as a vocation. Unlike many of that class, Lodge found it impractical to distinguish closely between public service and politics. He began his career as a reformer, and almost at the outset found it necessary to bolt his party: he voted for Tilden in 1876 because his choice for President, Benjamin Bristow, lost the nomination to Hayes. But when the crucial test came in 1884, his ambition to enter Congress and his responsibilities as chairman of the Republican State Committee determined his loyalty to the Republican standard, despite James G. Blaine and the Mulligan letters. Blaine carried Massachusetts that year, while Cabot Lodge lost not only his Congressional campaign but also the respect of his friends in the Massachusetts Reform Club.

The "Mugwump Campaign" of 1884 wrought great changes in Lodge. Where he had once viewed "character" and "the man" as the primary consideration in political campaigns, he now discovered that in politics men are subordinate to "principle." [12] Even before the Blaine episode he had decided, as he put it, "to make my fight inside the party because I can do more there than by going outside . . . I shall count for more in this way than in any other." [13] Rejection by his Mugwump friends drove him into the position of a party stalwart. He came to identify responsible government with party government. He adopted, moreover, an undying enmity toward "reformers."

When he finally reached Washington, he discovered that to achieve what he considered the objects of the "larger principles" required much acquiescence in dubious practices, and much cooperation with scoundrels. If he could ever have confronted his position entirely candidly he might have been spared both the pain of being cut by the reformers of his own social set and the label of "hypocrite" which sophisticated opposing politicians bestowed upon him. However well he learned to maneuver in rough political terrain, he pretended — in fact, convinced himself — that he never need do anything "vulgar." [14]

[12] John A. Garraty, *Henry Cabot Lodge: A Biography* (New York, 1953), p. 79.

[13] To Anna Lodge, April 18, 1880; quoted in Garraty, p. 76.

[14] Early during one senatorial term, Lodge asked his son-in-law, Augustus Peabody Gardner, whether a certain ambitious member of the General Court could be relied on to support him for re-election three years later if the same man were still in the legislature. Gardner blurted, "If you are ready to assist Shaw in nailing down the Presidency [of the Massachusetts Senate] and will let me hear from you to that effect, I shall be in a position to accomplish something." Lodge indignantly huffed, "I have never made a bargain with a man for his support, and I am not willing to begin." Lodge to Gardner, October 8, 1908, Gardner to Lodge, October 9, 1908, Lodge to Gardner, October 12, 1908 (Lodge MSS).

Although he leaned heavily upon Gardner in political campaigns — Lodge insisted sincerely that he owed more to his son-in-law than Gardner owed to him — he never could quite avow approval of his more forthright kinsman's methods. "You and he are . . . poles apart," Sturgis Bigelow assured him, "you standing for honesty in politics while he stands for corruption, and boasts of superior honesty because he avows it." W. Sturgis Bigelow to Lodge, May 4, 1912 (Lodge MSS). Actually, Lodge of course made many "bargains" during his career. He simply refused to call them that because they were not often explicit — just understandings among gentlemen.

Known as "the scholar in politics," Lodge savored the role quite as much as the deference he expected as a Brahmin. He had inherited a class pride, and though he followed a profession which demanded widespread loyalties, it was respect rather than popularity that he cherished. Beneath his mustache and neatly trimmed beard the corners of his mouth drooped sharply, suggesting a congenital hauteur which his manner of speaking reinforced. A reporter for the *Washington Post* once wrote that he had missed his calling when he became a politician instead of a clergyman: "There is always a reminiscence of burning incense, surpliced choirs, and of dimly lighted chancels when Senator Lodge gets up to speak." [15]

Lodge's break from an important segment of his social set in 1884 actually had deeper roots than his reluctant support of Blaine and his partisan regularity. Though, in common with many of the Mugwumps, his family fortune derived from mercantile activities, Lodge committed himself in theory and practice to the modern sources of wealth. "The true and lasting source of wealth," he said in 1894, "is production." [16] Correspondingly, he appears to have invested much of his wealth in copper mines, electric companies, railroads, and other modern industrial enterprises.[17]

He appears to have shared with the Mugwumps a distrust of the men who had made their wealth from the newer sources, but he rarely showed this attitude except when he was personally or politically affected. He fumed, for example, when businessmen opposed imperial expansion ("the vast, utterly selfish money interests represented by a few men are perilous guides"),[18] or when they gave financial aid to a rival politician

[15] Quoted in Festus P. Summers, *William L. Wilson and Tariff Reform* (New Brunswick, 1953), p. 86, where "surpliced" is given as "surplical."

[16] Quoted in William R. Allen, "Issues in Congressional Tariff Debates, 1890–1930," *Southern Journal of Economics*, 20:346 (April 1954).

[17] Karl Schriftgiesser, *The Gentleman from Massachusetts: Henry Cabot Lodge* (Boston, 1944), pp. 218n–219n. Schriftgiesser cites the *Boston Evening Transcript*, June 4, 1925.

[18] To President McKinley, quoted in Garraty, p. 187. Cf. "The old merchants of New England, from whom you and I are descended, would be pressing Congress to take vigorous action instead of trembling with fear

("A large number of 'businessmen' seem to be for him as he has made several — ten or more — millions in speculation in stocks. I sometimes think that 'the business man in politics' is too often one who has no business there").[19] Basically, Lodge defined class by wealth, not by social origins or sources of wealth, and in almost every contest between corporate wealth and civic reformers his trust in the former was more apparent than concealed.

Nevertheless — and perhaps paradoxically — Lodge differed sharply with the sentiments of both Mugwumps and industrialists on the legitimate function of the government as a regulator of the economy. He earned the Mugwumps' antagonism by his strong protectionist views. At the same time, where most protectionists in the business community appeared oblivious to the inconsistency in their demand for import duties and their pious pronouncements for *laissez faire* in all other respects,[20] Lodge took a more nearly Hamiltonian position. Protectionism was justifiable, he argued, because the government had an obligation to maintain a healthy manufacturing economy by actively excluding cheap goods. But it must also intervene in other ways — by restricting immigration, for example — to protect a particular standard of civilization, even if this made it more difficult for manufacturers to obtain cheap labor.[21] His ardor for a powerful and glorious nation, and consequently a strong navy, similarly antagonized both Mugwumps and businessmen, whose primary concern was with government economy. Finally, as we have noted, he refused to accept a divorcement of government responsibility from the activity of

---

lest we should do anything, as the present money power does" (Lodge to Thomas Wentworth Higginson, March 25, 1896, T. W. Higginson Papers, Houghton Library, Harvard University).

[19] To Roosevelt, September 25, 1902, *Correspondence*, I, 544.

[20] See Sidney Fine, *Laissez Faire and the General-Welfare State* (Ann Arbor, 1956), esp. chap. iv.

[21] Probably for political reasons, Lodge always carefully excluded the Irish from his public statements on immigration, and usually temporized on the French Canadians and Italians as well. See Edward N. Saveth, *American Historians and European Immigrants* (New York, 1948), pp. 57–58.

its creations, the corporations. He denied that "enlightened self-interest" ever adequately regulated economic intercourse: "If we could rely on enlightened self-interest, we should need very little law indeed. But . . . in the first place, men do not understand very well their real interest, and they are not enlightened about it very frequently when they think they understand it." [22] If Lodge often resisted particular proposed forms of government action, he always made it clear that it was a matter of policy, not principle.[23]

As a United States senator, Lodge exercised the usual control over federal appointments of persons from and in his home state, and on that basis alone he was able, when he chose, to exert considerable influence upon party policy in Massachusetts. Theodore Roosevelt's accession to the Presidency tended to strengthen Lodge's position in both state and national politics, though he was no Mark Hanna, as some of his contemporaries pretended to believe.[24] In addition, Lodge's unquestionable abilities inspired great admiration among the party faithful and naturally served to enhance his influence. ("What you say will go," wrote Boston Collector George H. Lyman in 1900. "Not only because it is pretty certain to be right, but because people have a way of thinking you are right, whether you are or not.")[25] Lodge's own conviction of his rightness made him intolerant toward opponents, and a venomous loser. His opinions of his opponents conspicuously lacked the tem-

[22] *Congressional Record,* 59 Cong., 1 Sess., June 12, 1906, p. 8323.
[23] "I have assumed," he declared in 1906 while opposing major features of the Hepburn railroad bill, "that railroads entered interstate commerce solely on the conditions and by permission of the Government of the United States. I have assumed that we could prohibit their engaging in interstate commerce if they violated the provisions that we laid down." "It is idle to say," he urged later in the same debate, "that we are unable to deal with [ownership by railroads of non-railroad business and properties] . . . or to stop it. If we are to be paralyzed in dealing with such an evil as this, then the interstate commerce clause in the Constitution is utterly vain." *Congressional Record,* 59 Cong., 1 Sess., May 7 and 8, 1906, pp. 6460 and 6509.
[24] See William E. Chandler, ex-Senator from New Hampshire, to Lodge, January 6, 1902 (Lodge MSS).
[25] Lyman to Lodge, February 12, 1900 (Lodge MSS).

perateness which might be expected from someone of his genteel pretensions. This personality trait led his critics to regard him as something of a tyrant. After the turn of the century, as the reformed press made "the boss" a symbol for what was wrong with democratic processes, the popular belief that Lodge "dominated" the Republican "machine" became a central issue in interparty and intraparty politics.

Nevertheless, even the strenuously anti-Lodge *Boston Herald* acknowledged in 1902: "Massachusetts is not a boss-ridden commonwealth, as certain other states notoriously are . . . Senator Lodge is very far from being able to do as he pleases." [26] Lodge's friends were sometimes painfully aware of that fact. On one occasion when Lodge strove to defeat the anti-imperialist forces within the G.O.P., his confidant, George Lyman, advised him: "You of course recognize that our Republicans are not like those in New York or Pennsylvania, and that they will stand no acknowledged authority. The only way to get your own way is to do it diplomatically." [27] During the McKinley administration, Lodge's influence over federal appointees was actually severely limited. Although former Massachusetts Governor John D. Long headed the United States Navy Department and thereby controlled the important patronage of the Charlestown Navy Yard, Lodge and Long had never been great friends. In 1900, Lodge complained sharply to Long that he could not place his followers in the Navy Yard and that more Democrats were benefiting from the Yard than Republicans.[28] In addition, during both the McKinley and Roosevelt administrations the Surveyor of the Port of Boston,

---

[26] *Boston Herald,* August 14, 1902. The statement was prompted by an editorial in the *Providence Journal* commending Massachusetts for its lack of a boss.

[27] Lyman to Lodge, March 20, 1900 (Lodge MSS).

[28] Lodge's original letter is unavailable, but see Long's trenchant reply, September 22, 1900 (Lodge MSS). Lodge's hostility to Long probably originated in Long's tepid view of America's imperialist ventures. When Theodore Roosevelt became President, Long was eased out of the Navy Department in favor of Congressman William Moody — a promotion which made room in the 6th Massachusetts congressional district for Lodge's son-in-law, Augustus P. Gardner.

who controlled considerable local patronage, was not only not Lodge's appointee but frequently used his influence to thwart Lodge's will; in 1899, for example, he helped defeat Lodge's candidate for the Republican nomination for lieutenant governor, Curtis Guild, Jr.[29]

In spite of gaining a friend in the White House after 1901, Lodge's influence in Massachusetts politics improved only a little. The reason for that was Winthrop Murray Crane: if anyone was a "boss" in Massachusetts, it was he. Throughout Crane's governorship (1900–1902) Lodge found it difficult to secure state appointments for his followers, as Crane chose an independent course.[30] In 1900, Crane refused to help Lodge gain the chairmanship of the Republican National Convention, leading Lodge to write Crane a letter which barely concealed his resentment. "I had always supposed," he wrote, "that you had a large control in the western part of Massachusetts, but I see now that it is passing into other hands . . . Perhaps by appealing to the rest of the state I may yet be able to secure the Chairmanship." [31] By the end of 1901, Lodge's bitterness began to show openly. "I called upon Senator Lodge," Congressman George P. Lawrence confided to Crane, ". . . and find he is a greatly changed man. He informed me that he knew who was boss in Massachusetts; that the only way he amounted to anything there was to find out what you wanted, and then hurry to express similar views." [32] Lodge's correspondence during the Progressive Era reveals that the Senator was forced to adjust himself more and more often to Murray Crane's positions.

[29] See Surveyor Jeremiah J. McCarthy to Lodge, January 28, 1901, Curtis Guild, Jr., to Lodge, March 16, 1901, and George Lyman–Henry Cabot Lodge correspondence for 1900 (Lodge MSS).

[30] See, e.g., Crane to Lodge, March 27, 1900 (Lodge MSS).

[31] Lodge to Crane, May 17, 1900 (Crane MSS).

[32] Lawrence to Crane, December 5, 1901 (Crane MSS). Lodge knew he could not do without Crane and consequently did not break openly with him. He frequently leaned upon Crane for political support and advice, as well as for advice on some business matters. I do not wish to make out a case for Crane as a "boss"; I merely wish to point out here the limitations on Lodge's power.

A frail, balding, jug-eared Yankee from Berkshire County in western Massachusetts, Murray Crane resembled Lodge in his political conservatism, party fealty, substantial wealth, and colonial heritage;[33] but he was Lodge's opposite in many striking ways. Crane never studied beyond high school, his family believing that formal education spoiled one's business sense. According to his biographer, "He was not bookish in his tastes, and there is nothing to indicate that he was outstanding in scholarship." [34] Cabot Lodge's influence hinged considerably upon his genealogical, intellectual, and oratorical luster, but Crane showed none of these qualities, and in fact, his taciturnity even exceeded that of his later protégé, Calvin Coolidge. As one contemporary wit cracked, "He never writes if he can talk, and he never talks if he can nod." [35] Many of his few surviving letters conclude with the sentence, "But I'll talk to you about it when I see you."

Nevertheless, Murray Crane was the most powerful single politician in Massachusetts for about twenty years. Nine of these years he was United States senator. "He was one of the wonders of the Senate," wrote Chauncey Depew in his memoirs; "he never made a speech. I do not remember that he made a motion. Yet he was the most influential member of that body." [36] Few people could fathom what made this small, odd-looking man so influential. Coolidge remarked, "His influence was very great, but it was of an intangible nature." [37]

[33] The first member of the Crane family to come to the new world was Henry Crane, who arrived in Dorchester in 1654. Following the War for Independence, the Cranes moved westward, settling in Dalton, where Zenas Crane, Murray's grandfather, founded the first of the family's paper mills in 1801. W. Murray Crane was born fifty-two years later. Though a Berkshire man, Crane nevertheless could claim Brahmin heritage through his maternal grandmother, who was descended from Charles Chauncey, second president of Harvard.

[34] Solomon B. Griffin, *W. Murray Crane, A Man and Brother* (Boston, 1926), p. 14.

[35] I am indebted to William V. Shannon, Washington correspondent of the *New York Post,* for the story.

[36] Chauncey Depew, *My Memories of Eighty Years* (New York, 1922), p. 183.

[37] From the foreword to Griffin, *Crane.*

Men of all kinds solicited his advice on matters ranging from personal or family affairs to business and political problems of the greatest moment. His inclination always was to moderate and smooth over conflicts, for which his enemies dubbed him "pussyfoot." [38] Often his response to a query detailed at great length was simply, "Do nothing." [39]

Perhaps the wellsprings of his influence were his restive energy, his attention to the personal characteristics of his associates, his frequently demonstrated personal kindliness, his great wealth, and, above all, his earned reputation as a sound and sharp businessman. Crane early showed his business acumen by capturing for the family mill the contract to manufacture the silk-thread paper for United States note currency. The family still has that monopoly. Soon afterward he married, and he appeared ready to settle down in the family manner in the Berkshires and devote himself to the paper business. But in four years his bride was dead, leaving him in search of some fulfilling activity.[40] He channeled his energy into business affairs, helping to expand the family business by 1890 into five mills, four in Dalton and one in Westfield. It was not in the paper business, however, that Crane made his fortune. Leaving the mills to his brother and cousin, Crane busied himself with the booming new enterprises of his time, especially the Otis Elevator Company and the American Telephone and Telegraph Company.[41]

As a man of wealth, and a member of a family employing an important part of the local population, Crane perforce par-

[38] I am indebted in part to John M. Blum and Claude M. Feuss for this information. According to Professor Blum, Theodore Roosevelt is credited with originating the epithet. The expression appears in at least one letter referring to Crane, that of W. Sturgis Bigelow to Lodge, December 15, 1916 (Lodge MSS).

[39] The Crane letters in the small collection in family hands appear to have survived because, among other reasons, the family wished to record the frequent requests made of him for advice. Among those letters, "Do nothing" and "I told so-and-so to do nothing" appear frequently. See, e.g., Crane to Lodge, November 26, 1903, to Calvin Coolidge, August 28, 1917. and to W. H. Taft, July 11, 1918 (Crane MSS).

[40] Griffin, *Crane,* p. 39.

[41] *Ibid.,* pp. 27–28; interview with W. Murray Crane, Jr., in August 1958.

ticipated in local public affairs. (In the past, three generations of Zenas Cranes, from his grandfather to his older brother, had served two years each on the Governor's Council.) He engaged extensively in private philanthropies, and there are many accounts of his aiding needy local citizens. When he entered state politics, he sometimes extended the same kind of aid to associates of all political shades.[42]

Crane's first taste of state politics occurred in 1892 when he went to Minneapolis as a delegate-at-large to the Republican National Convention. The Republican party in the state was currently undergoing one of those periodical adjustments in which the younger elements in the party sought to capture the positions of power preempted by the "Old Guard." Crane represented part of the "Young Republican" movement, though he served more in the rank and file than as a leader. In January the year before, Roger Wolcott, an 1884 Mugwump, Elihu B. Hayes, Cabot Lodge's campaign manager and political mentor, Boston reformer Edwin U. Curtis, and Curtis Guild, Jr., had organized the Young Men's Republican Club (later "Republican Club"), with Wolcott as president. The ostensible purpose of the Club was to counter the Democratic organization of a corresponding name which in 1890 had led the first successful gubernatorial campaign for the party in nearly a decade. But the Club was also to serve as a lever by which its members might gain control of the G.O.P., with Cabot Lodge as leader.[43]

That spring, "Old Guard" leader William W. Crapo of New

[42] Among his beneficiaries were such unlikely individuals as James Michael Curley and George Fred Williams. See Joseph F. Dineen, *The Purple Shamrock* (Boston, 1949), p. 90 — the late Mr. Curley verified the account for me in a personal interview in 1957; and Williams to Crane, January 24, 1902 (Crane MSS). Years later ex-Congressman Charles G. Washburn wrote to Crane's biographer: "You do not mention one very potent cause of his influence. He had more people under legitimate obligation to him than any man who had ever lived in Massachusetts." Washburn to Solomon B. Griffin, May 23, 1923 (C. G. Washburn MSS).

[43] Michael Hennessy, *Twenty-five Years of Massachusetts Politics* (Boston, 1917), pp. 15–16; Garraty, pp. 92, 95, 129–131.

Bedford was defeated for the Republican nomination for governor by the faction led by Lodge, Guild, George Meyer, and Eben S. Draper.[44] The Republican Club candidate lost the election to the popular "boy-governor," William E. Russell, but the Young Republican movement gained momentum.

At the Minneapolis convention, when Crapo resigned from his seat on the National Committee, Curtis and other Boston Republicans pushed Crane successfully to replace him,[45] probably because Crane was a wealthy, safe-and-sound businessman and the position was primarily a money-raising one. In

[44] Most of these men continued as leaders of the Republican party throughout the Progressive Era. It may be useful to sketch their careers at this point.

Edwin Upton Curtis (1861–1922) of Boston; lawyer; son of a lumber merchant; *not* related to George W. Curtis, the great civil service reformer; Bowdoin, A.B., 1882, A.M., 1885; entered municipal politics 1888; mayor 1894; Assistant U. S. Treasurer at Boston, 1906–1909; Collector of the Port of Boston, 1909–1913; Boston Police Commissioner (December 1918–1922) during the police strike which called national attention to Calvin Coolidge.

Curtis Guild, Jr. (1860–1915) of Boston; descended from John Guild (1676); son of the then well-known author-journalist; Harvard valedictorian, 1881, when he urged his classmates to imitate the English not only in dress and manner but in patriotic leadership as well — see Barbara Solomon, *Immigrants and Ancestors* (Cambridge, 1956), p. 98; appointed Brigadier General on the staff of Governor Wolcott, 1897; became sole owner and editor of the *Boston Commercial Bulletin* in 1902; president of the Republican Club, 1901–1902; Lieutenant-Governor, 1903–1905; Governor, 1906–1908; Ambassador to Russia, 1911–1913.

George von Lengerke Meyer (1858–1918) of Boston; wealthy investment banker, of a banking family; grandson of Germans prominent in finance and politics; owed his political prominence to his money and his fund-raising abilities, and to his socially successful wife; member Massachusetts House of Representatives, 1892–1896; Speaker, 1894–1896; Ambassador to Italy, 1900–1904, to Russia, 1904–1906; Secretary of the Navy, 1906–1909; Postmaster General, 1909–1913.

Eben S. Draper (1858–1914) of Hopedale; descended from James Draper (1648); manufacturer of cottons and cotton manufacturing machinery; younger brother of Gen. William F. Draper, extreme protectionist and sometime president of the Home Market Club and the American Protective Tariff League; an active Unitarian; member Republican State Committee, 1892, chairman, 1893–1895; Lodge's lieutenant in the fight for a gold plank at the Republican National Convention of 1896; president, Republican Club, 1903–1905; Lieutenant-Governor, 1906–1908; Governor, 1909–1910; married daughter of Benjamin Bristow.

[45] Griffin, *Crane,* p. 56.

addition, he held no controversial views, had no important
enemies, and was from "good family" background. In a word,
he was of the stuff of which governors are made.

Again the Republicans met defeat at the polls, Russell winning a third term, and Grover Cleveland ousting the Republicans from the White House (though Massachusetts gave
Harrison a plurality of 26,000). But as usual, the Republicans
captured the state legislature, which that winter had the task
of selecting a United States senator. The Young Republicans
demonstrated their strength to the faithful in the General Court
by electing Draper chairman of the state committee, so that
Cabot Lodge had clear sailing to his coveted prize. At the last
moment the Crapo forces, led by young William M. Butler of
New Bedford, made a brief protest, but in vain.[46]

In 1893 the Republicans regained the governorship. The
eastern party reformers put up Albert E. Pillsbury for governor,
but his Mugwump inclinations troubled Lodge's supporters.
Pillsbury bowed out gracefully before the state convention met.
In fact, he made the nominating speech for the winning candidate, a hack politician from Lowell with a poor election record,
but with the virtues of possessing many friends, few enemies,
and the type of oratorical pomposity which enchanted nineteenth-century audiences. The Young Republicans, however,
cooperated sufficiently with the Boston reform element to win
renomination for Lieutenant Governor Wolcott. "Billy" Russell's retirement and the Panic clinched the election for the
Republicans that year.

Biding his time, Crane secured himself within the party. In
characteristic fashion, he played on neither side of the intra-

[46] Garraty, pp. 131–132.
   William Morgan Butler (1861–1937); son of a Methodist minister; served
in the lower house of the General Court, 1890–1891, in the Senate, 1892–
1895, President of the Senate, 1894–1895; left the General Court to become
one of the leading lobbyists on Beacon Hill, and unofficial "lieutenant" of
Murray Crane in the eastern part of the State; re-entered public life when
Governor Channing Cox appointed him to fill the United States seat left
vacant by Cabot Lodge's death in 1924; became spokesman for President
Coolidge, and chairman of the Republican National Committee in 1924.

party fence. When he won the nomination for lieutenant governor in 1896 (with the understanding that he would move up to the gubernatorial nomination in 1898 or 1899), he had the support of the Lodge men, the Boston reform group represented by Curtis, and Crapo's protégé, William M. Butler (who in fact had become one of Crane's "inner circle"). Crane's "independence" of the intraparty factions made him the ideal candidate for the party which stressed *harmony* so strongly.

Meanwhile, the divisive "Silver" campaign of 1896 and the prosperity which followed the Republican triumph all but destroyed the Democratic party and assured Crane of an easy ride up the escalator in 1899. Crane won the governorship with 56 per cent of the state vote, and he took 59 per cent in 1900. These victories were not as overwhelming as Wolcott's had been, but they were still greater than any Republican ever received thereafter. Whether they resulted from Crane's quiet orthodoxy or the Democrats' not-so-quiet disorganization was hard to judge.

II

Since the Civil War, the Democratic party of Massachusetts had never been much more than an occasionally troublesome minority group. The party had had a hard time living down its foot-dragging during the war, especially because the state had taken so prominent a part in both the prewar antislavery crusade and in the actual fighting of the war. In addition, as the party became more and more the political haven of Irish-Americans, for whom the Civil War understandably took second place to their own social and economic struggles, it became decreasingly attractive to the Yankees. Until young William E. Russell won the first of three consecutive gubernatorial victories in 1890, the Democrats had captured the executive chair only twice since the Civil War, and no Democrat had ever won more than once. But even Russell carried no Democrats with him into important state office, and his own winning polls never topped 49 per cent of the total state vote. From that point,

Democratic fortunes plummeted. The panic of 1893 hurt them; the national campaign of 1896 was a positive disaster.

At the close of the old century, the Democrats constituted not a party but an aggregation of political clubs and associations whose influence often extended little further than ward lines. The local regulars, with no central organization to enforce party discipline with the powers of patronage, made whatever arrangements they could to maintain a satisfied following. This led often to rivalry with other Democratic organizations for the "good will" of local Republican organizations. Republican administrations could be persuaded to provide jobs, patronage, and "business opportunities" for particular Democratic leaders in exchange for continued control of the city government and a minimum of partisan obstructionism. It would be no great exaggeration to say that the securing of such political favors was the *raison d'être* of many Democratic ward organizations.

In Holyoke, for example, the Republican city organization found it possible to maintain control of the city in the interest of Yankee business ideals, despite a preponderant immigrant population. This was accomplished largely through a working arrangement with Democratic politicians who owned construction companies, saloons, and liquor stores. Republican politicos even helped to finance new liquor businesses for their Democratic colleagues, and arranged to secure licenses from the liquor commission.[47] Though the city usually gave majorities to Democratic gubernatorial candidates, it almost as regularly returned Republican city administrations.

In Boston, the party stronghold, ward leaders such as Joseph Corbett, James Donovan, John F. Fitzgerald, and Martin M. Lomasney vied for power. (In a few years, James Michael Curley would begin his extraordinary career, moving toward

[47] See Kenneth W. Underwood, *Protestant and Catholic: Religion and Social Interaction in an Industrial Community* (Boston, 1957), pp. 285–288, 292. From 1890 to 1910, the city gave Democratic gubernatorial candidates majorities fourteen times, and also returned Republican city administrations fourteen times, in seven cases in the same year.

his first major successes in his 1910 election to Congress and his mayoralty triumph in 1914.) At the beginning of the new century, Corbett and Donovan appeared temporarily to have the greatest power within the Democratic City Committee, working together with ex-Mayor Josiah Quincy's kitchen cabinet (dubbed the "Board of Strategy"). At the time, however, the Democrats were out of power in the Hub City, largely because Lomasney had thrown his support in 1899 to the Republican mayoralty candidate, Thomas Hart, against the Board of Strategy's candidate, Patrick A. Collins. Using patronage from his Republican ally, Lomasney built an opposition to the official Democratic organization which was sufficiently strong to dominate the City Council and Board of Aldermen. He appeared to be emerging as the leading "boss" of Boston. ("Lomasney," observed the *New York Sun* in September 1899, "must be considered politically, as a far bigger man than the Mayor.")[48] Lomasney's ascendency actually depended upon his ability to arrange alliances from year to year with rival ward bosses, including "Honey Fitz" himself; and during the Progressive Era, Fitzgerald often beat the so-called Mahatma of Ward 8 at his own game. In any case, at the turn of the century the maneuverings of the Boston ward leaders tended to cancel out. Consequently, leadership in the matter of state nominations usually came from beyond the ward districts.[49]

State leadership in the Democratic party devolved principally upon men of Yankee descent, despite the fact that the

[48] Quoted in Leslie G. Ainsley, *Boston Mahatma: Martin Lomasney* (Boston, 1949), p. 81.

[49] This account, as well as subsequent accounts of political alignments and factions in Massachusetts during the era, is based on a day-to-day study of Boston newspapers, especially the *Boston Evening Transcript* and the *Boston Herald*. Also helpful are the clippings from all the Boston newspapers, and most of the important newspapers throughout the state, collected in the Raymond Bridgman, the Charles F. Gettemy, and the Robert M. Washburn scrapbooks, in the State Library, State House, Boston. Both Bridgman and Gettemy were State House reporters. Gettemy later became secretary to Governor Curtis Guild (1906–1909), and the head of the State Bureau of Statistics. Washburn was a newspaperman and a legislator for many years during and after the Progressive Era.

party had come to depend increasingly on the non-Yankee wage-earning classes. That leadership included men like Nathan Matthews, Jr., who could claim as illustrious an ancestry as any Republican; Matthews had remained in the Democracy for the uncomplicated reason that his forebears had been among the party stalwarts since long before the Civil War. The party drew in addition from the old mercantile classes, centered mainly in Boston and organized in various boards of trade which carried into the twentieth century their traditional hostility to protective tariffs and an expensive national government; these classes produced the campaign funds and consequently played a dominating role in the party. Finally, the party attracted many of the highly principled genteel classes — the original Mugwumps — who periodically left the Republican party on particular issues, such as the Blaine nomination or imperialism. Like true rebels they would act through independent clubs, usually *ad hoc* campaign organizations. They often wielded considerable power across ward and town lines. But they found it difficult to cooperate with the "regulars," particularly the Irish-American ward leaders, when the candidates did not precisely fit their specifications.

At the turn of the century, George Fred Williams was the outstanding figure in the party. Born in Dedham, Massachusetts, in 1852, the son of a German stowaway who was adopted by a Cape Cod sea captain, Williams worked as a reporter for the *Boston Globe* before being called to the bar and becoming a successful lawyer. In 1884 he was one of a large group of reform-conscious New Englanders who left the Republican party to vote against James G. Blaine. In 1888 he won election to Congress as a Democrat and served two terms. He gained lasting renown in 1890 and 1891 by leading an investigation of illicit legislative influence by the West End Land Company, a speculative real estate venture headed by Henry M. Whitney. Williams later ran as the Democratic candidate for governor in 1895, 1896, and 1897.

While in Congress, Williams had led the fight among "gold"

Democrats to thwart the silverites in both parties.[50] At the National Convention of 1896 at Chicago, however, Williams converted to Bryan and to silver. His enemies claimed that he did it on the promise of receiving the nomination for Vice-President. From that point, Williams took a consistent Bryanite position on bimetallism, imperialism, labor, and the government's relations with corporations.

Williams carried a sizable portion of the Massachusetts Democracy with him, but many Democrats of Boston and other big industrial cities either would not campaign for Bryan or avowed their opposition. Bryan won the support of less than 106,000 voters in 1896, while McKinley polled 279,000 and carried even Boston by about 18,000. Williams, running for governor on four separate tickets including the Democratic and Populist, trailed Bryan with about 100,000 votes, less than 30 per cent of the total vote for governor.

In 1900 Williams led the Massachusetts Democracy to the National Convention to help nominate Bryan for a second try. He also wrote the state Democratic platform, which, among other things, condemned federal extravagance and imperialist and colonial policies, claimed all Massachusetts labor legislation for the Democrats, and endorsed the initiative and referendum, graduated income and inheritance taxes, and public ownership of public utilities. Bryan fared worse in the nation that year, though in Massachusetts he recaptured 40,000 Democratic votes.[51] He lost badly nevertheless, trailing McKinley 157,000 to 239,000, while the party's gubernatorial candidate, Robert Treat Paine, Jr., trailed the Republican nominee by 100,000 votes.

Without hope of state-wide or national success, Democratic

[50] See Williams to Edward A. Atkinson, February 5 and 27, 1892, Edward A. Atkinson papers, Massachusetts Historical Society, Boston.

[51] Bryan's stand against imperialism won back the support of many Mugwumps who had left the Democrats in 1896 over the currency issue. As one of them put it, no issue was more important than imperialism in 1900; see Mark A. de Wolfe Howe, *Portrait of an Independent: Moorfield Storey* (Boston, 1932), p. 205. In addition, party stalwarts, such as Richard Olney, decided to give the national ticket their support for the sake of unity.

leaders offered Williams little significant opposition. In 1898 he easily ousted the conservative National Committeeman[52] and held the position himself until 1902. Williams' residual power with the state Democrats depended largely on his vibrant personality and progressive political views, but probably also upon the fact that his good standing with the national party organization held promise of the rewards of office should the Democrats make a comeback nationally. In addition, the non-Bryan Democrats could find no suitable issues with which to confront the Republicans. Committed to Cleveland's kind of conservatism, they had no weapon against the McKinley Republicans.

Defeat in 1900 — the first time the Democrats had lost two successive presidential elections since 1880 — discredited and demoralized the Bryan-Williams faction. Charles Francis Adams, Jr., who had joined the Democrats on the imperialism issue, urged the party to jettison all its leaders and start anew.[53] Former Boston Mayor Nathan Matthews, Jr., demanded that the Democrats drop "populism" and adopt "patriotism" and the gold standard as their platform. John R. Thayer, who had won two terms in Congress from the solidly Republican city of Worcester by advocating protectionism and the gold standard, suggested that the Democrats might emphasize economy in government, anti-imperialism, and sound money.[54] The new state chairman, William S. McNary of Boston, expressed the conservatism of both the Irish and the Cleveland Democrats when he urged: "We should bring back to the party that great conservatism [which] . . . is now outside our ranks. We must keep socialistic tendencies out of our party . . ." [55] But Josiah Quincy, once a reform mayor of Boston and former Assistant Secretary of State under Cleveland, probably epitomized the conservative Democrats' attitude. The Democrats in Massachusetts, he believed, suffered mostly from dwelling on sharply

[52] Hennessy, *Twenty-five Years,* p. 81.
[53] *Boston Evening Transcript,* November 9, 1900.
[54] *Ibid.*
[55] *Ibid.,* June 27, 1901.

controversial issues. He urged that they "adopt a policy neither too radical nor too conservative — one of progress but of safety." "Personally," he added, "I sympathize fully with Bryan's position on the Philippine question, but if that is thought too radical, there is still ample basis for an issue with Republican policy . . ." [56] Williams was down, but the conservatives of the party had nothing to offer in his stead.

The Democratic party's ideological and structural weaknesses were not the only reasons for continued Republican dominance in the Bay State. The Republicans enjoyed a long history of responsibility for the administration of the state government. The Democrats by contrast suffered from a reputation of obstructionism, a common liability of a party long out of power. This doubtless reinforced the Republicanism of most old-time Yankees; the Grand Old Party stood for Respectability. The party's long incumbency must have impressed newcomers as well; it was perhaps one reason why heavy immigration failed to alter the G.O.P.'s dominant status. There were, however, two additional circumstances which guaranteed considerable immigrant support for the Yankee-oriented Republican party, despite the generally inhospitable reception which Republicans gave to immigrants.

In the first place, the influential old-stock and Mugwump element in the Democratic party was not beyond suspicion of an antiforeign animus. For example, George W. Anderson, a prominent Democrat and George Fred Williams' law partner, gained a reputation for bigotry while on the Boston School Board by inveighing against "the foreign element" and excessive Roman Catholic influence.[57] Charles Warren, Governor William E. Russell's private secretary, was one of the three founders of the Immigration Restriction League in 1894; and

[56] *Ibid.,* November 9, 1900.
[57] See, e.g., *Boston Evening Transcript,* November 15, 1901; also Democratic Congressman James A. Gallivan to Joseph Tumulty, September 14, 1914 (Wilson MSS). Wilson appointed Anderson United States District Attorney for Massachusetts, and later to the I.C.C. — over the strenuous opposition of many of the Irish-American Democratic leaders.

Robert Treat Paine, Jr., Democratic gubernatorial candidate in 1900 and 1901, was an active member of the League.[58]

In the second place, the Irish — the most powerful single element in the Democratic party — proved at least equally inhospitable to non-Irish immigrant groups. The same ethnic frictions which caused immigrants to establish their churches along nationalist rather than sectarian lines had its counterpart in politics. Geoffrey T. Blodgett, in his study of Democratic politics in Massachusetts in the late nineteenth century, has pointed out that while Irish-Americans resented being excluded from the prestige jobs by the Yankees, in fact the average Irish-American had reason for greater enmity toward other immigrant groups who represented a direct *threat* to him in the job market. No nativist could have expressed hostility toward European immigrants more heatedly than did an 1890 editorial in the *Boston Republic,* then the organ of P. J. Maguire, Boston's leading Irish Democrat at the time.[59]

[The Italians] are the very scourings of the slums of Italy . . . They are a dangerous as well as an undesirable element . . . Hungarians, Poles, and other pauperized nationalities also send in hordes of illiterate laborers who have no notion of permanent settlement and who never intend to become a part of our population. It is from these elements that the republic has reason to fear danger. The wave of socialism, communism, and atheism, which has been sweeping over Europe under the especial direction of Bismarck, Crispi, and others has inoculated this class of immigrants with notions about civil government that are a constant menace to all established forms and to public order.

In Lawrence, Lowell, Taunton, or New Bedford, Republican leaders did not have to exert themselves to persuade those French Canadians who voted at all to vote against the Irish-dominated Democratic city organizations.[60] Similarly, Polish

[58] Cf. Solomon, *Immigrants and Ancestors,* esp. pp. 102–104.

[59] Geoffrey T. Blodgett, "Massachusetts Democrats in the Cleveland Era," unpublished Ph.D. dissertation, Harvard University, 1960, pp. 211–212. See also Oscar Handlin, *The Uprooted* (Boston, 1951), chap. v.

[60] R. R. M. Lower, "The New France in New England," *New England Quarterly,* 2:289–290 (1929). Cf. Constance M. Green, *Holyoke, Massachusetts: A Case History of the Industrial Revolution in America* (New

immigrants strongly resented the seemingly superior attitude of the English-speaking Irish. Though normally disinclined to political activity, the Poles often rallied against Irish domination of local politics; they proved strong allies of the Yankee Republicans.[61] In Worcester, the Protestant Swedes (about 10 per cent of the population) and the Russian Jews (about 9 per cent) also may have found little in common with the Catholic Irish (about 25 per cent), and too often from the stalwart Democratic viewpoint the Democracy was identified with the Irish. Together with the French Canadians these groups helped to keep Worcester strongly and unfailingly in the Republican column, though 67 per cent of Worcester's adult male population in 1900 was of foreign birth, or of foreign or mixed parents. The same could be said of Fall River, where, though only 14 per cent of the adult male population was "older" than second generation, the electorate went Democratic only three times in the eleven years from 1890 to 1900.[62] In brief, because the Irish themselves aroused hostility among other ethnic groups, in many places they were more of a handicap to the Democrats than an asset.

However menacing the immigrants in Massachusetts may have appeared to the natives, and regardless of how hostile the Yankees appeared to immigrants, immigrant groups presented

---

Haven, 1939), p. 114. The best single study of "immigrant politics" in a Massachusetts city is Donald Barnard Cole, "Lawrence, Massachusetts: Immigrant City, 1845–1912," unpublished Ph.D. dissertation, Harvard University, 1956; now published, with less statistical material, as *Immigrant City* (Andover, Mass., 1963). With remarkable perseverance, Mr. Cole follows all the gerrymandering of ward lines in gathering his statistics on voting behavior. He comes up with no surprises, however. The Irish, he finds, were almost unanimously Democrats; the Germans and British were almost equally unanimously Republicans; the French Canadians were equivocal, but a smaller percentage of French Canadians than of any of the other major ethnic groups voted.

[61] Edmund de S. Brunner, *Immigrant Farmers and Their Children* (Garden City, 1929), esp. pp. 236–237.

[62] Based on my own computations from the U. S. Bureau of the Census, *Twelfth Census of the United States, 1900: Population* (Washington, D. C., 1902), Part I, pp. 620, 658–661, Part II, pp. 172–173, 222–225; MBSL, "Immigrant Population," *43rd Annual Report,* esp. pp. 33, 48, 63.

no solid front in politics. In particular, they offered no immediate threat to the Republican party, Yankeedom's special protector. Consequently, as the new century opened, the Grand Old Party remained securely in power in the old Commonwealth.

III

On January 4, 1900, thirty-seven year old Governor Winthrop Murray Crane quietly read his first inaugural address to the newly elected General Court. Characteristically, it was a brief and a conservative message. He warned the General Court against increasing the public debt ("It is time to call a halt"), though he conceded the worthiness of the projects to which state moneys had been applied in the past ("in almost every instance . . . the object is a worthy one"). It was simply that it was time to relax. ("The Commonwealth needs a breathing spell . . . No new work should be authorized.") He concluded by tapping the legislature on the wrist for its interference with the local affairs of cities and towns, and by asking the body to petition Congress for appropriations to widen and deepen Boston Harbor.[63]

Amidst the disquieting transformation of the American national character, Massachusetts appeared to greet the new century in a determined, staid fashion. Even the grumpy Mugwump *Boston Herald* applauded the new governor as one who promised to be "efficient" and "non-partisan." It delighted in the election of the Reform Club's James J. Meyers as Speaker of the House. And generally it predicted "no great struggles" ahead. "We are spared such things," it observed, "by the condition of politics in Massachusetts." [64]

[63] Massachusetts General Court, Senate Document No. 1 (Boston, 1900), pp. 30–32.
[64] *Boston Herald,* January 3, 1900.

CHAPTER THREE

REFORM AND CONSERVATISM
IN A CORPORATE AGE

This country has been developed by a wonderful people, flush with enthusiasm, imagination and speculation bent . . . Stifle that enthusiasm, deaden that imagination and prohibit that speculation by restrictive and cramping conservative law, and you tend to produce a moribund and conservative people and country.

E. H. Harriman*

BEHIND the serene aspect of partisan politics, Massachusetts stirred restively. The broad transformation of American society had opened many opportunities for power and wealth. The government especially had huge rewards to offer to the quick and the clever. Businessmen vied for the rights to serve the growing masses of city-dwellers — to supply them with coal and ice, with gas and electricity, with commuter and freight transportation. Such services would bring great fortunes, and the franchises for them were the gift of the state and municipal legislatures. With so much at stake, conflict was inevitable.

In harmony with developments elsewhere in the country, public-spirited individuals in the Bay State rallied to resist the inevitable maneuvers of self-interested businessmen and legislators. Massachusetts spawned municipal leagues, civic federations, reform clubs, and good government associations to defend "the public interest." Although the state took on an obstructionist role in federal politics during the Progressive Era, it did not lack men of good will to challenge fraud, extortion, and irresponsibility. Their function as "reformers," however, was undermined by the nation's economic transformation, and further complicated by their effort to maintain policies

* Quoted in Arthur M. Schlesinger, *New Viewpoints in American History* (New York, 1922), p. 96.

rooted in an old tradition rather than to create new and better policies. They functioned primarily as guardians or *conservators* of established standards of business and political behavior which men of comparable spirit in places like New Jersey, Wisconsin, and California strove to impose upon their communities. They carried on their struggle amidst a growing feeling within the state that the Commonwealth's advanced position had inflicted burdens upon its economy which appeared to jeopardize its ascendancy in the country. Massachusetts businessmen were haunted by the fact that although industry in the state continued to grow on all fronts (except in the foreign export-import business), it grew considerably more slowly than competing industries in other states.

In Louis Brandeis, Joseph Eastman, and the Public Franchise League, Massachusetts had some of the most effective fighters for progressive standards in the country. They demonstrated their power early in the Progressive Era in a struggle with the Boston Elevated Railway Company, one of the nation's largest traction syndicates. Significantly, they did not contend for *reforms;* they made their fight for the preservation of the traditional view of the Commonwealth's relationship to business and public service corporations.[1] Against the Elevated they succeeded. But their success only temporarily set back the tendency toward a revision or "modernization" of the state-corporation relationship in Massachusetts to bring it into line with that relationship in the rest of the country.

[1] That view held that the state bore the principal responsibility for enforcing the honest management and true valuation of corporate properties; it regarded capital stock as a measure of the owners' interests in a corporate enterprise as well as a guarantee fund for the corporation's creditors; it included in its definition of fraud the issuing of stock dividends, borrowing beyond existing capital stock, and operating a corporation before all the capital had been paid in. By 1900, Massachusetts stood almost alone in this interpretation of its responsibilities. The prevailing "modern" view held that capital stock represented a money-earning commodity which the investor purchased at his own risk; it contended that the state had no obligation to supervise corporate management beyond the general legal protection against fraud; it defined fraud solely as misrepresentation, and fixed the state's duty to be simply to require adequate publicity of corporate activities. See Stimson and Washburn, esp. pp. 21–22.

In the years after the climax of the Elevated battle, the state's business community was made acutely aware of the menace to its prosperity from interests outside the Commonwealth's borders and beyond the reach of its restraints. Out-of-state competitors took significantly greater shares of the boot-and-shoe and the cotton goods markets. Corporate consolidations elsewhere jeopardized the priority Massachusetts had enjoyed in the shipment of fuel, raw materials, and of commodities for export to Europe. As a consequence, while reformers in the country, encouraged by President Theodore Roosevelt, moved to place corporations under at least minimal restraints, Massachusetts began moving in the other direction. It was one of the paradoxes of Massachusetts' position during the Progressive Era.

I

Louis Dembitz Brandeis of Boston was clearly one of the most extraordinary men ever to appear on the American political scene. A corporation lawyer, millionaire, "people's attorney," civic reformer, adviser to a President, and Supreme Court Justice, he was a man of many careers and brilliant achievements. A leading progressive, Brandeis nevertheless contrasted sharply with the historians' model of the "composite progressive." [2] He was a second-generation American, a non-Protestant, and was already entering middle age at the start of the Progressive Era. Yet he virtually personified progressivism in at least one major form.

Although he was born in Louisville of German-Jewish immigrant parents, and had studied in Germany before he received his LL.B. from Harvard and settled in the Hub in 1879, Brandeis shared with "the classes" of his adopted city the traditional tenets of the American faith: that there are certain eternal

[2] See George E. Mowry, *Era of Roosevelt,* chap. v ("The Progressive Profile"), and *The California Progressives* (Berkeley, 1951), chap. iv ("What Manner of Men: The Progressive Mind"), as well as Alfred D. Chandler, Jr., "The Origins of Progressive Leadership," in Elting E. Morison, ed., *The Letters of Theodore Roosevelt* (Cambridge, 1951–1954), VIII, 1462–1465.

moral truths which inhere in the human soul, that men of all classes can agree on and have an interest in upholding these truths, and that America has a mission to cultivate the principles of goodness in all men. Fundamentally, Brandeis represented an advanced variety of the "Mugwump type." [3] Once the Mugwumps had thought character was enough; social conflict emanated, they believed, from dishonesty, irresponsibility, and ignorance. Many of them never became emancipated from this view. Others, like Brandeis, shifted their role from defenders of established moral values to critics of the social order, even while they continued to assume the validity of those values. [4]

Brandeis' social criticism focused on conditions which tended to subvert the established social order. Basically he was a conservative — inclined to preserve rather than to strike out for something new. Like others of his adopted class and city, Brandeis did not like the contemporary transformation of American society. Though he possessed a human sympathy and flexibility of mind which eventually enabled him to respect cultural and class attitudes alien to his own, during the Progressive Era, at least, his belief that there is only one truth convinced him that citizens of the most nearly perfect society must agree on moral principles. He strove to obviate the conflicts which jeopardized what he regarded as the established consensus. [5]

It was consistent that Brandeis did not regard himself as a Jew. His own professional and personal brilliance apparently shielded him from the disabilities which others of his religious origins often suffered. Eventually, social and political snubs, and the "hyphenate" problems arising from the World War, made Brandeis keenly aware of his own Jewishness: "It is the non-Jews who create . . . disabilities [for the Jews] and in

[3] See Richard Hofstadter, *The Age of Reform* (New York, 1956), esp. pp. 139–145, 148–149, 155–163. Cf. Henry F. May, *The End of American Innocence* (New York, 1959), esp. pp. 9, 16, 20, 30, and 52.

[4] Cf. Hofstadter, p. 149.

[5] See May, *End of Innocence*, chaps. iii–iv, esp. pp. 28–30, for a discussion of the "moral consensus" in the Progressive Era.

so doing give definition to the term Jews. These disabilities
. . . do not end with a renunciation of faith, however sincere." [6] But as late as 1905, Brandeis protested: "Habits of
living or of thought which tend to keep alive difference of
origin or to classify men according to their religious beliefs are
inconsistent with the American ideal of brotherhood, and are
disloyal." Whatever their national origins or religious beliefs,
Brandeis suggested, Americans must adjust their habits of living and of thought to the established patterns of American
culture.[7]

Brandeis also showed his essential unity with the orthodox
American mind in his emphasis upon personal initiative. In
the fashion of his time, Brandeis assumed the beneficence of
struggle. Struggle tested excellence, imposed responsibility,
developed character. "The great developer," he said, "is responsibility," and the development of the individual was the
objective of all effort.[8] He devoted his own life to the achievement of self-sufficiency, the essence of personal liberty.

It is no wonder that he opposed collectivist tendencies. They
threatened the very sort of individual freedom which was his
own lifelong objective. His reforming zeal gained much from
his fear that the excesses of the "great captains of industry and
of finance . . . [are] the chief makers of socialism." [9] He
endorsed labor's efforts to organize on the ground that unions
would serve partially to counterbalance the power of the new
business consolidations which threatened American individualism. He noted, however, that unless they too were checked,
unions might subvert the public interest in the same way. He
had a genuine sympathy for workers, and regarded unions as
legitimate weapons to secure for them a fairer share of the
fruits of their labor. But he rejected the closed shop as "op-

[6] Louis D. Brandeis, quoted in Horace M. Kallen, *Zionism and World
Politics* (Garden City, 1921), p. 139.

[7] Speech before the Boston Century Club, November 28, 1905 (Brandeis
MSS).

[8] See Alpheus T. Mason, *Brandeis: A Free Man's Life* (New York, 1946),
pp. 585, 438.

[9] Quoted in *ibid.*, p. 104.

posed to our ideas of liberty," [10] and he urged incorporation of unions in order to subject them to the same responsibilities and restraints as business. "The plea for [sic] trades unions for immunity," he argued, "be it from injunction or from liability for damages, is as fallacious as the plea of the lynchers." [11]

Brandeis came to participate actively in civic and political affairs relatively late in life. He was nominally a Republican until 1884 when he joined in the rebellion against James G. Blaine. But party politics did not interest him much. He did enlist with the Massachusetts Reform Club in the fight for civil service reform, engaged periodically in local reform campaigns, and lent financial aid to investigations of public utility and liquor industry lobbying at the State House. For the most part, however, his corporate law practice monopolized his time and attention as he strove to become a "free man" by earning financial independence.

He was already a millionaire and approaching middle age when he became diverted by problems of labor and management relations. ("I think it was the affair at Homestead which first set me thinking seriously about the labor problems.")[12] He began to see that the prevailing interpretations of law had rigged the American system of justice in favor of the strong and well-to-do. As he later expressed it, able lawyers had allowed themselves to become servants of great corporations and powerful individuals, "instead of holding a position of independence, between the wealthy and the people, prepared to curb the excesses of either . . ." [13] He wondered whether there was justification "for the great inequalities in the distribution of wealth, for the rapid creation of fortunes, more

[10] Quoted in Alpheus T. Mason, *Brandeis: Lawyer and Judge in the Modern State* (Princeton, 1933), p. 59.

[11] "Should Trade Unions Be Incorporated? — Joint Debate Between Gompers and Brandeis," *Boston Post,* December 5, 1902. Together with many socially conscious Bostonians, Brandeis also opposed extending the franchise to women. See Arthur Mann, *Yankee Reformers in an Urban Age* (Cambridge, 1954), p. 211.

[12] Quoted in Mason, *Free Man's Life,* p. 87.

[13] Quoted in Mason, *Lawyer and Judge,* p. 22; see also Mason, *Free Man's Life,* p. 101

mysterious than the deeds of Aladdin's lamp." [14] With such thoughts, Brandeis entered upon a new career as "the people's attorney" to correct social abuses and excesses which jeopardized the traditional American faith in individualism, self-help, and self-government.

In this career, Brandeis achieved remarkable success. Without the aid of a political party, he influenced public policy in matters ranging from savings bank insurance plans to public utility franchise legislation. He did this by perfecting pressure group and propaganda techniques. "Most of the world is in more or less a hypnotic state," he once wrote, "and it is comparatively easy to make people believe anything, particularly right." [15] Brandeis worked to persuade the electorate to evince its will, after he had helped to shape that will. In this way he expected to thwart the influence of money: "Our country is, after all," he pointed out, "not a country of dollars, but of ballots." [16]

Brandeis' most successful instrument for action was the Public Franchise League. Together with several public-spirited businessmen, including Edward Albert Filene, the erratic but well-meaning department store magnate and philanthropist, Brandeis organized the Public Franchise League in 1900 for the purpose of maintaining public control over franchise grants. Despite its grandiose title, the League remained something of a one-man organization. Until 1905, when Joseph B. Eastman became executive secretary, Brandeis virtually *was* the League. Other men, of course, occasionally participated in its deliberations and financing, but unless Brandeis acted, the League was inert.

When Brandeis moved to other scenes, Eastman replaced him as prime mover. Eastman was one of those rare individuals who find meaning in life only through service to others. A bachelor, the son of a minister, and a member of an old Amer-

[14] Quoted in Mason, *Free Man's Life*, p. 104.
[15] *Ibid.*, p. 108.
[16] *Ibid.*, p. 104.

ican family whose name is conspicuous in the history of education and photography, Eastman was recommended to Brandeis by the renowned Boston social reformer, Robert A. Woods of South End House.[17] Like Brandeis, Eastman believed that the people, when informed, can distinguish "right" from "wrong" and will uphold "right." "Corruption breeds," he contended, "when the public is inert, and not when people are awake and alive to the issue at stake . . . The public can, if it will, protect itself and maintain its rights against the greed of corporate wealth and power." [18]

Devoting all his time to the Public Franchise League, Eastman sometimes had barely enough to live on. Filene provided him with most of his salary, which apparently never exceeded $1,000.[19] Brandeis regularly contributed 20 per cent of the operating funds for the P.F.L., though occasionally he was wheedled into contributing more. At the end of each year's report, Eastman appended an urgent, even pitiful, plea for funds. On one occasion, while the League was in the midst of a nationally publicized legislative battle, Eastman was forced to remark that most of the men currently in the League had agreed to work with it on the understanding that they would not be called upon to finance it; consequently, there was not enough money to pay even his own meager salary. ("[Some] members of the League have loaned me personally $535, which has helped me to get through the winter. At the present time, however, my finances are at low water mark.")[20]

Despite these conditions, the League had phenomenal success in its role as a pressure group for the public interest. In 1905, for example, the League concluded an arrangement with the Boston Consolidated Gas Company whereby the Company could offer higher dividends to its stockholders only after it

[17] Claude M. Fuess has written a competent biography of Eastman — *Joseph B. Eastman: Servant of the People* (New York, 1952). For Woods's career, see Mann, esp. pp. 115–123.

[18] Robert A. Woods and Joseph B. Eastman, "The Boston Franchise Contest," *Outlook,* 82:841 (April 14, 1906).

[19] Fuess, *Eastman,* p. 48.

[20] Eastman to Brandeis, June 10, 1910 (Eastman MSS).

reduced gas rates. The General Court enacted the plan into law in 1906. The settlement followed a two-year public controversy initiated by the P.F.L., which charged the Company with overcapitalization. Emulating the practice of certain British and Canadian cities, the Boston plan was the first of its kind in the United States. Within two years, Boston gas rates dropped 20 per cent.[21] "If the demand for municipal ownership in America can be stayed," observed Brandeis, "it will be by such wise legislation as the Public Franchise League has promoted, and by such public service as Mr. [James L.] Richards [President of the Company] and his associates are rendering in the management of a private corporation." [22]

In 1907, representatives of Kidder, Peabody and Company, which financed the Gas Company, deferred to the League so far as to consult it in advance on a proposed bill to merge the Boston Elevated Railway Company with the West End Railway Company, both also financed by the great investment house. The League approved the merger idea but found other provisions of the bill objectionable. The Elevated separated the merger provisions from the objectionable ones, and introduced the controversial provisions in the legislature as a separate bill. The League appeared at hearings to oppose it, whereupon the Elevated offered to improve the bill by giving the Railroad Commissioners supervisory powers. The League, however, maintained its opposition and finally forced the Elevated to withdraw.[23]

The secret of the League's power lay primarily in the in-

---

[21] The plan's details and history are adequately treated in Irvin Bussing, *Public Utility Regulation and the So-Called Sliding Scale* (New York, 1936), chap. v ("The Sliding Scale in Boston"); see also Mason, *Free Man's Life,* chap. ix ("The Sliding Scale Rate Principle, 1904–1907"), and Louis D. Brandeis, "How Boston Solved the Gas Problem," *Review of Reviews,* 36:594–598 (November 1907).

[22] Brandeis, "Gas Problem," p. 598.

[23] Though the Company introduced a similar bill later in the legislative session, it did not get beyond the earlier stages required for passage. The legislative part of the contest can be followed in the daily newspapers for February through June of 1907. For a summary, see Eastman's 1907 annual report for the P.F.L., in both the Eastman and Brandeis MSS.

genuity of its two principal members, Brandeis and Eastman. Each was capable of making the most detailed analysis of financial points of controversy to meet the corporations' own "experts" at legislative hearings. In addition, they had the direct support of some of the most influential newspapers in Boston. Edward H. Clement, an editor of the *Boston Evening Transcript,* regularly worked with the League, and John H. Fahey, publisher and editor of the *Boston Traveler,* served for a time as treasurer of the League. Edward A. Grozier, publisher and editor of the *Boston Post,* and Samuel Bowles, owner and editor of the *Springfield Republican,* consistently cooperated with the League, though apparently they did not attend its meetings as Clement and Fahey did.

Since the League's economic philosophy was essentially traditionalist, it won the support of a great many of the established interests in the Massachusetts business community. It attracted especially those who believed themselves confronted by a class which had only recently achieved affluence by means of the new financial and corporate techniques. For the old-timers, traditional political theory on corporations had tangible business meaning. Thus, as Brandeis and the League moved to do battle with what they tended to regard as the forces of greed and corruption, they did not lack friends among powerful and not altogether disinterested forces.

II

The Public Franchise League entered its first major campaign against the aspirations of a traction syndicate led by Henry M. Whitney. Whitney had long been suspect in the Massachusetts business community for his novel financial techniques and for the methods he used to influence the legislature on behalf of his many business ventures. He had scandalized the public in 1890 by admitting to a legislative investigation committee that he had spent $50,000 to secure the passage of certain legislation. His "revelations" led to a "corrupt practices" act (1892) — one of the first in the country — which required the registration of all lobbyists with the General Court and provided for penalties in cases of "improper" influence on legislators.

Like his more famous brother, William C. Whitney, who managed Grover Cleveland's presidential campaigns and served in his first administration as Secretary of the Navy, Henry Whitney got into street railway finance by way of real estate speculation. Having purchased lands in Brighton and Brookline, to the west of Boston, Whitney projected a street railway there from the center of the Hub in order to enhance land values: no great profits could be expected from the horse-drawn railway itself. In 1888, however, after viewing Frank J. Sprague's novel electric railway system in Richmond, Virginia, Whitney became inspired by the financial possibilities of city traction. He returned to Boston to purchase and consolidate in the West End Street Railway Company the franchises of seven of the city's eight railways. The purchased properties comprised 212 miles of track, 1700 cars, and 8000 horses — the largest such system in the United States.

Before the end of 1889 Whitney, working with Sprague, created the first major electric railway system in the country.[24] Within a decade, the electric railway revolutionized urban and interurban traffic.[25] Many railroad lines dependent primarily on passenger traffic fought a steadily losing battle against its competition. "If the electric street railway had been discovered 30 or 40 years earlier," wrote the Massachusetts railroad commissioners in 1896, "doubtless some of the auxiliary railroad lines now in existence would never have been projected." [26]

[24] Harold C. Passer, *The Electrical Manufacturers, 1875–1900* (Cambridge, 1953), pp. 214–247, and "Frank Julian Sprague," in William Miller, ed., *Men in Business* (Cambridge, 1952).

[25] "When the largest street-railway system in the United States [i.e., the West End] decided to invest several millions in electric traction, the smaller street railways were no longer hesitant about electrifying." Passer, *Electrical Manufacturers,* p. 339.

[26] Mass. Board R.R. Commissioners, *28th Annual Report* (Boston, 1897), p. 9. From 1893 to 1904, "the entire natural increase in population and the use of means of transportation went . . . to the street railways": Walter S. Allen, "Street Railway Franchises in Massachusetts," *Annals of the American Academy of Political and Social Science,* XXVII (January 1906), 107.

In 1894 a syndicate, including Whitney and J. P. Morgan and Company of New York, received from the Massachusetts legislature a charter for a new corporation, the Boston Elevated Railway Company. The new company was to extend Boston's transit system by building elevated tracks downtown. A referendum in Boston that fall ratified the charter. Three years later, the legislature authorized the Boston Elevated to lease the West End Street Railway Company for ninety-nine years subject to approval by the Railroad Commission.

The Commission, however, refused the lease on two grounds. It had investigated the assets of the West End and discovered that its stock was watered. Despite the high market price of the company's common stock, the Commission argued that its real value was impaired by about 8 per cent.[27] This meant that the $8.00 per share rental which the Elevated was to pay the West End stockholders amounted in actual value to an 11 or 12 per cent dividend. The Commission could not find justification for the guarantee of such high dividends (or rental) — especially because the trend until 1897 indicated continuing reduction of dividend rates on the par value of most conservative corporate stocks to an average slightly less than 8 per cent.[28] In the second place, the Commission found that the proposed lease was "wholly discordant with public policy," not only in the guarantees which included immunity from legislative interference and protection against any reduction of fares, but in the fact that the lease ran "for a term of years quadruple the length of the longest term that the legislature has [previously] consented to sanction." [29] Ultimately the Company acceded to the demands of the Commissioners. It agreed to reduce the fixed dividend from 8 per cent to 7 per cent and the term of the lease from ninety-nine years to about twenty-

[27] The Commissioners used replacement cost, the then accepted Massachusetts standard of valuation, to determine the integrity of the Company's outstanding stock.

[28] See Mass. Board R.R. Commissioners, *29th Annual Report* (Boston, 1898), p. 147.

[29] *Ibid.*, p. 149.

five, so as to expire when the Boston Elevated franchise expired.[30]

Many conservative elements in Boston, however, regarded the lease as a victory for the Company. Three things particularly disturbed them: (1) the Boston Elevated Railway Company had nearly completed consolidation of the railway lines in the Boston metropolitan area, thereby raising before conservatives the specters of "conspiracy" and "monopoly"; (2) it sought guarantees, in long-term franchise and immunity from fare reductions, that its investments would not be impaired by public interference; (3) the lease arrangement would give to West End stockholders a guaranteed return on corporate securities — in short, it made the legislature appear privy to a coup for stock speculators. Each aspect smelled of corporate arrogance.[31]

Speaking at the end of the year before the Massachusetts Reform Club (a society of Mugwump origins and proclivities), the Club's secretary, Charles Warren, noted "a demand from the conservative voices of the people for government interference with quasi-public corporations to the extent of more rigid restrictions and control in giving of franchises and privileges to such corporations." Warren described the Club as united "in a broad way on one principle, namely: that that government is best whose interference is least, and least often felt." But, alluding to the Elevated controversy, he wondered whether government interference "may not really be more beneficial to the public than the present system of ruinous competition between private companies or oppressive, prejudicial,

[30] *Ibid.*, p. 155.
[31] On the last point, see the draft of a letter (undated, in the Brandeis MSS) from the Municipal League of Boston to the Railroad Commission, written by Louis Brandeis in 1897 before the Commission's decision on the issue. Brandeis argued, in part, that the earnings of the West End Company before 1896 did not warrant even the 6 to 8 per cent dividends paid out by the Company — a fact apparently supported by the Commission's findings that the capital of the Company was impaired. He believed, moreover, that even a guaranteed 7 per cent dividend would be too high and would set a precedent for other public service corporations in future leases of consolidations.

and corrupting combinations of corporate capital." "The recent action of the Massachusetts Railroad Commissioners," he
concluded, "has undoubtedly the assent of a large majority of
the people of the Commonwealth." [32]

When the Elevated moved in 1899 to enhance its control
over Boston transportation, the opposition was better organized. The city itself owned a key section of the rapid transit
system, a subway leading into the downtown area and joining
two principal sections of the West End system. The elevated,
which rented the section from the city, succeeded in persuading the General Court to pass a bill which granted the Company outright ownership of the subway. Governor Roger Wolcott, however, insisted that the legislature include a referendum provision in the bill. That fall the Boston voters defeated
the measure by a two to one majority, after a spirited campaign in the city newspapers and public assemblies conducted
by elements of the Reform Club, the Municipal League, and
the Associated Board of Trade.[33]

The battle reopened in 1900. To alleviate traffic conditions
in the narrow neck of the business section, the city of Boston
had begun construction on a second subway, which it planned
to lease to the Elevated. The Company warned that it would
refuse the lease. It presented a bill of its own to give it the right
to build and own the proposed subway outright. The bill provided (a) that the Elevated undertake construction and operation of the new subway entirely at its own expense, and (b)
that the city of Boston assume ownership, if it chose, on condition (c) that the Company be given exclusive rights in and
to the subway for fifty years (later reduced to forty).

The Associated Board of Trade, leading the opposition, responded by hiring Louis Brandeis, who had participated in
the earlier fights against the Company, to represent the Board
at legislative hearings. He was instructed to seek amendment of

---

[32] Massachusetts Reform Club, *Annual Report*, 1897 (Boston, 1898), pp.
6, 12.
[33] Woods and Eastman, pp. 835–841. The vote was 51,585 to 26,354.

the Elevated's bill to accord with past franchise arrangements. Brandeis mobilized forces from every constituent association of the Board of Trade. He arranged with eight financiers — including ex-Mayor Morton Prince, Franklin Haven of the Merchants National Bank, and Francis Lee Higginson, a former director of the West End — to stand ready to take a lease of the subway on the Board's terms if the Elevated refused. In that way he provided a reasonable alternative for legislators who feared that it was either the Elevated's bill or no subway. He drafted a substitute bill which Grozier, Clement, and William Brigham (top correspondent for the *Transcript*) publicized in the pages of the *Boston Post* and the *Boston Evening Transcript*. In addition, Brandeis had the assistance of Representative Charles P. Keith, a brother of Benjamin F. Keith of the Board of Trade, who served on the joint legislative committee which handled the subway bill. By May 28 the Elevated signified capitulation by urging the committee to postpone action on the issue for a year.[34]

Having regrouped its forces, the Elevated made a determined assault in 1901. It soon appeared that the Company had overwhelming support in the legislature, especially among the Bostonians — despite the opposition of the titular leaders of both parties (except the Republican mayor). The Boston ward leaders of both parties, but particularly the Democrats

[34] There is a complete file in the Brandeis MSS detailing the fight against the Elevated. See especially Robert S. Boit (president of the Boston Associated Board of Trade) to Brandeis, March 21, 1900; E. H. Clement to Brandeis, March 26, 1900; Brandeis to Clement, April 18, 1900; Brandeis to A. A. Maxwell (chairman of the Committee on Metropolitan Affairs), April 24, 1900; Lawrence Minot to Brandeis, April 27, 1900; and C. P. Keith to B. F. Keith, May 4, 1900. Mason's *Free Man's Life* covers the contest in some detail, but the treatment suggests that Brandeis was Boy David, representing Good, challenging Goliath Elevated, representing Evil. This, in my opinion, is an inadequate, even inaccurate, description of the issue. That the lines drawn were not quite so simple I can suggest here merely by pointing out that some of Brandeis' own associates in civic causes before, during, and after 1900 opposed Brandeis and the Board of Trade in this contest. See e.g., John Mason Little to Brandeis, March 21, 1900 (Brandeis MSS). Helping to finance the Boston Elevated were Kidder, Peabody, and the National Shawmut Bank of Boston; their rivals included Lee Higginson & Co. and the Merchants National Bank.

who could not expect much patronage from a state organization, supported the Railway Company, for the Company supplied the jobs which their party could not. Charles Warren of
the Reform Club did not exaggerate much when he fumed
that "there is not a single position in the Boston Elevated Railway Company's service as employee that can be obtained by
any man unless he has the backing of some member of the city
government." [35]

The power of the local political leaders depended very
largely on their ability to get jobs for their constituents. As
intermediaries between workers and employers, they preempted the normal position of union leaders. The situation
suited both employers and politicians, and it accounts in large
part for the lack of a genuine labor movement in Massachusetts, as well as for the opposition of the Boston Central Labor
Union to the position of the Boston politicians on this bill. For
its part, the Elevated was a major employer which often
needed favors from politicians. The Elevated bill was a case in
point.[36]

Many Democratic ward leaders welcomed an alliance with
the backers of the Elevated Railway Company for reasons
other than patronage. Among the directors of the Company
were Democrats such as Henry Whitney and William A.
Gaston, president of the National Shawmut Bank and son of a
former Massachusetts governor. Only such men could supply
the funds and the "respectable" names to compete successfully
with the regular organization in state-wide elections, and thus
help to depose the Williams faction of the party.[37] Democrats
in other parts of the state shared the anti-organization motive
of the Bostonians. The old faction of anti-Bryan Democrats,

[35] Massachusetts Reform Club, *Annual Report,* 1901 (Boston, 1902), p. 15.
Rev. Frederic O. MacCartney, the Socialist member from Rockland, de-
clared on the floor that one member had said he could not vote against the
Elevated's bill because he had 300 constituents working for the Company.
Boston Evening Transcript, June 6, 1901.

[36] Cf. Robert A. Woods, ed., *Americans in Process* (Boston, 1902), pp.
360–361.

[37] Gaston openly aspired to follow in his father's political footsteps.

headed by John W. Corcoran, had its spokesman in the General Court in Corcoran's young cousin, David I. Walsh, then serving his first term as a member from Clinton. Walsh led the floor fight for the Company's bill and inserted a "sleeper" provision limiting the Company's expenditure on the subway to $6 million.[38]

It would be a mistake, however, to attempt to account for all the pro-Elevated votes by dwelling on the cunning maneuvers of the railway speculators and the political needs of legislators. It is clear that some supported the Elevated because it appeared ready to provide a necessary public improvement without increasing the municipal debt. The support which many independent and disinterested Republicans gave to the bill suggests that this was a persuasive argument.[39]

Though the Boston Chamber of Commerce, the Boston Central Labor Union, the new Public Franchise League, and most of the titular leaders of the Democratic party joined with the Board of Trade in the fight, on June 5 the House passed the Elevated's bill, 169 to 55, after defeating a referendum rider, 162 to 62.[40] Board of Trade forces despaired, but Morton Prince wrote hastily to Brandeis: "We are not to give up yet. We are not beaten til the Gov. signs. We know, I think I know, the Gov.'s opinion to this bill. He may be willing to veto." [41] On June 6, Governor Crane announced that he would veto the bill if it omitted a referendum provision. He called the bill the most important issue before the legislature in half a century.[42] Ignoring the warning, the Senate killed a referendum amendment, 27 to 9, and then passed the bill, 26 to 13.[43] A week later the Governor vetoed it, and the House upheld him.

[38] Brandeis to Representative Charles R. Saunders of Boston, June 4, 1901 (Brandeis MSS).

[39] Cf. the "Legislative Summary," in the *Boston Evening Transcript,* January 1, 1902.

[40] Massachusetts General Court, *Journal of the House of Representatives,* June 5, 1901, pp. 1284–1286. Tallies include pairs.

[41] Prince to Brandeis, June 6, 1901 (Brandeis MSS).

[42] *Boston Evening Transcript,* June 7, 1901.

[43] Massachusetts General Court, *Journal of the Senate,* June 9, 1901, p. 1028.

The bill itself was a bipartisan measure in the sense that neither party took an official position on it, and that the votes were scrambled. Even on the vote to uphold the veto, almost exactly the same proportion of Democrats as Republicans (33 per cent) changed sides. Legislators from all parts of the state voted for the bill, but support for it was especially heavy in Boston, where Democrats in the House voted 28 to 1 for it, and Republicans voted 18 to 3 the same way.[44]

Crane justified his veto by pointing out that though the Company promised to absorb all costs for forty years, section 10 of the bill limited stock and bond issues to $6 million; this would leave the city nearly helpless to force the improvements which would be needed over a forty-year period. Second, he argued that the bill violated the spirit of the anti-stock-watering laws by arranging for the Company to pay the rental to the city in stock, with no provision for retirement of the stock at the end of the forty years, and not even a pretense that the stock would represent tangible assets. The omission of the referendum, moreover, placed the citizens of Boston in an inferior position to the Company, which, according to the bill, had a three-month option on accepting it. Crane concluded by declaring the long term of the franchise contrary to established state policy.[45]

Certainly the Elevated people were attempting to get away with as much as they possibly could. But it is important to add that they sought only what businessmen in most parts of the country had customarily obtained without meeting significant resistance. Moreover, a large and important segment of the American business community argued for long-term and even irrevocable franchises, such as the Elevated demanded, on the ground that with the uncertainties of short and revocable franchises public utilities could not continue to attract sufficient capital.

[44] *MHRJ,* June 5, 1901, pp. 1284–1286.
[45] *MHRJ,* June 17, 1901, pp. 1331–36; *Boston Evening Transcript,* June 18, 1901.

The chief policy makers of the state at the time — namely, the Governor and the Railroad Commission, and, in the end, the legislature also — regarded that argument as inadequate. Though the state's right to revoke franchises might theoretically discourage investment, the Commission maintained: "Nothing can better attest the *essential* permanency of street railway franchises than the faith which conservative businessmen express in them by their readiness to purchase the stocks and bonds and to loan money to the companies at moderate rates of interest." [46] The only possible justification for more liberal franchises was that corporations in other states were able to get them.[47]

III

Although contemporary reformers tended to believe that the Elevated franchise contest was noteworthy as an example of the struggle between public opinion and corporate power — or in the popular vernacular, the People and the Trusts — it was more significantly a contest between a dynamic, speculative element in the business community which aspired to exploit modern financial techniques, and a conservative element which cherished traditional business methods and the traditional state-corporation relationship. For the Elevated people, the contest was simply a business matter. The Company ended the fight when it failed to persuade the representatives of the public that a long-term franchise was necessary to attract adequate capital to support an efficient subway system. By accepting the lease on traditional, more restrictive terms in 1902, the Company in effect verified Brandeis' prediction that it would do so "if it will find that the Legislature will not grant even better terms." [48] For the opposition the issue was largely a

[46] Mass. Board R.R. Commissioners, *32nd Annual Report* (for 1900), pp. 87–88. I have inserted the emphasis here to preserve the tone of the original.

[47] See Allen, "Street Railway Franchises," esp. p. 108.

[48] Statement made before the Joint Committee on Metropolitan Affairs, April 26, 1902 (copy in Brandeis MSS). The Brandeis-sponsored bill passed the House 127 to 93 on June 26, 1902 (*MHRJ*, pp. 1317–1319). There was no roll call in the Senate.

moral one. It was not only that the Brandeisians believed the
corporation had "corrupted" the legislature. ("In our subway
fight, we found the great evil that we had to deal with was the
influence of the corporation, due largely to the patronage
which it exerts . . . This we find to be the most serious and
widespread form of corruption.")[49] What was more important
was that the "traction trust" had attempted to "steal" the public
thoroughfare from the people by seeking a long-term franchise
in the face of venerated state tradition, and had sought permission, moreover, to issue securities unsupported by tangible
assets, also in defiance of state law and tradition.[50]

Yet even the Board of Trade and Public Franchise League
recognized the great popularity and value of the recently completed elevated railway system, organized as it was by modern
finance techniques. Early in 1901 they fretted over the possibility that William Gaston, executive director of the Company,
might run for governor and make the election tantamount to a
referendum on the Company's bill. They tacitly conceded that
the new transit system represented an attractive advertisement
for the new corporate and financial techniques.[51]

The League and its allies were able to hold the line against
the encroaching web of modern finance capitalism largely because of circumstances peculiar to the years before 1897. Business conservatives tended to stress the experience of falling
utility rates and steady dividends over the past thirty years.
Thus, in rejecting the original lease of the West End Railway

[49] Brandeis to W. H. McElwain, June 18, 1902 (Brandeis MSS).

[50] At stake secondarily was control of the commuter routes into downtown
Boston. The downtown merchants held a weapon over the railway managers
as long as the government maintained control and as long as the merchants
continued to participate in government policy making through associations
like the P.F.L. Some merchants, on the other hand, held the view that only
if the managers had a virtually free hand would the railway properties
obtain the investments necessary to maintain the most efficient commuter
service.

[51] See George B. Upham to Brandeis, February 26, 1901, and Laurence
Minot to Upham, March 3, 1901 (Brandeis MSS). The Upham–Brandeis
letter was a reply to a letter in which Brandeis expressed similar misgivings.

Company, the Railroad Commissioners argued: "Whatever future accepted rate of return, *hitherto tending downward,* on capital invested in public-service corporations . . . the rate here fixed would run on to the end of the lease without diminution or power of revision." [52] With these premises, it was easy to regard any effort to fix utility rates by statute and permanent franchises as a legislative-corporate cabal. Similarly, so long as a secular deflation had made the state's utility securities attractive investments, conservatives continued to regard efforts to permit corporations to issue stock on intangible assets simply as attempts to perpetrate fraud.

But when industrial securities offered high returns after 1897, the restricted public service corporations found it hard to obtain fresh capital for maintenance and improvements.[53] And when out-of-state interests threatened Massachusetts' economic ascendancy in the country, the call for a reappraisal of the state's traditional corporation policies became insistent. Consequently, although the Public Franchise League's victory over the Elevated in 1902 possibly helped to safeguard against the excessively liberal corporate charters common in other states, it was something of a rearguard action. Thereafter, the traditionalists gave way gradually before the pressure for fewer controls on corporate activity in the state.

For several decades, entrepreneurs in sections of the country nearer the domestic markets and sources of supply had labored to overcome the industrial and commercial pre-eminence of New England. By the Progressive Era they had had significant success. In 1890, for example, New England had produced 43

[52] Mass. Board R.R. Commissioners, *29th Annual Report* (Boston, 1898), p. 147. My emphasis.

[53] For example, in 1906 the Boston & Maine Railroad, despite its reputedly solid financial condition, failed to market a new issue of $6 million of stock. (See Chapter Eight.) It was only after 1897 that industrial securities entered the capital market in significant volume and thereby presented serious competition to the securities of utility corporations. See Thomas R. Navin and Marian V. Sears, "The Rise of a Market for Industrial Securities, 1887–1902," *Business History Review,* 29:105–138 (June 1955).

per cent of all coarse cotton yarns, 86 per cent of medium yarns, and all the fine yarns. The section's chief competitor in cotton textiles was the South, which had produced 41 per cent and 3 per cent of the country's coarse and medium yarns respectively. Within the next twenty years, the South had leaped ahead of New England in coarse yarns, producing 62 per cent to New England's 29 per cent, had almost caught up in mediums, producing 42 to New England's 53 per cent, and had made severe inroads on New England's monopoly of fine yarns, producing almost a quarter of the country's total. By 1900, the South's production of sheeting, duck, twine, and other coarser cotton products had exceeded New England's in value and quantity, and by 1904 it had overtaken the northern section in denims, ticks, and toweling, and was not far behind in bags and bagging. The South had made similar inroads in the manufacture of cotton print cloth.[54]

Massachusetts shoe manufacturers also watched nervously as Ohio, Illinois, Wisconsin, and Missouri captured increasing shares of the national shoe market; from 6.6 per cent of the national output in 1879, those states were producing almost 17 per cent by 1900. Reduced transportation costs had enabled eastern manufacturers to reach the continental market; but these advantages were available to the western manufacturers, too, and the agitation for increased federal regulation of railroads after 1900 threatened to undermine the special rates which New England manufacturers enjoyed.[55] Perhaps more foreboding was the fact that the growth of the meat-packing industry in the West meant plentiful hides there. After 1900 New England shoe manufacturers (who were centered within thirty miles of Boston) had to depend increasingly on imported

[54] Seymour L. Wolfbein, *The Decline of a Cotton Textile City: A Study of New Bedford* (New York, 1944), p. 61; Thomas Russell Smith, *Cotton Textile Industry of Fall River, Massachusetts: A Study of Industrial Localization* (New York, 1944), pp. 80–85, 104–105, 120–121.

[55] Thomas L. Norton, *Trade Union Policies in the Massachusetts Shoe Industry* (New York, 1932), p. 29. See also Elmore W. Sanderson, "Boots and Shoes," Department of Labor, *Bureau of the Census Bulletins* (Washington, D. C., 1907), p. 15.

leather.[56] Despite a tariff of 15 per cent imposed upon hides in 1897, hide imports between 1899 and 1903 rose 12 per cent over the preceding five years.

In addition, incursions into Massachusetts by "foreign" financiers, such as Morgan, Rockefeller, and Vanderbilt, aroused concern among Bay State commercial leaders that Massachusetts might become an economic "colony" to New York, akin to some southern and western states. The larger corporations operating in Massachusetts tended to incorporate under more liberal state laws elsewhere, which aroused anxieties about effective state control over the local economy. As we have already noted,[57] in 1901 almost twice as many corporations doing business in Massachusetts incorporated under "foreign" charters as under Massachusetts laws. In 1900, Governor Crane won high praise by arranging for the Boston & Maine Railroad, a Massachusetts corporation, to absorb the Fitchburg Railroad, after Vanderbilt's New York Central succeeded in leasing the Boston & Albany. Both the Fitchburg and the Boston & Albany ran the length of the state from junctions at the Hudson River to terminals in Boston. Commercial leaders hoped that by attaching the Fitchburg to a stronger railroad, it could provide healthy competition for the Boston & Albany–New York Central combination.

A disastrous drop in Boston port activity in 1902, especially in exports, served to highlight the dangers of foreign-controlled properties in Massachusetts. Compared to $130 million in exports in 1901, Boston handled only $86 million in 1902, the lowest since 1894. The decline, which continued for several years, dropped Boston below New Orleans to third place in total port activity for the first time in generations.[58] The loss reflected an increase in the domestic consumption of American

---

[56] Sanderson, "Boots and Shoes," p. 24. See also Frederick S. Hall, "The Localization of Industry," *Twelfth Census,* vol. VII, *Manufactures,* part 1, 1902, pp. cxc–ccxiv.

[57] See Chapter One.

[58] Boston Chamber of Commerce, *18th Annual Report* (Boston, 1904), p. 21, and graph on p. 181.

products, especially food; the big reduction in exports for Boston was in breadstuffs, which in three years dropped 80 per cent below the 1901 total of almost $29 million. A shortage of railroad cars, the failure of the corn crop in 1901, and a Canadian drive to develop the port of Montreal by diverting goods usually destined for Boston over the Grand Trunk and Boston & Maine Railroads — all these factors contributed to the collapse of 1902.

But Massachusetts businessmen focused upon still another cause of the decline. When a railroad glut developed in 1902, merchants and manufacturers alike found that business centers in other states with direct railroad connections westward received goods before shipments trickled through to Massachusetts. It appeared, at least, that New York financiers, who controlled many of the ship lines as well as the railroads which fed the New England lines, looked after their own interests in New York before fulfilling their obligations to the north.[59] The business community felt the discrimination most acutely following the coal strike settlement in October 1902, when a second railroad jam prolonged the fuel famine in Massachusetts.

Before the end of the year, still another blow fell. In December, J. P. Morgan completed consolidation of the major transatlantic ship lines to form the International Mercantile Marine Company (I.M.M.). The consolidation absorbed the Leyland, Dominion, and Wilson-Furness-Leyland Lines, all operating out of Boston. This left the port with no independent services actively seeking to attract freight to the port. In addition, the I.M.M. fixed uniform rates for its lines at all ports for both eastbound and westbound traffic across the Atlantic. While shippers could send goods from any of the five major Atlantic ports to Liverpool at exactly the same cost, Philadelphia, Baltimore, and Norfolk enjoyed railroad rate differentials which made the shipping of goods from any point in the American interior to those ports less expensive than to New York or Bos-

[60] *Ibid.,* p. 22.

ton. The differentials, arranged originally by the railroads in the 1880's to end rate wars, served ostensibly to equalize the cost of traffic from the American interior through all the major Atlantic ports to Liverpool. By eliminating the cost advantages which Boston had enjoyed on transatlantic voyages, Morgan's I.M.M. almost crippled Boston's export business.[60]

These were the circumstances under which Massachusetts undertook to reconsider the traditional view of business corporations in the Commonwealth.

In 1903, a special committee on corporation laws, set up earlier by the General Court, reported that "the more important provisions of the present law [in Massachusetts] regulating the organization and conduct of business corporations and the liability of its stockholders and officers are unsuited to modern business conditions"; the committee urged repeal.[61] Consequently, just as Theodore Roosevelt and the federal government were taking the first major steps toward control of business corporations, the Massachusetts General Court was engaged in loosening its corporation controls. Repeal passed without a roll call and with little debate.[62]

The new law ended the requirement that all capital be paid in before business could commence, and it deprived the state commissioner of corporations of the responsibility for determining the valuation of corporate properties and the amount

[60] Though Boston and New York suffered the same disadvantages, New York had harbor and rail facilities, plus financial connections, which placed it in a special category above all other ports. "There are two sorts of seaport along the Atlantic Coast: New York and all others." Edwin J. Clapp, *The Port of Boston: A Study and a Solution of the Traffic and Operating Problems of Boston, and Its Place in the Competition of the North Atlantic Seaports* (New Haven, 1916), p. 24.

[61] Stimson and Washburn, p. 20.

[62] See Hans Thorelli, *The Federal Anti-Trust Policy: Origination of an American Tradition* (Baltimore, 1955), pp. 560ff; Arthur M. Johnson, "Theodore Roosevelt and the Bureau of Corporations," *Mississippi Valley Historical Review,* 45:571–590 (March 1959). In his first annual message, December 3, 1901, Roosevelt suggested that "supervision of corporations by the National Government need not go so far as . . . the supervision . . . by so conservative a State as Massachusetts, in order to produce excellent results.

of capital stock which could be issued upon it. It permitted directors to include "good will," patents, and intangible properties in determining valuation. Finally, it closed to the public the list of corporation stockholders, and removed all personal liability for legally incurred corporate debts, except for operatives' wages up to six months. Although the law applied only to non-public corporations, within the decade the state eased the laws governing utilities as well.

It is worth noting that while the federal government focused on publicity as the primary means of *restraint* on business corporations ("Publicity is the only sure remedy which we can now invoke," the President said),[63] in the Bay State the ostensible adequacy of publicity served as the justification for *relaxing* state controls. ("The State's duty ends," the corporation committee argued, "in providing clearly that creditors and stockholders shall at all times be precisely informed . . . and particularly that there should be full publicity given to all details of the original organization.")[64] As the contemporary economist and reformer William Z. Ripley pointed out, moreover, Massachusetts continued to lead the country in regulatory techniques even after the passage of the new law:

A brief outline of *possible remedies* for the present evils of the industrial situation may properly begin with the assumption that so far as individual repressive action by the separate states is concerned, the limit of legislative activity has about been reached . . . The utmost that the separate states can do is perhaps indicated by the laws of Massachusetts, making provision for publicity and general supervision.[65]

Ripley suggested that really effective remedies for the prevalent evils of corporate activities had to come from the federal government. As the Federal Bureau of Corporations reported in 1904, the granting of state charters to corporations had resulted in "an inevitable tendency of state legislation toward the lowest level of lax regulation." "Matters which rightly affect the

[63] Quoted in Johnson, "Theodore Roosevelt," p. 572.
[64] Stimson and Washburn, p. 22.
[65] Ripley, pp. xxvi–xxvii.

whole," the Bureau continued, "are . . . directed and shaped by a *small* part of the community. The net result of this State system is thoroughly vicious." [66] The Massachusetts Corporation Law of 1903 was itself a consequence of the failure of the federal government to regulate corporations effectively.

IV

For Massachusetts, what was new was not control, but official acknowledgement of the conception of the corporation as an instrument primarily for private profit rather than for public service, with minimal obligations to the community which granted its privileges. The Boston traction contest illustrated the state's resistance to the insurgency of modern business views and practices. The resistance stemmed from both a quasi-moral repugnance for the unorthodox practices and a fear of their proved competitive force. Ultimately, the regional situation rendered impotent the traditionalist, civic-reform veto groups. As the *Boston Evening Transcript* was forced to remark late in 1902, "The people of Massachusetts seem to have come to believe that they have pressed the corporations too far now in the otherwise praiseworthy effort to squeeze the water out." [67]

[66] U. S. Bureau of Corporations, *First Annual Report* (Washington, 1904), p. 8.
[67] *Boston Evening Transcript,* August 2, 1902.

CHAPTER FOUR

A STILLNESS IN MASSACHUSETTS

In the United States of today everyone is middle class. The resort to force, the wild talk of the 'nineties are over. Everyone is busily, happily getting ahead.

Boston Herald, December 31, 1904

IN the year that William McKinley won a second term in the White House, Wisconsin elevated to the governorship the insurgent, Robert M. LaFollette. The following year, single-taxer Tom Johnson began his outstanding career as mayor of Cleveland, and tariff critic Albert Cummins trounced the Republican machine candidate for governor in Iowa. These men joined a small but increasing number of political upstarts, like William S. U'Ren of Oregon, Samuel "Golden Rule" Jones of Toledo, and Hazen S. Pingree of Detroit, who had already gained national attention for their attacks on privilege, corruption, and boss-dominated government. After Theodore Roosevelt acceded to the Presidency, the diffuse progressive spirit found a national focus.

Although Massachusetts shared in the country's growing sensitivity to bossism, corruption, and the aggressiveness of corporate wealth, it gave no direct political expression to that feeling during these early years. The Boston Elevated Railway contest suggested a struggle for advantage within the political economy, but it never gained status as a strictly political issue. In 1902, a big strike in the West Virginia and Pennsylvania coal mines caused some popular rumblings in the Bay State, motivated by the fear of a cold, fuelless winter, but when the strike was abruptly settled before election time, virtually by decree of President Roosevelt and J. P. Morgan, the noises disappeared and partisans failed to make effective use of them for political purposes. Groping for an issue with which to confront the Republicans, Democrats revived the proposals for a reciprocity treaty with Canada; but, although the issue restored a semblance of unity to the Democracy and stirred certain segments of the Boston electorate, it contributed little to reform sentiment in the state.

Massachusetts seemed, indeed, to be moving in another direction from the rest of the country. As we have already noted, the Commonwealth began retrenchment in its corporation policies during these years. At the same time, the Socialist party, which had shown such promise in the last years of the old century, went into decline in Massachusetts even while the national party grew to striking proportions behind Eugene V. Debs. While the coal miners of Pennsylvania and West Virginia successfully wrung concessions from the mine owners, Massachusetts textile workers fought a losing defensive battle with their employers. Finally, in the years when the American people began to respond to the revelations of the muckrakers, to experiment with new administrative, legislative, and electoral techniques, and to adopt as their heroes men who declared for an end to the Old Order, Massachusetts sat at the feet of a man who epitomized conservatism, compromise, and — stillness.

I

Nearly everyone in Massachusetts, it seemed, liked Murray Crane. Businessmen praised him for the "business methods" and economy which marked his administration. Mugwumps and many Democrats lauded him for his honesty and "nonpartisanship." His veto of the Boston Elevated Railway Company bill endeared him to the civic guardians, while the Company expressed its respect for him by explaining that it had accepted the P.F.L.'s "onerous" terms only at Crane's personal request.[1] Labor men trusted him to arbitrate disputes; his settlement of a teamster strike early in 1902 was considered by many the high spot of his administration. He earned even the

[1] *Boston Herald,* June 6, 1902.

affection of many Irish-Americans when he became the first
Republican to name an Irish Catholic to the State Superior
Court. Finally, his evident aloofness from the influence of the
presumed "boss" of the party, Lodge, endowed him with an
enduring reputation (despite the facts) as an "independent"
— which in the Progressive Era was pure blandiloquence.
The Massachusetts electorate expressed its affection for the
Governor by re-electing him twice with near-record majorities
in the annual elections.

Crusades were not in Murray Crane's line. "It is more important," he declared, expressing his political credo, "that the
law be permanently fixed . . . than that experiments in new
legislation should be constantly tried." [2] With the cooperation
of the state senate, Crane repressed efforts to improve labor
conditions, revise election laws, and experiment with municipal ownership of public utilities. He permitted only an amendment to a three-year-old law which forbade commercial bank
directors to sit on savings bank boards, and he encouraged the
lease of the Fitchburg to the Boston & Maine Railroad after
the New York Central had leased the Boston & Albany. With
Senator Lodge, Crane quashed efforts to institute direct primaries for state officials, though he finally acquiesced in a bill
which established the system for most elective Boston city officials.[3] Above all, he insisted on "economy." He opposed even
the efforts of Senator Lodge, responding to pressure from the
Boston Chamber of Commerce and other groups, to improve
Boston harbor with combined federal and state appropriations.[4] Although during the somewhat restive year of 1902 —
Crane's last in office — State House reporters noted an "in-

[2] Quoted in Hennessy, *Twenty-five Years*, p. 98.

[3] Lodge to Crane, February 27, 1902, and Crane to Lodge, April 15, 1902
(Lodge MSS). The Luce Direct Primary Bill passed June 28, 1902, without
a roll call in either house. Robert Luce, a Republican from Somerville,
worked with gradual success for more than a decade to establish direct
primaries in the state. See Chapter Seven.

[4] Lodge specifically urged Crane not to let his economy program interfere
with the pressing needs of Boston commerce, but Crane would not yield.
Lodge to Crane, November 13 and 22, 1901 (Lodge MSS).

creasing disposition of the members of both old parties in the popular branch of the General Court not to be frightened by the bugaboo of socialism," and "the willingness of an interesting number of members of the legislature to cast aside any natural prejudices they may have once cherished toward everything bearing a Socialistic label," [5] Crane gave these propensities little chance to develop. In the end, the General Court passed all but one of Governor Crane's recommendations, while reporters agreed that the legislature during his administration was "not memorable — a dead legislature rather than a weak one." [6]

Crane's conservatism clearly captured the spirit of the Massachusetts electorate during those years. His popularity left the Democrats without a tittle of hope for an election victory so long as he was the Republican standard bearer. Under the circumstances, the Democracy slipped into the hands of "Colonel" William A. Gaston of the National Shawmut Bank and Boston Elevated Railway Company. Gaston promised at least to provide the party with campaign funds.

II

There is no doubt that Gaston could have bought the nomination for governor in 1901. But, although he formally announced his candidacy early in the year, he was persuaded to withdraw. In the first place, although the Bryanite Williams faction had acquiesced in its temporary relegation to oblivion, it made clear its determination to fight openly a candidacy so closely identified with modern finance capitalism as Gaston's. ("Might as well nominate J. P. Morgan," fumed ex-candidate Robert Treat Paine, Jr.)[7] On the other hand, there is evidence which suggests that the House of Morgan applied pressure to

---

[5] *Springfield Republican,* June 15, 1902; *Boston Herald,* May 25, 1902.
[6] The quotation is from the legislative summary of Charles S. Groves in the *Boston Globe,* June 30, 1902. Groves later became the private secretary of Governor Curtis Guild, Jr., in 1907, and he was executive secretary of the Republican State Committee from 1908 to 1913.
[7] *Boston Evening Transcript,* August 22, 1901.

force Gaston to withdraw his candidacy on the ground that it
would embarrass the Elevated Railway Company in its fight
for a liberal franchise.[8] In addition, Gaston did not have the
united support of the Cleveland or "Gold" Democrats, many of
whom urged Charles Sumner Hamlin, former Assistant Secretary of the Treasury under Cleveland, to run; Hamlin seemed
assured of the support of the revived Young Men's Democratic
Club, the Mugwumpish organization which had boomed William E. Russell, but which had become moribund since the
Williams-Bryan coup in 1896. In any event, Gaston knew he
could not beat Crane.

Consequently, Gaston used the opportunity to pose as the
magnanimous benefactor of the party. He offered to finance
the campaign of anyone whom the party might nominate. At
the same time, he maneuvered to control the nomination. For
his decoy, Gaston chose Josiah Quincy, the retired Boston
reform mayor who had escaped intraparty squabbles by living
in Europe since his retirement. Quincy, who had served as
Assistant Secretary of State under Cleveland, was clearly
acceptable to the Mugwump wing of the party, and Gaston
already had sewed up the support of the Boston ward leaders.
He then got Quincy's old lieutenants in the Boston city organization to persuade Hamlin that he ought to withhold his candidacy on the ground that only Quincy could heal the rifts in
the party.

On August 31, Quincy returned from Europe and went immediately into conference with Gaston. Two days later, Quincy
lunched with Hamlin and informed him that he had told
Gaston he had no wish to run. Still unaware that Gaston and
Quincy were playing the game together, Hamlin offered to
withdraw if Quincy would run. He pleaded the good of the
party and the necessity of stopping Gaston. Quincy stayed coy
for twenty-four hours, and then telephoned Hamlin that he
would run.[9] It took Hamlin only seventy-two hours more to

[8] See Diary of Charles Sumner Hamlin, August 7, 1901 (Hamlin MSS).
[9] *Boston Evening Transcript* and *Boston Herald,* August 26 through September 4, 1901; Hamlin Diary, August 30, September 2 and 3, 1901.

discover that he had been duped: "Gaston," he wrote in his diary, "is dominating the situation and is simply using Q as a stop gap for a year." [10]

At the state convention, nevertheless, the party put on a show of harmony. Although it was common knowledge by then that Quincy would throw his support to Gaston in 1902, the Bryanites and Young Democrats decided to make no fight — especially since Gaston appeared to let them run the proceedings. On Hamlin's recommendation, a former Gold Democrat was chosen permanent chairman. Hamlin himself made the nominating speech for Quincy, and John W. Coughlin of Fall River, a Hamlin backer, took second place on the ticket with Gaston's blessings. The convention appointed one of George Fred Williams' lieutenants chairman of the resolutions committee, and gave him the privilege of writing a platform for a losing campaign.

Gaston apparently made no effort to modify the language of the platform. It contained the usual condemnation of railroad rebates, imperialism, and legislative interference with municipal government, and it urged direct election of United States senators, direct primaries, the right of the public to demand a referendum on any legislation, municipal ownership of public utilities, tariff reciprocity (especially with Canada), and improved labor legislation. Its principal target, however, was corporate consolidation: "The communism of capital must be met by State control . . . If financial socialism for private profit is not met by reasonable measures of legislative socialism to protect the public interest, it will control the State and destroy individualism." In general, the platform sounded like a Populist manifesto; it expressed the widespread concern in America that the "trust" movement would soon require a radical reassessment of traditional social and political assumptions.[11]

Confident of victory, the Republicans wrote a brief platform which touched state issues at only two points. Obviously allud-

[10] Hamlin Diary, September 6, 1901.
[11] *Boston Evening Transcript,* October 3, 1901.

ing to the current Elevated Railway franchise fight, it called
for mandatory referenda on local issues, and it declared that
the public highways belonged to the people and ought not to
be leased to private interests without proper compensation.
Otherwise, it reiterated the Republican stand for a protective
tariff (modified perhaps by carefully drawn reciprocity agree-
ments), and the maintenance of the gold standard; it urged
construction of an isthmian canal, and improvement of Boston
harbor with federal funds; finally, it called for Congressional
action to regulate hours of labor, in order to end the disadvantage to industry in states (such as Massachusetts) which had
advanced labor legislation.[12]

Quincy put up a fairly decent show against Crane. He had
no illusions about the campaign, and publicly acknowledged
that the nomination was "obviously a call to party leadership,
and not to public office." [13] His principal function, which he
did well, was to reconcile the warring Boston factions. He
carried Boston by the largest margin since William Russell's
victory by 14,000 in 1892, and prepared the way for the
December mayoralty election, when the reunited Democrats
swept back into power behind Patrick A. Collins. But, though
Governor Crane did not make a single speech, he took the
state by 70,000, a margin more than double what either candidate had anticipated. The Republicans took back the mayoralty from the Socialists in Brockton, and though they lost
Cambridge for the first time in thirty years, and a dozen seats
in the lower house of the General Court, they cut the Democratic minority in the Senate from 9 to 7, and generally
remained confidently in command of the Commonwealth.
"Everything in the state is in good condition," exulted the Republican State Chairman. "We had several hard Senatorial
fights, but pulled them out all right, and everything seems to
be peaceful." [14]

[12] *Ibid.*, October 4, 1901.
[13] *Ibid.*, September 25, 1901.
[14] A. H. Goetting to George von L. Meyer, November 25, 1901 (Meyer
MSS).

III

Tranquillity did not endure uninterrupted. The turbulence beneath the surface in 1901 inevitably agitated the placid political waters. When J. P. Morgan capped the swift movement toward corporate consolidation by organizing the United States Steel Corporation, which represented the most colossal aggregation of capital in the world, he stunned the most insensitive men of the business community. Even the staid and proper *Boston Herald* was moved to remark: "If a limited financial group shall come to represent the capitalistic end of industry, the perils of socialism, even if brought about by some rude, because forcible, taking of the instruments of industry, may be looked upon by even intelligent people as possibly the lesser of two evils." [15] Before the end of the year President McKinley was assassinated by an anarchist. The new Chief Executive pledged himself to maintain the slain President's policies; but hopeful men anticipated that the rambunctious ex-Police Commissioner and Rough Rider would give fresh attention to long-standing social problems, while timid men feared that chaos was only around the corner. Roosevelt's personality suggested freshness; the expectation itself helped prepare the country for change.

The following year the Republicans suffered their first small fright of the new century. Campaign exhortations that year to "stand pat" (Mark Hanna) and "stand by the status" (Speaker Joe Cannon) only revealed how precarious "the status" really was. Both the nation and the Bay State continued prosperous, but the full dinner pail was not enough when it appeared to many that others were getting more. The subtle pressures of the rising cost of living created a feeling of vague discontent[16] which was soon to focus on specific objectives, particularly corporations and the tariff.[17]

[15] *Boston Herald,* October 3, 1901.
[16] See MBSL, "The Causes of High Prices," *35th Annual Report* (Boston 1905), pp. 81–130.
[17] At the midpoint of the year (1902), the wholesale price index was up 10 per cent over prices at the same time the year before, a jump unmatched

In March 1902 the federal administration filed suit against J. P. Morgan's Northern Securities Company. It was the first significant step taken by the central government against the trusts since Grover Cleveland's second administration. The President followed this action, however, with a speaking tour designed not only to publicize the need for *some* checks against corporate abuses, but also to reassure the nervous financial community that the action did not mean a change in the cautious and conservative course he had plotted in his first annual message. To many Massachusetts civic and commercial leaders, Roosevelt's "assurance" probably appeared more a threat than a promise. They had been calling for federal controls for years, so that, to quote Curtis Guild, Jr., editor of the *Boston Commercial Bulletin* and president of the Massachusetts Republican Club, "what is stockwatering in Massachusetts may not be finance in New Jersey." [18] They had reason to fear that the efforts toward federal control of corporations, already late, would also be too little.

Roosevelt's Northern Securities action nevertheless set him on the road to the "trust-buster" title. However much he wished to preserve a restrained attitude toward the trusts, he excited those long eager to settle a score with their supposed chief nemesis. Willy-nilly, "trusts" were an issue. Political professionals, such as Henry Cabot Lodge, feared that the agitation might indeed set off a whirlwind which could disrupt the Republican party. Writing in April to George Meyer, an important party financier, Lodge noted that though conditions still seemed good, he foresaw "serious dangers ahead growing out of the blind hostility to the trusts and the feeling of dissatisfaction as to the tariff." [19]

---

in any year since the Civil War. Average wholesale prices for the entire year were up about 4 per cent, also a recent record. *Report of the [Massachusetts] Commission on the Cost of Living,* House Document 1750 (Boston, 1910), pp. 15, 18, 59.

[18] Guild's inaugural address as president of the Massachusetts Republican Club, in *Boston Evening Transcript,* January 29, 1901. See also Guild's statement in the *Boston Herald,* October 21, 1902.

[19] Lodge to Meyer, April 5, 1902 (Meyer MSS).

Although Massachusetts businessmen and consumers responded to the collectivization of American economic life in much the same manner as businessmen and consumers elsewhere in the country, they tended to regard the Roosevelt administration's antitrust program with some skepticism. When the President delivered a eulogy in Boston on the Massachusetts corporation laws in August 1902,[20] he enjoyed a mixed reception. Massachusetts was already preparing to make concessions to the corporation movement along the lines suggested by its special committee on corporation law. Besides, as the *Springfield Republican* observed, G.O.P. orators had exercised orally against "trusts" for more than a decade without consequence, and there was no reason to believe that Roosevelt's remarks forecast anything different. In the absence of federal action, therefore, the traditionalist, individualist Springfield paper argued (in the face of the President's encomium) that business was "unduly restricted in Massachusetts." [21]

On this theme, William Gaston made his delayed bid for the governorship. He charged that business was "being driven out of Massachusetts by foolish, antiquated laws." He promised to save the Bay State economy by giving corporations a better break — without, of course, imitating "the loose laws of our neighbors." [22] In 1902, Gaston's corporation affiliations were no handicap. His role in promoting the National Shawmut Bank and Boston Elevated Railway consolidations served him well with businessmen looking for someone to spark Massachusetts' apparently lagging economy. To win the Democratic nomination against Charles S. Hamlin, Gaston routed the party faction which prepared to make war on "commercialism in politics" and the "increased aggressiveness of corporate wealth." [23] His nomination removed from the campaign whatever there was of a corporation issue in Massachusetts.

[20] See Chapter One, note 26.
[21] *Springfield Republican,* August 28 and June 30, 1902.
[22] Campaign leaflet, dated August 15, 1902, in the Gettemy Scrapbooks.
[23] Hamlin Diary, June 2, 1902, and *Boston Herald,* July 24, 1902. At the Democratic State Convention, Gaston forces successfully beat down the

The tariff issue was another matter. No tariff act has ever pleased all business groups. The opposition to the Dingley tariff of 1897 had taken form almost immediately, not least among Massachusetts commercial interests and shoe and leather manufacturers.[24] By 1900, even the National Association of Manufacturers had begun to suggest revision, ostensibly to facilitate the opening of new markets for America's expanding productive capacity. McKinley's death, however, had created among business leaders a "don't rock the boat" sentiment, which the new President's first annual message reflected. "There is," Roosevelt contended, "general acquiescence in our present tariff system as a national policy . . . Nothing could be more unwise than to disturb the business interests of the country by any general tariff change at this time."[25] But businessmen affected by import duties refused to acquiesce. The rising cost of living, moreover, focused consumers' attention upon "protectionism," whose purpose, after all, was to raise domestic prices.

When, in May 1902, the anthracite coal miners went on strike, the issue sharpened. By the end of July the *New York Tribune,* a stalwart Republican paper, acknowledged "convincing evidence of a certain change in popular temper" toward the tariff over the past year. When a Republican convention in Iowa, dominated by the insurgent Albert Cummins, committed the state party to immediate revision of the tariff,

---

platform written by George Fred Williams, chairman of the resolutions committee, which began: "A heartless capitalism, born of greed and nourished by law, is perverting our institutions and morals, invading press, pulpit and college, and oppressing labor and trade. Its system has one aim, to increase the hoards of the wealthy out of the toil of the people. Its method is to secure grants or immunities of privileges, and it is rapidly bringing trade, lands, money and inventions under monopolistic control, and its hand guides the helm of government. Its reign is not longer endurable." *Boston Herald,* September 17, 1902.

[24] See, e.g., *Boston Herald,* May 11, 1899: report of a New England Shoe & Leather Association dinner, attended by several Republican and Democratic Congressmen, at which a formal campaign for repeal of the 15 per cent duty on hides was begun. See also the annual reports of the Boston Chamber of Commerce.

[25] *Congressional Record,* 57 Cong., 1 Sess., December 3, 1901, p. 83.

Republican newspapers throughout the country began to make similar discoveries about the changed temper of the American public.[26] As the coal strike dragged on, the tension mounted. "Trusts," Cabot Lodge wrote to his friend in the White House, "thanks to you, we can manage . . . Tariff revision we can discuss . . . But the rise in the price of coal we cannot argue with." [27] Roosevelt agreed that the strike had created "a good deal of formless and vague uneasiness . . . in favor of tariff revision." "The tariff," he continued, "of course, has nothing whatever to do with the matter [the rise in coal prices], as there is no tariff on anthracite coal." [28] But he confessed, "All this is aside from the immediate political effect." The high prices had created "an unreasoning feeling" against the government and the tariff, and he expected the public to "visit upon our heads responsibility for the shortage of coal." [29]

By the end of September, the *Boston Herald* observed: "The evidence is increasing that there is something very like a tariff reform wave started in this country . . . It has been prevalent, and we may add powerful, in Iowa; it has been much in evidence in Wisconsin and Minnesota, and it has certainly affected the tone of the press in . . . [Chicago], if it has gone no farther. We are more interested just at present in the fact that it has reached Massachusetts, and is seriously affecting public opinion in the Republican party of this state." [30] Responding to the pressures of their constituencies, three of Massachusetts' ten Republican Congressmen came out for revi-

[26] See Richard C. Baker, *The Tariff Under Roosevelt and Taft* (Hastings, Nebraska, 1941), pp. 30–32.

[27] Lodge to Roosevelt, September 22, 1902, in *Correspondence*, I, 528–529.

[28] Roosevelt was mistaken. The Dingley Act's definition of "anthracite coal" actually classified all available anthracite as dutiable. See H. C. Gauss (confidential clerk for Secretary of the Navy William H. Moody) to Congressman James T. McCleary of Minnesota, October 17, 1902 (Moody MSS). McCleary had protested a speech by Moody in which the former Massachusetts Congressman had said that the 67¢ per ton duty on anthracite "was smuggled into the tariff act in a sneaking and cowardly manner." *Boston Herald,* October 11, 1902.

[29] Roosevelt to Lodge, September 27, 1902, in *Correspondence*, I, 532–533; Roosevelt to Mark Hanna, September 27, 1902, quoted in Henry F. Pringle, *Theodore Roosevelt, A Biography* (New York, 1931), p. 189.

[30] *Boston Herald,* September 27, 1902.

sion of the tariff. This was sufficient cause for alarm among stalwart protectionists. But what the *Herald* had particularly in mind was the disturbance created in Boston's new Back Bay Congressional district by one Eugene Noble Foss.

Foss was a manufacturer who had risen from rather plebeian origins to great wealth in the classic manner, by marrying the boss's daughter. He had never participated directly in politics until 1900, when he assisted in his brother's election to Congress in Michigan. Meanwhile, he had earned the distrust of conservatives in the business community by his speculation in stocks and real estate (occasionally in collaboration with the suspect Henry Whitney). In 1902, to the chagrin of the regular Republican organization, Foss announced his candidacy against the party's choice for Congress. His program was "free wool, free coal, free iron, free hides," and reciprocity with Canada — or, as Senator Lodge grumpily, but fairly accurately, described it, "free trade in everything Massachusetts buys and protection for all she makes." [31] "My desire to go to Congress," Foss declared, "is because I am a New England manufacturing man . . . and because I have invested money here." He thanked Iowa for reviving the tariff revision issue, because revision, he contended, was "an absolute necessity to the manufacturing men of this district." New England's natural market, he argued, was to the north, not in the American West; New England businessmen must secure a reciprocal trade agreement with Canada. To those who deplored the influence of business in politics, Foss retorted, "I say let us have more commercialism; . . . we are reaching a point where a few businessmen are needed to leaven up the politicians." [32]

[31] Lodge to Roosevelt, September 25, 1902, *Correspondence*, I, 530.

[32] *Boston Record*, August 5, 1902. In a speech made later in the same month, Foss pointed out that only two of Massachusetts' fifteen representatives in the Capitol were businessmen; it was time, he said, that there were more businessmen — like Mark Hanna — in Washington. *Boston Herald*, August 26, 1902. See also *Boston Evening Transcript*, September 20, 1902. For purposes of comparison: of New York's 34 Congressmen and Senators, 20 described themselves as businessmen; in Pennsylvania, 13 of 28; in Ohio, 9 of 21; in New Jersey, 6 of 10; in Connecticut, 5 of 6; and in Rhode Island, all 4. *Congressional Directory*, 57th Congress.

In the open caucus balloting on September 24, Foss carried the 11th congressional district by a small margin. Regulars reckoned Foss's victory against the all-out efforts of the party organization as a measure of the discontent within the state over high prices, particularly of coal. As Foss's own campaign manager had said when asked whether "the people" really cared about tariff revision, "They may not know all the details of these [tariff] questions, but they, for instance, know that coal is $12 a ton." [33] Something of a megalomaniac, Foss attempted to turn his nomination victory into a springboard for control of the party. He announced that at the state convention he would substitute his own revisionist platform for the party's protectionism. ("He is mad . . . apparently," said Lodge, only slightly amused.) [34] Under the circumstances, there appeared to be some chance that Foss might succeed in cracking the façade of Republican solidarity.

But at the convention during the first week of October, the party brass stopped the revisionist "revolt." Senator Lodge, in a stirring oratorical performance, urged the faithful to recognize that Massachusetts' strength lay in loyalty to the national party's principles; the tiny state could not expect to retain its pre-eminence if it went its own way. The welfare of the state's labor and industry, he declared, depended on protectionism; protectionism would fail if each state's party organization demanded exemptions on its behalf. In the *regular* manner, and by working with the party *regulars,* Lodge pledged he would seek some form of tariff agreement with the countries to the north.[35]

[33] *Boston Herald,* September 20, 1902.
[34] Lodge to Roosevelt, September 25, 1902, *Correspondence,* I, 530.
[35] *Boston Herald,* October 3 and 4, 1902. The Boston Chamber of Commerce expressed its confidence in Lodge's sincerity: "While no further progress has been made toward securing a general treaty of reciprocity with . . . Canada . . . the coal famine with which we are confronted has created an irresistible demand for at least a limited treaty of reciprocity, that will provide for placing coal upon the free list in return for similar action by Canada. A bill designed to accomplish this has been introduced by Senator Lodge and should be law." *17th Annual Report* (Boston, 1903), p. 18. Lodge's bill not only failed to become law, but the Senator was at that very

Lodge, of course, worried less that high coal prices might breach the walls of protectionism than that they might overturn the party in Massachusetts. He fretted particularly over the possibility that the strike might cause the defeat of his son-in-law, Augustus P. Gardner, who had just won a hard-fought open caucus election for the Republican congressional nomination in the Gloucester-Haverhill district. In a near panic, Lodge sputtered against the "insensate folly . . . of the operators" who, in refusing a settlement, jeopardized Republican power and "created socialists." [36] "If no settlement is reached it means political disaster in New England and especially in this State," he wrote to Roosevelt. "We shall lose the three close districts which will give the Democrats five, and Gus [son-in-law Gardner] and George Lawrence will both be in serious peril. Our vote on the Governor will fall to the danger point." Lodge assumed that the President did not have authority to intervene officially in the strike, but he pleaded, "Is there anything we can appear to do?" [37]

Some three weeks before election time, the chief threat to Republican success was removed. While Lodge wrung his hands in helpless exasperation, Murray Crane stepped in with the practical suggestion that the President summon both sides to Washington, where Roosevelt might offer recommendations to both groups jointly. Since the suggestion came from so conservative and eminent a businessman as Crane, Roosevelt believed he could accept the idea without risking the stigma of radical. The principals to the dispute arrived in Washington on October 3, and within two weeks Roosevelt, with the aid of Mark Hanna and J. P. Morgan, convinced the operators

---

time in the process of sabotaging Secretary of State John Hay's reciprocity treaty with Newfoundland. See Chapter Five.

[36] Lodge to Roosevelt, September 25, 1902, *Correspondence*, I, 530; and Lodge to William H. Moody, October 6, 1902 (Moody MSS). Just like the Populists, whom he detested, Lodge chose America's favorite bogyman as the target of his fury: "Such insolence and arrogance [he raged] . . . I firmly believe Morgan is behind them." To Roosevelt, October 11, 1902, *Correspondence*, I, 538.

[37] Lodge to Roosevelt, September 27, 1902, *Correspondence*, I, 531–532.

that unless they consented to an arbitrated settlement they would have to bear the responsibility for "socialistic" intervention by the government in the coal mines, and probably the defeat of the Republican party at election time. On October 16, the country learned of the end of the strike, and Republicans breathed easier. "Well, we have got it thru!" Roosevelt exulted in a note to Crane. "I am very thankful that you came on to see me about it. But, heavens and earth it has been a struggle!" [38]

"The settlement of the coal strike," Lodge observed, more to the point, "has changed the complexion of the campaign here entirely . . . We shall have decreased majorities, of course, for it is an off year and we have a new candidate for Governor, but we shall elect Bates, who is making a most admirable campaign." "His speeches," Lodge added, "are strong and manly, and he has displayed a grasp of both State and National questions that I hardly anticipated." [39]

IV

John L. Bates, lieutenant governor and Republican candidate for governor in 1902, had worked his way into party eminence partly in spite of the efforts of the senator who now condescendingly admired his campaign behavior. After a two-year apprenticeship on the Boston Common Council, he had won election in 1894 to the lower house of the General Court; three years later he had astonished the politicos by taking the Speakership of the House without machine support. Then, in 1899, he had upset the Republican organization at the state convention by challenging and defeating Curtis Guild, Jr., Cabot Lodge's protégé, in an open contest for the lieutenant-governor nomination. In the interest of party harmony, the organization had fallen in behind Bates, and Guild had waited patiently another three years for the second place nomination. Lodge himself had placed no obstacles in Bates's way to the

[38] Roosevelt to Crane, October 17, 1902 (Crane MSS).
[39] Lodge to Meyer, October 20, 1902 (Meyer MSS); Lodge to Roosevelt, October 20, 1902, *Correspondence*, I, 542.

top of the escalator as Murray Crane's successor in 1902; indeed, he had huffily deplored the fact that hostility to Bates was based "on the profound idea of a certain element . . . 'that he is not our kind.' " [40]

But young Jack Bates of East Boston won few smiles on Beacon Street and in the Back Bay. It was true that he was of colonial descent, on *both* parents' lines; he had even served for four years as Supreme Governor of the United Order of the Pilgrim Fathers. His family, however, was not one of wealth. His father was a notorious finger-wagging Methodist minister-evangelist. To win a position in politics, Bates had to rely on ward-heeler support, often from among his father's following, and some of his supporters were definitely not the "right sort." As the prospective successor to the beloved Murray Crane, he evoked a bipartisan sniff from the genteel set. "I should hate to run against so sincere, honest, and clearminded a man as Murray Crane," former Democratic candidate John E. Russell had written to Charles Hamlin in 1901. "When that Cheap Jack, rattling Methodist, Bates comes up it will be different." [41] In many of the somber and aseptic social clubs around the state, Republicans harrumphed that a vote for "Gaston and Guild" would be about the best decision at election time in 1902. [42]

Nevertheless, as Lodge had predicted, Bates beat Gaston handily, though his plurality was some 20,000 votes smaller than Guild's plurality over the Democrats' second-slot candidate. That many Republicans did vote for Gaston and Guild is evident from the returns in the Back Bay congressional district, which Gaston carried by 600 votes, though Guild carried the district by over 1,000. But what Gaston gained from Republican snobs he appears to have lost among Bryanite Democrats. He pulled the Democratic vote up about 4 per cent

[40] Lodge to Roosevelt, November 3, 1902, *Correspondence,* I, 545.
[41] Russell to Hamlin, August 18, 1901 (Hamlin MSS).
[42] *Boston Record,* August 15, 1902; *Springfield Republican,* September 21, 1902; Lodge to Roosevelt, October 27, 1902, *Correspondence,* I, 544.

(to 39 per cent of the total), but fell short of Bates's total by 37,000 votes, a gap 25,000 larger than even pessimistic Democrats had anticipated. In the city of Boston, Gaston did worse than Quincy had the year before; the Republicans also reduced the Boston delegation in the House by one.

Agitation during the year over the coal strike and tariff produced no striking changes in the relative strength of the two major parties.[43] The principal tariff agitator, Eugene Foss, went down to defeat in the new congressional district which the Republican legislature had purportedly made "safe." Although there is some evidence that the regular Republicans deliberately cut the pugnacious interloper (Murray Crane, for example, allowed his name to be linked with Foss's Democratic rival), the fact that Foss lost most heavily in the wards which had supported him in the open caucus election indicated that he owed his nomination as much to Democrats crossing into the Republican caucus as to his stand for tariff revision.[44] Only in the Socialist and Socialist Labor party columns did the electorate manifest any sharp disaffection toward the *status quo*. The combined Socialist vote for governor increased by more than 20,000 (a more than 100 per cent increase), and the Socialist percentage of the total vote in the state rose from 6 to 10 per cent. In addition, the Socialist Democratic party elected a third member to the lower house of the General Court, this one from Brockton. Since the two Socialist candidates for lieutenant governor polled 25 per cent more votes than the gubernatorial candidates, it is safe to assume that those who voted the Socialist tickets did not do so out of pique against Bates. The Socialists did, however, draw their greatest new strength from usually Republican wards. The vote

[43] The Democrats regained the two state senate seats they had lost the previous year, and ten seats in the lower house; they also took four of the fourteen congressional elections, two more than they were expected to take, including the new district.

[44] The same districts which supported the machine candidate in the caucus gave Foss majorities. But Foss lost even his own ward in the November polls, and most of the other wards he had carried in September.

probably reflected a reaction, accentuated by the coal strike
and charges of a "coal trust," against the great business consolidations of the previous year.

By the following year, the "crisis" of 1902 was ancient history. Little protest arose, for example, when the legislature
rejected the findings of its own investigation into coal price-
fixing; bills to permit municipalities to purchase and own coal
yards ultimately failed, though in the House they had attracted
considerable support early in the session. In the hot days at the
close of the session, the Senate shelved a bill to regulate the
sale of coal, coke, and charcoal, without attracting more than
squib attention in the press.[45]

Even the agitation for tariff revision subsided, as it did
throughout the country. Although during 1903 Roosevelt kept
up with public opinion by pushing through Congress three
moderate acts to limit corporate activities,[46] he worked closely
with Old Guard leaders — like Senator Nelson Aldrich of
Rhode Island — to put the clamps on any further tariff agitation. Publicly and privately he used every effort to stifle revisionist sentiment, which he feared might divide the party and
jeopardize his election in 1904. In his public addresses Roosevelt became the spokesman for the standpat view.[47] Meanwhile,
he chided confidants who criticized the Old Guard's stiff-
backed opposition to the reconsideration of existing tariff
schedules; the Old Guard senators, he averred, were all "broad-
minded and patriotic, as well as sagacious, skillful and reso-
lute." [48] "My feeling about this tariff question," he confided,
"is, of course, that it is one of expediency and not of moral-

[45] *MSJ,* June 9, 1903, pp. 1057–1058. The General Court ultimately
passed a weak bill requiring coal dealers to be licensed. *MHRJ,* June 16,
1903, pp. 1455–1457; *MSJ,* June 22, 1903, pp. 1128–1129, June 26, 1903,
pp. 1152–1153.

[46] The acts were the Elkins anti-rebate bill, the establishment of a Department of Commerce and Labor which included a Bureau of Corporations,
and the Expedition Act, which was to facilitate antitrust prosecutions. The
latter two had possibilities but did not nearly meet existing demands.

[47] See Roosevelt to Elihu Root, April 22, 1903, in Baker, p. 38; Roosevelt
to Grenville M. Dodge, April 22, 1903, in Morison, III, 466.

[48] Roosevelt to William Howard Taft, March 19, 1903, in Baker, p. 39.

ity." He would therefore gauge his policy according to "how fast or slow it is necessary to go in view of public sentiments."[49]

Republican party organizations in the states during 1903 followed the President's lead. Even the Iowa party trimmed its demands, in effect repudiating the insurgent Governor Albert Cummins.[50] There was no dissent at the Massachusetts State Convention when the Resolutions Committee wrote a platform which opposed revision.

Under Gaston's leadership, the Democrats meanwhile fell into internecine warfare as serious as that which followed the 1896 campaign. Gaston himself precipitated one major schism by charging that the state committee did not use his money to the best purposes in the 1902 campaign. He broke with the committee and alienated a powerful segment of the Boston Democracy led by Chairman William S. McNary. In selecting his own campaign manager in 1903 to direct his second try for the governorship, Gaston could hardly have made a worse choice. His man, Edward F. McSweeney, was a former deputy commissioner of immigration at Ellis Island, whom President Roosevelt had dismissed the year before on suspicion of corruption. George Fred Williams, who had "given up politics" after the defeat of his platform at the 1902 convention, came out of his tent long enough to denounce McSweeney and to send incriminating information about him to President Roosevelt.[51] Despite Gaston's lavish use of money, the rank and file behind both Williams and McNary sat on their hands throughout the campaign.

Gaston suffered in addition from a lack of issues. When the 1903 campaign got under way, he tried for a time to capitalize on the current post office scandals, but his employment of McSweeney undermined the effectiveness of the issue since McSweeney had been charged with much the same kind of mis-

[49] Roosevelt to J. B. Bishop, April 22, 1903, quoted *ibid.*, pp. 39–40.
[50] *Ibid.*, p. 40.
[51] Roosevelt to Lodge, October 23, 1903, *Correspondence*, II, 70; Roosevelt to Curtis Guild, Jr., October 20, 1903, in Morison, III, 633–34.

conduct. In addition, it was not an issue which would easily excite voters in an off-year state election. On state matters, the Democratic platform touched only three issues: (1) the alleged extravagance of the Bates administration, (2) the passage of the new Corporation Law, and (3) Bates's rigid enforcement of blue laws and liquor regulations (at least in Boston). Governmental extravagance might perhaps have been an attractive issue to a business-oriented electorate, but it was not one to stimulate mass enthusiasm, and in any case, both parties could (and did) produce their own figures on the extent of the state debt. An attack on the Corporation Law might have had a powerful effect under different circumstances. But in 1903 it bordered on the ludicrous. As Senator Hoar declared at the Republican State Convention, since the Democrats had selected the principal author of the law (Frederic J Stimson) to write the Democratic platform, they were in no position to cause the Republicans discomfort.[52] Stimson, who had served on the special committee of 1902, never denied Bates's statement that he had indicated no dissatisfaction with the law during consultations with the Governor, or until the time that Gaston invited him to write the Democratic platform. But whether or not the Republican leaders had significantly edited the Committee's bill, as the Democrats charged, since Gaston was heading the ticket the protestations appeared a mockery. Only the third point proved mildly effective, if a bit dishonest. As Bates argued, "The complaint of the invasion of personal liberty of citizens [which was the way the Democrats phrased the issue] seems like the blind appeal of men who have not the courage in their platform to ask for the repeal of the laws, the enforcement of which they condemn, and who therefore place themselves in the inevitable light of men who appeal for votes on the ground that, if elected, the laws will not be enforced." [53] The appeal was nevertheless popular, but it was limited to Boston.

[52] Hennessy, *Twenty-five Years*, p. 11.

[53] Bates's comment on the Democratic platform, in the *Boston Herald*, October 4, 1903.

It was unfortunate for the Democrats that their disunity and the character of their leading candidate left them in a poor position to take advantage of a fine election opportunity, for Jack Bates's record as a governor and as a politician exposed him to considerable criticism, most of it sound. Most Republican leaders believed throughout the campaign that Bates was in serious trouble. The state committee sounded the alarm, and the top men of the party rallied to the rescue. The committee recruited Murray Crane to write the platform ("a model of brevity [chortled one committeeman] . . . guaranteed to be . . . as harmless as the editorial page of the [Boston] Transcript");[54] Senator Lodge hurried home from London where he had been negotiating a boundary between Canada and Alaska; old Senator George Frisbie Hoar was persuaded to make the nomination speech for Bates; Guild and Crane prevailed upon Secretary of the Navy William H. Moody to campaign in his home state and to make one of the other nominating speeches at the convention;[55] and President Roosevelt persuaded several Congressmen, including Senator Joseph B. Foraker of Ohio, to make a few speeches in the Bay State.

Bates's principal weakness lay in his neglect of his early supporters among the rank and file in his effort to make his peace with the organization leaders. Immediately after the 1902 election, and again after the inauguration, Curtis Guild reported that Bates had proved unexpectedly friendly and, indeed, appeared ready to settle down as a "regular." [56] Some time later, one of the party's "regular" financiers exulted that Bates was "making a very good Governor" and had "got clear of the gang who had supported him." [57] But other party workers perceived that this development might ruin Bates. "The Bates situation is one that I do not believe ever existed in the State before," confided one member of the state committee.

[54] J. B. Reynolds to Lodge, September 26, 1903 (Lodge MSS).
[55] See letters from Crane and Guild in 1903 (Moody MSS).
[56] Guild to George Meyer, November 28, 1902 (Meyer MSS); Guild to Lodge, January 12, 1903 (Lodge MSS).
[57] George Meyer to Lodge, September 15, 1903 (Lodge MSS).

Bates's friends had deserted him, and were attacking him. He was "absolutely dependent now and in the future upon the persons who [had] fought him for Lieutenant Governor [in 1899]." He had only the formal support of the machine.[58]

While abandoning his friends, Bates did not go over completely to the organization leaders. He maintained his independence especially in his appointments. He ignored not only Lodge, which did not surprise even the Senator, but also Murray Crane, the still important Crapo faction in southern Massachusetts, and William H. Moody.[59] In itself, this practice might not have hurt him, since the machine would have stayed with him rather than create a fight to oust him. But Bates's selections were sometimes truly astonishing. For example, he came near creating a public uproar when he indicated that he would name to the state superior court the attorney for Thomas W. Lawson, the erratic millionaire-muckraker; luckily for the party, the nominee declined to be considered.[60] Luck did not intervene, however, in Bates's appointment of a chief of the Boston Police Commission. It was his Police Commissioner's activities which gave rise to the Democrats' complaints about interference with "personal liberty." In defending the appointment, one party official lamented that Bates did not realize "how much disgust communities have for a man who sticks his nose into all parts of the city with a corps of reporters and newspaper artists at his heels." [61]

[58] J. B. Reynolds to Lodge, September 26, 1903 (Lodge MSS).
[59] See Walter Clifford to Moody, July 1 and 6, 1903 (Moody MSS); Crane to Lodge, April 13, 1903 (Lodge MSS).
[60] George Meyer to Lodge, September 15, 1903 (Lodge MSS).
[61] J. B. Reynolds to Lodge, September 26, 1903 (Lodge MSS). Cf. *Boston Herald,* August 23, 1903. Although the genteel Democratic newspapers and the major candidates did not choose to make a major issue of it, Bates was also tainted by something of a personal scandal. Even his best friends had a hard time explaining his acceptance of a $3000 personal loan from the notorious professional lobbyist, Walter Holden, during his first term as lieutenant governor in 1900. Holden had been one of Bates's financial angels during the Governor's climb to the top; he apparently deserted Bates when Bates refused to name Holden's man to the Boston Police Commission. The *Springfield Republican,* which supported Bates as a lesser evil than Gaston,

The elections that fall proved only that the electorate was in no mood for change. Gaston's liabilities evidently outweighed Bates's, and the embattled incumbent was re-elected by almost exactly the same margin as in 1902. In the General Court contests, the Democrats won exactly the same number of seats in each house as the previous year. Significantly, the Socialists were the only losers: despite the weaknesses of the major party candidates, the combined Socialist vote for governor dropped 10,000 votes, or 50 per cent; it never again showed noteworthy strength. Politically, Massachusetts had returned to the apparent placidity of early 1901; the stresses and strains of American society in the early part of the Progressive Era, though quite real, had so far made no impact on the state's politics.

V

The following year the Republicans finally forfeited their hold on the governorship. Bates had learned nothing from his troubles in 1903, and his intraparty relations worsened. The state's economy meanwhile suffered a serious setback, thereby compounding the Governor's political woes.

From the beginning of the year, Bates showed his inability to command the support of his party in the General Court. The legislature not only rejected the Governor's recommendations, it demonstrated positive delight in repudiating him. He hurt his own cause by recommending that the legislature strengthen the Sunday entertainment laws; the suggestion only compounded the difficulties caused by his meticulous police commissioner in Boston. He alienated state farm groups by recommending the reorganization of the state Board of Agriculture in order to centralize responsibility and enforcement of inspection and grading laws. (Some of the farmers' organs, reported one newspaper, "are saying that if this were not a

---

"explained" (October 26, 1903) that obtaining money from men like Holden was necessary since the hostile party machinery had precluded his obtaining money from more "legitimate" sources.

presidential year the Governor's course in this matter would jeopardize his reelection.")[62] His request for a bill to increase the state's share of the revenue from local liquor licenses from 25 per cent to 50 per cent gave rebellious Republican legislators an opportunity to play to their local constituents.[63]

More frequently, however, the legislators used their own ingenuity to embarrass the Governor. Against his wishes, the General Court passed a bill prohibiting overtime employment of women and children (under eighteen) in textile mills, and then sustained the Governor's veto by only a small margin. The same bill had been introduced regularly for about ten years; this was the first time the party leaders allowed it to go to the Governor. Since Bates had vetoed a bill in 1903 to reduce the legal day's work on all public projects to eight hours at the prevailing local wage rates, the second veto marked him as the special enemy of labor.

The hostility to the Governor reached a high pitch on the final day of the legislative session. Bates had vetoed a bill to grant a bounty of $125 to every veteran of the Civil War who had not yet received any gratuity from the state.[64] By a vote of 151 to 47 in the House and 25 to 8 in the Senate, the General Court overrode the veto amidst tumultuous shouting and excitement, which was capped by a parade out of the State House and down the steps to Beacon Street below with two legislators bearing the author of the bill on their shoulders.[65]

That summer, 30,000 cotton textile workers in Fall River jolted Bates's hopes for re-election when they struck against a proposed 12½ per cent reduction in wages. The workers

[62] *Boston Herald,* May 12, 1904.

[63] On February 26, the lower house smashed Bates's request on the liquor licenses by a vote of 153 to 23. *Boston Herald,* February 27, 1903.

[64] In 1903 President Roosevelt signed an act which provided for bonuses to all veterans between the ages of 62 and 70. Pringle, *Roosevelt,* p. 242.

[65] *MHRJ,* June 9, 1904, pp. 1202–1204; *MSJ,* June 9, 1904, pp. 974–975; *Boston Herald,* June 10, 1904. The law was disallowed later by the state supreme court on the ground that a vote of two thirds of the entire legislature, not merely two thirds of those voting, was necessary to override; the court also declared that the use of public funds for private purposes violated the state constitution.

had already absorbed a 10 per cent cut in order to enable the operators to meet a sharp rise in raw cotton prices beginning in the latter part of 1903.[66] The paralysis in this major industry exacerbated workers' feelings about the eight-hour bill and overtime bill vetoes, as well as the widening gap between wage levels and the cost of living.

Later that summer, the Democrats received the kindest gift of all. Angered by the state committee's demands for full control of the 1904 campaign, "Colonel" Gaston withdrew from politics. The petulant banker never served the Democracy so well.[67] Democrats soon found a new financier for their campaign when William L. Douglas of Brockton stepped in to offer his candidacy and his bank roll.

Douglas, a native of Plymouth, Massachusetts, was a self-made man who had earned a fortune in the manufacture and sale of cheap shoes. He attributed his success to intensive sales promotion. Advertisements for "Douglas Shoes," accompanied by a sketch of the manufacturer's mustachioed countenance, appeared daily in most major newspapers throughout the East. Douglas had participated periodically in local and state politics and had served two terms in each house of the General Court. He had attended every national convention of the Democratic party as a delegate since 1884 (except for 1896).[68] Consequently, Douglas enjoyed ample publicity in advance of his campaign for governor in 1904.[69] A conservative who had voted for Palmer and Buckner in 1896, he nevertheless stood well with the labor interests. In 1886 he had helped push through the bill which created the Massachusetts Board of Arbitration and Conciliation, and later he had contributed

[66] MBSL, *Labor Bulletin No. 41* (Boston, May 1906) pp. 191–196.

[67] *Boston Evening Transcript,* September 15, 1904; J. O. Lyford to George H. Lyman (Collector of the Port of Boston), September 15, 1904, in the George H. Lyman Papers, Massachusetts Historical Society, Boston.

[68] In 1904 he attended as a delegate at large, for which privilege he had donated $5,000 to the party campaign chest. Hamlin Diary, January 10 and March 23, 1904.

[69] Michael Hennessy estimates that Douglas was probably the most widely known citizen in Massachusetts (*Twenty-five Years,* p. 129).

significantly to the movement for laws to enforce the weekly payment of wages — both pioneer achievements in the nation.

Douglas struck a single theme in his campaign in 1904: reciprocity with Canada, with an emphasis on "free hides" and "free coal." It was sound Democratic dogma which alienated few in the party and served to attract those who had left because of emphases on political innovations, labor legislation, and — most recently — greater freedom for corporations. In addition, Douglas capitalized on his reputation in labor circles. In the manner of an elder statesman, he urged the striking workers of Fall River to end their walkout, and recommended that the companies take back the workers without discrimination; meanwhile, he promised to set up an investigation of the manufacturers' profits on which he would base a recommendation to the workers on what wages they might reasonably demand. Douglas' offer of personal mediation proved highly popular among the hard-pressed strikers and their sympathizers throughout the state. Meanwhile, trade union leaders contributed to Douglas' cause among the working classes by organizing "Flying Wedges" (as they were popularly called) to conduct intensive anti-Bates campaigns in each of the industrial centers of the state.

Douglas ignored all election contests besides the gubernatorial, and he saw to it that little money was spent in Massachusetts to aid the presidential campaign of Alton Parker against Theodore Roosevelt. "It is not far from the truth," wrote the *Boston Herald* political reporter, "to say that the managers of the Democratic campaign have abandoned the attempt to get votes for Judge Parker in Massachusetts . . . and no fault is being found with those Democrats who indicate their intention of voting for Roosevelt and Douglas." [70] The Democratic Club declined to accept one member's proffered resignation from its executive committee, although he wrote, "I find myself obliged to follow the course of . . . many other

[70] *Boston Herald,* October 30, 1904; see also Hennessy, *Twenty-five Years,* p. 129.

Democrats of long standing, and to support the candidacy of President Roosevelt." [71] The sentiment appeared widespread.

On election day, William Douglas polled the largest popular vote for governor (235,000) since Roger Wolcott's landslide victory over George Fred Williams in 1896; he overwhelmed Bates by more than 35,000. It was entirely a personal victory, for the Democratic party suffered setbacks in every other sector. Theodore Roosevelt swept the Bay State by 92,000 votes (258,000 to 166,000); Lieutenant Governor Curtis Guild won a third term with a 30,000 vote plurality; and in addition, the Republicans reduced the Democrats' congressional delegation by one, their state senate representation by three, and their lower house membership by fifteen.

Many interested observers saw in the results a victory for the cause of reciprocity with Canada, and for tariff reform generally.[72] Others, like George Fred Williams, argued that Parker's defeat, Douglas' success, and gubernatorial victories by reform Democrats such as Joseph W. Folk of Missouri and John A. Johnson of Minnesota proved that the country was in a radical mood and that the Democrats could win only on a "progressive" platform.[73] But whatever may be true about Parker, or Minnesota, or midwestern states where young insurgents defeated the old guard Republican factions, in Massachusetts the Democratic gubernatorial victory proved nothing more than Douglas' popularity and Bates's unpopularity.[74] The same voters in Fall River who gave the Democratic gubernatorial nominee a thumping 3,000 vote plurality — the first time a Democrat had carried the city in twelve years — also gave the Republican congressional candidate a 2,000 vote plurality and returned the same number of Republicans to the legislature (five out of seven) as they had in 1903. The same was true

[71] Prescott F. Hall to William H. Brown (secretary of the Club), September 8, 1904 (Democratic Club MSS). Hall had served as chairman of the executive committee until July of 1904.

[72] See Baker, p. 44; Baker agrees with that judgment.

[73] *Boston Herald*, November 10, 1904.

[74] Cf. Hennessy, *Twenty-five Years*, p. 131.

of Fitchburg, Brockton, Lynn, and five other cities, where voters boomed Douglas but returned the usual number of Democrats (or fewer) to the General Court. Moreover, they were to give no other Democratic gubernatorial candidate a plurality for at least five more years. Meanwhile, Eugene N. Foss, who made his second bid for election to Congress as the Republican nominee, took a worse drubbing than in 1902: Massachusetts had no taste, evidently, for Republican insurgents such as those who had been stirring the Midwest for the past four years.[75]

VI

In sum, as reform movements throughout the country began to set a national mood during the early years of the new century, Massachusetts seemed disinclined to share that mood. Well-worn Democratic proposals to extend the popular character of government by such devices as the initiative and referendum inspired little enthusiasm within the state. For a time during these years, the Socialists had won considerable respect in the Bay State, but by 1904 their political power had already dwindled. The combined Socialist poll that year plummeted to 13,600, or 3 per cent, the lowest in the history of the two parties: contrary to the national trend, Massachusetts Socialists were on the wane. At the same time, while reformers elsewhere launched campaigns against corporate freedom and irresponsibility, Massachusetts found it necessary to withdraw from advanced positions which it had held against abuses by corporations. The state also resisted the extension of laws to protect its workers (especially women and children) from exploitation. The nonviolent but prolonged labor agitation which shook the state in 1904 represented not increased aggressiveness but defensive action by workers against reduced wages.

Only the efforts of Democrat Douglas and Republican Foss, together with various commercial groups, for reciprocity with Canada and a general tariff revision suggested that Massa-

[75] See Mowry, *Era of Roosevelt,* p. 75.

chusetts might have something to contribute to the reform spirit. For a time during 1904, indeed, the Republican hierarchy fretted about the revisionist noises which emanated from the Bay State; that was not the corner of the country from which protectionists expected such sounds. Lieutenant Governor Guild pleaded with Lodge early that year that the "critical" condition of the party, caused by revisionist sentiment, required that the party issue an official declaration in favor of reciprocity.[76] President Roosevelt noted that Navy Secretary William H. Moody, too, was "much impressed by the Massachusetts reciprocity movement." [77]

But Foss and his allies met defeat at the polls. William Douglas' gubernatorial victory had no general significance, and the state electorate returned heavy Republican majorities to the General Court, thereby guaranteeing the return of the revisionists' nemesis, Senator Lodge, who was up for re-election that January. All in all, Massachusetts was out of step with the nation.

[76] Guild to Lodge, February 26, 1904 (Lodge MSS). Lodge replied that he did not think the situation so "dark" but that he might make such a gesture anyway. Lodge to Guild, March 10, 1904 (*ibid.*).

[77] Roosevelt to Lodge, June 2, 1904, in Morison, IV, 813.

CHAPTER FIVE

TARIFF TINKERING AND RAILROAD REFORM

The great development of industrialism means that there must
be an increase in the supervision exercised by the Government
over business enterprise.

Theodore Roosevelt, 1905

In 1905, Theodore Roosevelt came into the Presidency "in
his own right," and reformers hopefully prepared to watch his
smoke. The President chose as his prime target the railroads,
whose iniquities had long been trumpeted by small and large
business groups across the country. In addition, although he
sought to evade the issue, Roosevelt faced rising demands for
a reshuffling of tariff advantages among the nation's business
interests. As the progressive movement began to gain momentum, tariff revision and railroad reform became the issues on
which both the drive for an improved political economy and
the challenge to Republican party leadership centered.

On these issues Massachusetts appeared in an ambivalent
role. Large sections of its business community, for example,
dominated the movement for tariff reform, but the state's senators usually spoke for the well-taken-care-of interests, and
thus helped to thwart reform. The state's advanced legislation
had admittedly hobbled its corporations in their competition
with corporations chartered by other states, and political leaders such as Curtis Guild had demanded uniform national corporation laws to remove the handicap, but when the federal
government finally made a significant move to control the railroads, the most conspicuous of interstate corporations, the
state again appeared on the conservative side.

I

Although the Republican national platform of 1904 had
offered little to encourage those who hoped for revision of the

Dingley tariff, revision was widely regarded as the first order of business for the new administration. The Dingley tariff was the first since the Civil War to survive eight years without revision — that may have accounted at least in part for the revisionist agitation. In addition, many business enterprises possessed a vital interest in tariff reform. In any case, a few days after the election the *Boston Evening Transcript* (November 11) bluntly predicted that Roosevelt would call a special session of Congress which would deal exclusively with the tariff, the *Washington Star* (November 15) considered it "open to little doubt" that the new Congress would enact a new tariff law, and the *New York Journal of Commerce* (November 19) said plainly, "The tariff must be revised." [1] At the same time, Roosevelt's closest cabinet adviser, Elihu Root, suggested to him privately that there was "a widespread conviction that . . . the present tariff is too high," and added that even many manufacturers did not believe their industries required the existing duties.[2]

But Roosevelt knew that though existing tariff schedules might handicap and antagonize some businesses, revision would surely antagonize others and perhaps not even reconcile those originally alienated; meanwhile, revision would irritate those businessmen who were not directly affected by the schedules but who would nevertheless have to make troublesome adjustments in their plans and expectations. The President's response to all the revisionist advice and agitation was to huddle with Speaker Joseph ("stand by the status") Cannon — and three days later the President's secretary informed the press that there would be no mention of the tariff in the annual message that December. There was none. ("Whence comes this so-called demand for tariff-tinkering?" Cannon wanted to know.)[3]

Roosevelt nevertheless did work for one tariff measure in

[1] Quoted in Baker, pp. 45–46; see Baker also for many additional editorials throughout the country.
[2] Philip C. Jessup, *Elihu Root* (New York, 1938), II, 214.
[3] Quoted in Pringle, *Roosevelt,* p. 292.

which at least a limited segment of the economy had an interest: a reciprocity treaty with Newfoundland which exchanged free entry into the United States of Newfoundland-cured fish for free entry into Newfoundland of some American manufactured goods and the right of American fishermen to use Newfoundland waters. The treaty partly met the rising demands for reciprocity with Canada by such business organizations as the National Association of Manufacturers and the National and New England Reciprocity Leagues. In addition, trade experts pointed out that the Newfoundland treaty represented a first break in the British Commonwealth preferential tariff arrangement; Prime Minister Sir Robert Bond of Newfoundland had had to overcome vehement Canadian opposition to obtain permission from Great Britain for the negotiations. The treaty had encountered, however, the stubborn opposition of the Gloucester (Massachusetts) fishermen, who feared it would ruin their industry. And the fishermen had the passionate support of Massachusetts' Senator Lodge, the second-ranking Republican on the Foreign Relations Committee. Although in 1902 Secretary of State John Hay had proceeded with the lengthy negotiations with Bond only after Lodge had told him that he believed the treaty would not injure Gloucester (since Gloucester dealt primarily in fresh, not cured, fish), Lodge later got word of opposition from Gloucester and proceeded to pigeonhole the agreement. No plea of vital national or even Massachusetts benefit could move him. There the matter stood when Roosevelt made his post-election move.

A few days after his election, Roosevelt wrote to Lodge: "I feel that you and [Murray] Crane should get together and agree on what amendments are indispensably necessary to that treaty, and . . . [then] report it out . . . Of course remember that the Gloucester people cannot be trusted to establish the minimum they ought to receive . . ." [4] On the same day, the President wrote to Crane, whom Governor Bates had appointed in October to the seat of the late Senator Hoar, urging

[4] Roosevelt to Lodge, November 12, 1904, in Morison, IV, 103.

him to use his influence with the state's senior senator: "Amend the Newfoundland reciprocity treaty as . . . necessary," he pleaded, "but . . . get the treaty out." The whole success of Canadian reciprocity negotiations, he added, depended on the good faith shown in the Newfoundland case.[5]

But Lodge remained intransigent. He was moved partly by sentiment. ("I have been brought up among these fishermen," he once wrote to his mother when a similar issue arose; ". . . I do not propose to stand by in silence and see their rights sacrificed.")[6] But the fact that son-in-law Gardner needed Gloucester's support to stay in Congress surely reinforced his determination. Lodge permitted the treaty to pass the Senate in January, but with such amendments as to make it worthless to Newfoundland. For that country it was a poor anticlimax to the years of effort its leader had exerted to arrange amicable trade relations with the United States. When the treaty's terms became known early in February, the *Boston Evening Transcript* lamented, "No American would have the effrontery to ask Sir Robert Bond to accept it," while Secretary Hay raged privately, "It seems to me as stupid a piece of bad manners as any country has ever been guilty of."[7]

As expected, Newfoundland rejected the revised agreement with bad feelings. That same month, Roosevelt's efforts to revive negotiations with Canada for a reciprocity treaty also broke down. For the rest of the year, far from establishing amicable trade relations with our neighbors to the north, Roosevelt sweated out a series of armed conflicts which broke out between Newfoundland and Gloucester fishermen. In May, Roosevelt wrote sadly to Lodge, "Inasmuch as our fisherfolk conduct their fisheries under circumstances which give the Newfoundlanders and Canadians a chance to harass them, it was obviously unwise to undertake a negotiation which our own people would insist upon having carried on in a way that

[5] Roosevelt to Crane, November 12, 1904 (Crane MSS).
[6] See Garraty, p. 235.
[7] Quoted in Charles C. Tansill, *Canadian-American Relations, 1875–1911* (New Haven, 1943), p. 95.

inevitably inflamed and exasperated the other side." There was perhaps a touch of reproof in his carefully chosen words to his friend.[8]

Although there may have been abstruse reasons for Lodge's steadfast loyalty to the Gloucester fishermen, his opposition to the Hay-Bond Treaty represented accurately his general reluctance to undo a vested interest; although the prosperity of the tiny Gloucester fisheries depended upon the "artificial" protection of the import duties, which duties interfered with the possible prosperity of other businesses, the fact that the Gloucester interest *existed* gave it rights against any positive governmental action.[9] To the conservative mind, this outweighed most arguments for action on behalf of interests on the make. Gloucester, of course, did not stand alone; many larger industries could claim the rights of a vested interest, such as the woolens, worsted, and cotton textile industries. Each opposed all gestures toward tariff adjustments because they might jeopardize its protected position in world competition. In addition, that large section of the business community which feared the disrupting effect of any tariff revision seconded the pleas for inaction.

Curiously, although Massachusetts' leaders in Washington killed reciprocity, it was nevertheless the noisy segment of the Massachusetts business community, which had dominated the revision campaign during the past year, that Roosevelt had specifically hoped to mollify by pressing the Hay-Bond Treaty. The Massachusetts shoe and boot industry, largest in the nation and employing the state's second largest labor force, led the general demand for tariff revision; it aimed at the removal of the Dingley Act's 15 per cent duty on cattle hides. The newspaper industry gave reciprocity a strong boost, hoping for cheaper pulp and newsprint from Canada, while Nova Scotia

[8] Roosevelt to Lodge, May 15, 1905, in Morison, IV, 118. Lodge had just urged the President to consider purchasing Greenland from Denmark to outflank the Canadians and Newfoundlanders: Lodge to Roosevelt, May 12, 1905, in *Correspondence*, II, 119–120.

[9] Lodge stated his position in just this way in correspondence with Henry M. Whitney in December 1904 (Lodge MSS).

coal interested both coal users and those Massachusetts businessmen, like Henry M. Whitney, who had money in Nova
Scotia mines. Such interests had exasperated Roosevelt during
the campaign of 1904, and he had accused them of the fatuous
desire to exploit cheap raw materials from abroad while they
enjoyed tariff protection for their manufactured products. "The
feeling in Massachusetts about the tariff is absolutely unreasonable," he had fumed earlier that year, "and it is out of the
question to pander to it. Massachusetts owes everything to the
tariff." He pressed for the Hay-Bond Treaty only because he
feared that there was "a sentiment which demands a revision,"
which he could not ignore. "I am meeting not a material need
but a mental attitude," he wrote privately.[10]

The pre-eminence of the Massachusetts Board of Trade, the
Boston Chamber of Commerce, the National Shawmut Bank,
and other merchant and finance leaders among the tariff revisionists suggested that there was more at issue than the President knew or was willing to concede. Eugene Foss had his own
drum to beat, but he also spoke for many who were beginning
to look to the North for markets and raw materials to replace
those they had lost or provide substitutes for those they could
not win in the West. President Lucius Tuttle of the Boston
& Maine Railroad endorsed this viewpoint, as did leading
Republicans such as Curtis Guild and senior Congressman
Samuel Powers. President Charles Mellen of the New Haven
Railroad summed up the issue in May 1904 in a letter to
Henry Whitney, then president of the Boston Chamber of
Commerce:[11]

No one subject is fraught with more of importance to industrial
New England [than reciprocity]. With the center of population in
this country continually moving further westward, with the establishment of manufacturing industries closely following, with cheaper fuel
and cheaper raw materials often available elsewhere, New England will

[10] Roosevelt to N. M. Butler, August 22, 1904, in Morison, IV, 899;
Roosevelt to Butler, December 2, 1904, *ibid.*, 1056.
[11] Letter dated May 15, 1904, printed in the *Springfield Republican,* May
17, 1904.

feel seriously the loss of [its] markets . . . which is inevitable . . .
It is important New England should lead in a policy calculated to
replace those lost markets by others naturally tributary to it, than which
[none is more important than] . . . our northern neighbor . . . Having had part personally during the past six years in directing the establishment of industries elsewhere, knowing the many disadvantages under
which New England labors, I can only wonder at so many being . . .
misled as to their true interests.

II

During 1905, the reciprocity interests made strenuous efforts
to commit the Republican party to their cause. A group of
commercial leaders called the Committee of 100 circulated a
petition among Republican businessmen to demand that the
Republican platform include a resolution which favored reciprocity with Canada and "free" hides, coal, iron, lumber, ore,
and wood pulp. Sidestepping the controversial Eugene Foss,
the Committee publicly endorsed Lieutenant Governor Curtis
Guild and businessman Fred S. Hall to head the Republican
slate that fall, despite Murray Crane's efforts to prevent any
endorsement.[12] Curtis Guild, both as Lieutenant Governor and
formerly as editor of the *Boston Commercial Bulletin,* had long
supported the cause. Leading Republican Congressmen such
as William Lovering of New Bedford and Fred Gillett of
Springfield had urged reciprocity in Congress the previous
year. In January the pressure impelled Lodge to call for an
inquiry "to ascertain whether a tariff revision is desirable at
the present time" (bringing grumbles from the Home Market
Club that the Senator had failed to indicate what conditions
required the opening of such an issue).[13] In August Lodge and
Crane announced that they would support a tariff revision if
it contained a "maximum and minimum" provision.[14]

[12] Crane to Lodge, July 12, 1905 (Lodge MSS); *Boston Herald,* September
6, 1905.
[13] In *Boston Herald,* January 21, 1905.
[14] For the Senators' decision on tariff policy, see Lodge-Crane correspondence, August 11, 18, 19, 1905 (Lodge MSS). The "maximum-minimum"
idea, later incorporated in the Payne-Aldrich Tariff, provided for minimum
duties to be set by the Congress for trade with countries which afforded the

At the state convention in October, however, Lodge and Crane successfully downed the "reciprocitarians." In a trenchant speech, Lodge denounced the Committee of 100's petition as a "Five Cent Resolution," [15] and though he maneuvered to include favorable comment on tariff revision in the party platform it was clear to all that the leadership opposed action at that time. The party also blocked the revisionists' effort to name the second-place candidate. Eben S. Draper, arch-protectionist, manufacturer, and president of the Republican Club, took the nomination by an overwhelming majority over his two opponents.

The nominations illustrated the operation of the Republican party. Years in advance, the organization had designated both Guild and Draper for their position on the state ticket.[16] That Guild's political and social views differed from Draper's more extremely than they did from those of, say, Democratic Governor Douglas, or even from those of Wisconsin insurgent Robert LaFollette, did not merit consideration. The party simply recognized the claim of each candidate to his position on the ticket. As president of the Republican Club, a regular donor to the party treasury, and an avowed aspirant for the governorship, Draper had established a solid stake in the second-place nomination for 1905.

Guild's claim was of even longer standing. He had entered politics as the protégé of Cabot Lodge during the 1890's when Lodge's state power was at its height. Through Lodge's influence, Guild had become one of the four delegates at large to the Republican National Convention in 1896, and had obtained a military commission during the Spanish War. A minor revolt against Lodge's domination of the party in 1899 had

United States "favored nation" treatment; the President was authorized, however, to raise duties to a maximum against countries which "discriminated" against American products.

[15] Lodge later explained that he was referring to the fact that the Committee offered five cents to anyone who filled out a newspaper coupon advertisement for reciprocity. *Boston Herald,* October 25, 1905.

[16] See Francis C. Lowell to George Meyer, April 26, 1905, and Draper to Meyer, May 22, 1905 (Meyer MSS).

helped to defeat Guild's bid for lieutenant governor that year. But Lodge boosted Guild's stock once again by persuading Theodore Roosevelt to take him along on the vice-presidential campaign in 1900. In 1901, Lodge had helped Guild to reorganize the Massachusetts Republican Club, at least partly as a vehicle for Guild's political advancement.[17]

The Lodge-Guild relationship resembled the Lodge-Roosevelt one; in both, the conservative Senator promoted the political interests of a younger, more reform-minded and energetic man of his own social class. The political philosophy of the three men did not differ much, but Roosevelt and Guild had a greater inclination to translate that philosophy into governmental policy. The difference was largely one of style: each lambasted "big business" on special occasions, but Lodge usually confined his hostility to private letters or conversation, while Roosevelt went so far as to condemn publicly the "malefactors of great wealth," and the still more excitable Guild was capable of denouncing J. P. Morgan as a "beefy, red-faced, thick-necked financial bully drunk with wealth and power." [18] More positively, Guild urged improved state and national child labor legislation, and as early as 1901 he went on record for a national incorporation act to provide more effective control of all interstate corporations.[19] Conservatives like Murray Crane, of course, regarded him as "impetuous." [20] Nevertheless, Guild had no opposition when he followed Bates into the lieutenant governorship in 1903, for to squelch Guild's aspirations a second time would have meant to disrupt the organization, which in the 1902 campaign the Republicans did not believe

[17] Lodge to Roosevelt, June 29, 1900, in *Correspondence,* I, 466, and Guild to Lodge, February 13, 1913 (Lodge MSS). Presidency of the Republican Club became a regular step in the political escalator; Guild, Draper, and Louis A. Frothingham each served as president before becoming the party's nominee for lieutenant governor.

[18] Quoted from Guild's *Commercial Bulletin,* which was quoted in the *Fitchburg Sentinel* and other papers, February 21, 1910.

[19] *Boston Evening Transcript,* January 29, 1901.

[20] See Crane to Lodge, July 12, 1905 (Lodge MSS).

they could afford. In 1905 the organization moved him "automatically" to the head of the ticket.[21]

III

Conditions within the Democratic party were the reverse of those in the Republican party. While the G.O.P. was too prosperous a concern to be seriously affected by either political winds or the self-propelled ambitions of wealthy individuals who might finance their own campaigns, the Democrats were too weak and disorganized to resist such influences. Despite William Douglas' victory in 1904, the Democrats still lacked the firm organizational grass roots of an integrated state political party. They remained prey to private money and special interests, in this case those of the reciprocitarians.

Douglas' policies after his inauguration did little to reward the principal party workers around whom an integral organization could be built. He had never sympathized with the leader of the state committee, which caused the regulars to distrust him. Although they accepted Douglas' nominee as chairman of the state committee, they stripped that man of his appointive powers.[22] The Governor's own appointments exasperated the regulars, while within the party councils he strove to reduce the power and prominence of the Irish.[23] Before his administration was very old, Democrats openly accused Douglas of being anti-Catholic. Boston's mayoralty-aspirant John F. Fitzgerald published a list of Douglas' appointees in his newspaper, *The Republic,* in the spring of 1905, showing that the Governor had named 662 non-Catholics and only 54 Catholics to offices throughout the state.[24] Even Douglas' supporter,

[21] So striking was the emphasis upon the smoothly operating promotional mechanism within the party that former State Committee chairman Albert Goetting campaigned for the lieutenant-governor nomination against Draper on the promise that he would break the party escalator by refusing elevation to first place after Guild's tenure; he was the stronger of Draper's two rivals.

[22] *Boston Herald,* December 10, 1904; Hamlin Diary, June 19, 1905.

[23] Hamlin Diary, June 19, 1905.

[24] See also Fitzgerald's editorial in *The Republic,* May 13, 1905.

Charles S. Hamlin, wrote in his diary, "Governor D if not an A.P.A. comes as near to it as any one in my memory." [25] And Eben S. Draper wrote privately that Douglas had "lost a large voting support from the Democratic machine in Boston, and further, from the Irish-American democrats." "It really seems," Draper continued, "as if he had gone out of his way to avoid appointing any of them to office." [26]

Douglas ended all possibilities that he might help to consolidate the party's small gains when he suddenly announced early in 1905 that he was not a candidate for re-election. According to Charles Hamlin, Douglas was induced to withdraw upon the threat of a personal scandal. Late in the 1904 campaign it became known to both Democratic and Republican leaders that during the Civil War Douglas had accepted a bounty to serve as a substitute, and had subsequently deserted; years later, according to Hamlin's informants, he had paid several thousand dollars to obtain a fraudulent honorable discharge and conceal his desertion. With or without Douglas' knowledge, his campaign manager made a deal with Senators Crane and Lodge that Douglas would never run again if they would keep the story from the press.[27] The deal was kept, and on May 26, 1905, the day of the legislature's adjournment, Douglas announced his retirement.[28]

Douglas explained publicly that he had not expected to be elected in 1904 and that, though he was grateful for the public's trust, he preferred private life. Political pundits who did not know about the desertion story guessed that the Governor had become fed up with running battles with the Boston organization led by William Gaston and John F. Fitzgerald; the fact that a majority of the Democrats in the legislature had voted with the Republicans to override several vetoes lent substance

[25] Hamlin Diary, June 19, 1905. "A.P.A." refers to the American Protective Association, an anti-immigrant, particularly anti-Catholic, group which flourished during the 1890's.

[26] Draper to George Meyer, May 22, 1905 (Meyer MSS).

[27] Hamlin Diary, November 29, 1904, and October 30, 1907.

[28] *Boston Herald,* May 27, 1905.

to this view.[29] Many Democratic leaders openly welcomed Douglas' retirement, while George Fred Williams thought that Douglas had been stabbed in the back.[30]

Douglas' exit once more left the Democrats leaderless. The Governor himself tried to get Charles S. Hamlin to run for the nomination, and although Henry M. Whitney and ex-Secretary of State Richard Olney visited Hamlin for the same purpose, he refused to run because Gaston was sure to fight him.[31] Douglas' money, $25,000 according to Hamlin,[32] ultimately went to support Charles W. Bartlett, a likable lawyer from Newton who held the rank of "General" in the state militia but was politically unknown. Bartlett won the nomination without serious opposition.

The Democratic second-place "choice" — the word must be used with some reservation — indicated how thoroughly the reciprocitarians had come to dominate the party that year. Henry Whitney, who put up his own money and thus might have had the first-place spot had he fought for it, became the candidate for lieutenant governor instead. The reason was clear. A triumph over Curtis Guild would mean nothing for Canadian reciprocity since Guild supported that fight. On the other hand, if Whitney could beat Draper, reciprocity would indeed have scored a striking victory. Although there were many, like George Fred Williams, who would have stressed needed labor legislation, the reciprocity forces wrote into the Democratic platform, "The paramount issue at this time before the people of Massachusetts is relief from tariff restrictions." The platform charged that Republican protectionism had "cut Massachusetts from its natural markets of sale and purchase." [33]

[29] See, e.g., votes on a new soldier's bounty bill, May 17 and 25, *MSJ,* 1905, pp. 821, 873–876, *MHRJ,* 1905, pp. 1093–1095, 1099–1101, and votes on other vetoes, *MSJ,* 1905, pp. 846, 861, *MHRJ,* 1905, pp. 906–907, 1072–1074, 1084–1086.
[30] *Boston Herald,* July 18, 1905.
[31] Hamlin Diary, September 13, 1905.
[32] *Ibid.,* October 19, 1905.
[33] *Boston Herald,* October 8, 1905. The platform indicated that the Democrats, too, accepted the "maximum-minimum" principle for a new tariff act.

The Republicans attempted to turn Whitney's candidacy to their advantage. Inspired by Whitney's shady career as a corporation builder, they tried to shift attention from tariff revision to the fight against irresponsible corporations. "Luck has come to you in the nomination of Whitney," former Senator William E. Chandler wrote to Lodge. "It changes the issue on everything; especially that of corporation control." [34] "There is really only one question," Cabot Lodge declared to a campaign audience, "and that is whether the measures used by Mr. Whitney to secure passage of the West End [Railway] bill in [1890] . . . were methods which Massachusetts desires to approve by electing Mr. Whitney to office." [35] George Fred Williams thought so, too, and denounced the Democratic slate.[36]

But the old charges against Whitney proved disappointing, and the tariff issue bobbed up clear. The Democrats contended that if Whitney's expenditures in 1890 indicated that he had used corrupting techniques to promote his company, it also proved that the Republican legislature was corruptible. The point hit home, and, halfway through the campaign, Draper's campaign manager persuaded him to drop the issue. ("It's lucky that it wasn't gone into," Draper's manager wrote later; " — if others know what I knew and apparently he [Draper] didn't.")[37] Whitney meanwhile attempted to claim President Roosevelt's support for reciprocity, and he cited his visit to the President with other Boston businessmen in December 1904 when Roosevelt (according to Whitney) agreed that "continental free trade" was an objective of his administration. Roosevelt would not deny the contention publicly, though he allowed Lodge to make a disavowal for him.[38] Whitney got the

---

[34] Chandler to Lodge, October 16, 1905 (Lodge MSS).

[35] *Boston Herald,* October 20, 1905.

[36] *Ibid.,* October 13, 1905.

[37] William D. Sohier to Stephen P. O'Meara, December 21, 1905 (O'Meara MSS).

[38] Roosevelt to Lodge, October 31, 1905, in *Correspondence,* II, 207–208. Roosevelt did some weasling in this letter. "I regard Whitney as a peculiarly obnoxious specimen of a very obnoxious class and Draper as a fine fellow," he began irrelevantly. "But how far I can go in answering [Thomas] Talbot

better of the exchange, and in addition he pinned a charge of bad faith on Lodge in the Newfoundland negotiation. Whitney's two associates in the December visit to Washington supported him, and one asserted that the late Secretary Hay had warned him privately not to trust Lodge's verbal endorsement of reciprocity.[39]

The election results showed the effectiveness of the tariff issue. Curtis Guild, supported by the reciprocitarians, eased into the governor's seat with a 22,000 plurality over Bartlett. Although he took only 50 per cent of the total vote, he recaptured every one of the usually Republican cities, including Fall River, which Bates had lost to Douglas in 1904. But Whitney made the big point for the tariff reformers by coming within 2,000 votes of becoming the state's first Democratic lieutenant governor since the Civil War.

The experience may have frightened the Republicans, but they would make no concession to the tariff reformers. Noting that even the pro-Republican newspapers in Boston continued to drum for tariff reform, thus lending aid to Whitney's campaign, Lodge, Crane, and Congressman A. P. Gardner entered negotiations to purchase a city newspaper to serve as the party organ. They aimed at first for the *Herald* (in which the United Shoe Machinery Company held a dominant interest), but the

---

[Republican State Chairman, who had asked Roosevelt for an explicit denial] I do not know. It seems to me he ought not to bring the President into a question of personal veracity . . . I do not remember my exact language and it is possible that I may have said something that could be construed as having such meaning." For Lodge's and Talbot's letters, see RMA MSS. After the campaign, Roosevelt wrote privately to the editor of the *Boston Advertiser:* "Mr. Whitney lies by intention; and the other two [who had supported Whitney's story], I suppose, merely because they are fools." Nevertheless, Roosevelt confessed, "The conversation [at the White House] was a very long one, and no one could pretend to give it all from memory." Roosevelt to Guild A. Copeland, November 18, 1905, in reply to Copeland's inquiry, November 17, 1905, in RMA MSS; the correspondence was marked, "Not for publication."

[39] James M. W. Hall (former Republican mayor of Cambridge) to F. F. Tripp (Secretary of the Independent Committee of Business Men), November 2, 1905, printed in the *Boston Herald,* November 4, 1905. Cf. Tyler Dennett, *John Hay: From Poetry to Politics* (New York, 1933), pp. 423–429.

price was too high. (Gardner, always the Machiavellian, suggested that William A. Wood, president of the American Wool Manufacturers Association, should have put up the money, considering how well the party had provided for the wool manufacturers' tariff needs.)[40] They found John H. Fahey, the Boston civic reformer, willing to sell his 55 per cent interest in the *Traveller* for $300,000 but ultimately that fell through too (apparently because Gaston outbid the Republicans).[41] The Republicans thus were required to hold the tariff line in the face of a generally hostile press.

Guild alone among the top leaders publicly interpreted the election results as support for his demand that Congress act to revise the tariff immediately. In a letter to Roosevelt, Guild contended that the Republicans in Massachusetts "would have been overwhelmingly defeated" had not the state platform endorsed "immediate tariff revision."[42] But the governor-elect received a private rebuke from Lodge for his trouble. "As a matter of fact," Lodge wrote, "nobody here [in Washington] seems to have the slightest interest or have the least desire to undertake a revision of the tariff. The sentiment in favor is confined to our State, so far as I can judge, and I have been talking with a great many people." The President, Lodge informed Guild, wished that everyone would simply let Congress handle the tariff issue.[43]

IV

Roosevelt, meantime, while lacking any genuine interest in tariff reform, was willing to use it as a bludgeon to force conservative Congressional leaders to establish more effective con-

[40] Lodge to Draper, December 4, 1905 (Lodge MSS). See also Lodge to Draper, November 27, 1905 (*ibid.*).

[41] The Republicans' purpose was ultimately served by the appointment of Robert Lincoln O'Brien as chief editor of the *Boston Evening Transcript* in 1906. O'Brien appears to have been in close contact with Lodge on most important issues, and, if he did not always follow Lodge's advice, he at least shared many of the same opinions. This was particularly true concerning the tariff.

[42] Quoted by Champ Clark in Congress, January 9, 1906, *Congressional Record,* 59th Cong., 1 Sess., p. 868.

[43] Lodge to Guild, December 8, 1905 (Lodge MSS).

trol of the nation's railroads.[44] As he moved closer to that objective, he grew increasingly impatient with the revisionists. To friendly acquaintances interested in revision, such as Jacob Riis, he complained that he was "up to his ears" in legislative problems and had no time for the tariff issue. To closer confidants, such as Lodge, he excoriated what he called "the idiot revision feeling" in various parts of the country.[45] Meanwhile he spelled out his program to extend I.C.C. coverage to all forms of transportation, to eliminate discriminatory practices, and to give that agency power to establish maximum rates upon complaint and "subject to judicial review." [46]

In Massachusetts, the railroad control issue did not claim much attention. The state had strong laws of its own which had given its business community adequate protection against irresponsible management and discriminatory rates. In 1905 the New Haven Railroad, under new (out-of-state) management, had successfully evaded the laws by purchasing street railways through the holding company device without the legislature's sanction. But the division of opinion in the long and bitter controversy which ensued lay *within* the state's parties rather than between them. More important, that controversy led to no appreciable demand, even by the New Haven's adversaries, for increased federal control over the nation's railways. No federal action then conceived of could have solved the New Haven problem — except perhaps antitrust action, and the government already had that weapon. In general,

[44] This, at least, is the thesis of Professor John M. Blum in his "Theodore Roosevelt and the Hepburn Act: Toward an Orderly System of Control," in Morison, VI, 1558–1571; in his "Theodore Roosevelt and the Legislative Process: Tariff Revision and Railroad Regulation, 1904–1906," *ibid.*, IV, 1333–1342; and in *The Republican Roosevelt* (Cambridge, 1954), esp. chap. vi. I would quarrel principally with Blum's contention — minor for his general argument, but major here — that the same business interests which advocated tariff revision also sought greater federal control over the railroads ("The Legislative Process," p. 1337; *Republican Roosevelt,* p. 80). In Massachusetts, at least, this was not true.

[45] Pringle, *Roosevelt,* p. 292; Roosevelt to Lodge, August 9, 1906, in *Correspondence,* II, 224.

[46] Blum, "The Hepburn Act," pp. 1558–1560. The quoted words are Roosevelt's.

Massachusetts businessmen had no important quarrel with the railroads. They certainly did not suffer the exorbitant or discriminatory rates that stirred up shippers, manufacturers, and farmers elsewhere in the country. The New England railroads provided Massachusetts with highly favorable rates, sometimes even in defiance of I.C.C. arbitration rulings. In such rulings, the I.C.C. had enjoined New England railroads from *lowering* their rates — the precise opposite of its efforts with most of the nation's railroads.

In general, therefore, the Massachusetts business community responded to the President's proposals with slightly skeptical support. The Boston Chamber of Commerce — which had led the fight for tariff reform — expressed probably the most serious doubts. During 1904, eastern railroads had engaged in a rate war which the New England railroads had initiated in order to recapture export trade diverted through the more southerly ports. Subsequently the I.C.C. rendered an arbitration settlement that only moderately reduced those rate differentials which, allegedly, gave the southern ports an advantage. The Boston Chamber, regarding the decision as only "a partial victory," argued that as long as transatlantic shipping rates remained uniform from all Atlantic ports, *any* interior rate differential handicapped New England.[47] New England merchants refused to regard the decision, the second in six years in which the I.C.C. had "disappointed" them, as a final settlement, and they hinted that the New England railroads might soon have to violate the agreement. Consequently, the Chamber's report for 1905 expressed anxiety about possibly greater I.C.C. power, especially if business interests elsewhere in the country should ultimately persuade the federal government to equalize all railroad rates on a mileage basis, to the distinct disadvantage of the distant New Englanders.[48]

---

[47] New York was assigned the same rates as Boston, but its extraordinary port and financial facilities easily overcame that handicap.

[48] Boston Chamber of Commerce, *20th Annual Report*, 1905 (Boston, 1906), pp. 20–21. In 1909 the New England railroads did repudiate the settlement and another rate war began. See discussion in Clapp, pp. 98–100.

Since Roosevelt had asked Congress to give the I.C.C. power to establish only maximum rates, New England's special low rates on domestic commerce remained secure, and, in general, Massachusetts' legislative leaders looked favorably on the President's program. (In the Senate, Cabot Lodge expressed the merchants' anticipatory anxieties in a lecture on how New England would suffer if railroads were not free to lower rates to accommodate competing market areas, but he conceded — when Senator Nelson of Minnesota interrupted — that his remarks had no direct bearing on the proposed legislation.)[49] Murray Crane approved the effort to crack down on rebates, on private railroad car abuses, and on other forms of discrimination.[50] The very conservative Speaker of the Massachusetts House, Louis A. Frothingham, praised Roosevelt's policies as designed to bring the nation's railroads up to the standards which Massachusetts had set.[51] And Cabot Lodge, who had defended Roosevelt's proposal as a conservative measure which would thwart the movement for public ownership, ultimately was responsible for several strengthening amendments to the administration's bill. Lodge's amendments placed oil pipe lines under I.C.C. surveillance, prohibited railroads from owning enterprises which produced the freight which they carried (such as coal and iron), raised the commissioners' pay, prohibited them from outside employment while they served the I.C.C., disqualified railroad directors and stockholders from commission appointments, and gave President Roosevelt an opportunity to name an entirely new board of commissioners to enforce the new legislation.[52] Curiously, only Congressman Samuel McCall, the darling of the state's Mugwump reformers, denounced the rate-control provision as a violation

[49] *Congressional Record,* 59 Cong., 1 Sess., March 22, 1906, pp. 4111–4112.
[50] Crane to Lodge, August 11, 1905 (Lodge MSS).
[51] *Boston Herald,* February 1, 1905.
[52] *Congressional Record,* 59 Cong., 1 Sess., March 22, May 7, 8, 14, 15, 1906, pp. 411–412, 6460, 6509, 6625, 6824, 6882.

of the rights of private property and voted against the Hepburn bill.[53]

To the insurgent reformers in the country, Massachusetts nevertheless appeared aligned with the "reactionary" opponents of effective railroad legislation; for the opposition concentrated on the judicial review issue, and that question united both cynical "railroad legislators" who hoped to cripple the I.C.C. with broad court review, and conservatives for whom court review represented a necessary bulwark for minority rights against the arbitrary tendencies of majorities. By the middle of the twentieth century, liberals could appreciate the salubrious effect of a restraining judiciary, especially in civil liberties cases, but the early reformers more usually had had experience with stodgy and bigoted judges who followed an antiquated legal tradition. On the other hand, modern liberals would not regard as disconcerting the establishment of federal commissions to check the activities of private power, but in 1906, as John M. Blum has pointed out, "men of disinterested conviction as well as those who were sheer obstructionists questioned the legality of combining in one body the quasi-legislative power of determining rates, even maximum rates, the quasi-judicial authority of deciding upon the validity of the rates, and the quasi-executive function of investigation and enforcement." [54]

It is difficult to judge how much the Massachusetts senators' demands for broad judicial review were due to their genuine fear for individual liberty and how much to a class-conscious bias that the best interests of the country properly lay in the unfettered hands of the private businessmen who then controlled the country. The balance of evidence suggests that the latter had greater weight, especially in the case of Senator Crane. As for Lodge, with the "proper" conservative limitations, he generally approved Theodore Roosevelt's effort to balance private power with government power; he gagged

---

[53] *Congressional Record,* 58 Cong., 3 Sess., February 7, 9, 1905, pp. 2027–2028, 2205–2206.

[54] Blum, *Republican Roosevelt,* p. 96.

only on the unpredictable consequences of a limited judiciary. But whatever the private motivations, Massachusetts won the reputation in the Progressive Era of being "opposed" to effective railroad legislation — in spite of its almost unanimous endorsement of the Hepburn Act on the final votes, in spite of its sponsorship of important invigorating amendments to the President's bill, and in spite of its record on railroad legislation within its own borders.

CHAPTER SIX

REFORMERS AND JACOBINS

The first and central faith in the national credo was, as it always had been, the reality, certainty, and eternity of moral values. Words like truth, justice, patriotism, unselfishness, and decency, were used constantly without embarrassment, and ordinarily without any suggestion that their meaning might be only of a time and place.

Henry F. May

On the moral side, the working classes . . . are not held together with the established and comfortable classes in a single great spiritual communion standing ever for common humanity. The two sections of society are in separate and opposite religious bodies. The force of these divergent loyalties is distinctly anti-social . . . It is a melancholy reflection that when any serious moral crisis arises . . . the old-established religious life of the city is almost utterly without authority or power . . . in shaping the issue.

Robert A. Woods*

B Y 1906 progressive reform was in full swing throughout the country. The Hepburn, Meat Inspection, and Pure Food and Drug acts of 1906 represented the largest spate of major reform legislation from any single Congress since the Reconstruction Era. Robert LaFollette had shifted his reform energies to the United States Senate, and the muckrakers had invaded Washington.[1] President Roosevelt had helped to build up the national zest for change, and Charles Evans Hughes' exposure of the New York insurance companies had acted as a catalyst (like "a dash of cold water upon the face after a

---

* The quotations are from May, *The End of American Innocence: A Study of the First Years of Our Own Time* (New York, 1959), p. 9, and Woods, *Americans in Process* (Boston, 1902), p. 370.

[1] Lincoln Steffens published his first article on national politics in January, and later that year David Graham Phillips completed his "Treason of the Senate."

time of moral drowsiness")[2] for many who were still indis-
posed to action. More and more reform groups inaugurated
campaigns against vested political and economic interests: in
New Hampshire, insurgents challenged the power of the Boston & Maine Railroad in state affairs; across the country, Californians opened a drive against the Southern Pacific Railroad;
in New Jersey, the "New Idea" was born. In Missouri, Joseph
Folk; in Kansas, William Stubbs; in Alabama, Braxton Comer;
in Georgia, Hoke Smith; in North Carolina, Robert Glenn:
each used the governor's office to war on the alliance between
the politicians and the powerful corporations and to stimulate
civic improvements. The urge for change even invaded the
stolid corners of Vermont and Maine.[3]

In Massachusetts, too, reform activities picked up impetus.
During the years 1905 to 1908, a loose army of civic leaders
informally generaled by Louis Brandeis intensified its efforts
"to awaken the public conscience and self-respect."[4] The
movement radiated from municipal to state affairs, as the state
appeared to share in the general "moral awakening" which
stimulated reform elsewhere in the country. In Curtis Guild,
the state enjoyed a governor at least as progressive (if not so
sensational) as any in the country. During Guild's three-year
administration the state built up a record of progressive legislation probably unmatched anywhere in the country. The General Court enacted a state inheritance tax, introduced the
nation to compulsory medical inspection for all school children, passed a corrupt practices bill which outlawed corpora-

[2] Editorial in *Outlook,* November 4, 1905, quoted in Merlo J. Pusey,
Charles Evans Hughes (New York, 1952), I, 165.

[3] For special studies which mark 1906 as the initial year for progressive
activity, see George E. Mowry, *The California Progressives,* p. 55; Leon B.
Richardson, *William E. Chandler; Republican* (New York, 1940), pp. 679–
680; Ransom E. Noble, *New Jersey Progressivism Before Wilson* (Princeton, 1946), p. 70. See also Herbert Rosenthal, "The Progressive Movement
in New York State, 1906–1914," unpublished doctoral dissertation, Harvard
University, 1955; Winston A. Flint, *The Progressive Movement in Vermont*
(Washington, D. C., 1941).

[4] From an open letter of the Boston Good Government Association, in the
Boston Herald, December 5, 1903.

tion contributions to political campaigns, reinforced the eight-hour day for all employees doing government work, outlawed the type of contract which the United Shoe Machinery Company used to force manufacturers to lease all their machinery in order to lease any, prohibited night work for women and children, founded a free employment service, strengthened laws requiring inspection of factories for health and child labor violations, placed telephone, telegraph, and express companies under commission regulation, pioneered in controls on the profits of gas companies, and established savings bank insurance. The Governor added his voice, moreover, to those from the Middle West demanding a revision of the tariff.

Curiously, this reform activity failed to quicken the nation's pulse; it barely even caught the nation's eye. In part this was due to the conservative position that the state's Congressmen appeared to take on the tariff and railroad reform issues. But it was also because most of the state's reforms, while refreshing and noteworthy when they occurred in previously unenlightened states like California and Wisconsin, were rather "old hat" in the Bay State. Californians could get excited over the organization in 1907 of the Lincoln-Roosevelt Republican League, which aimed to end the Southern Pacific's strangle hold on the Sunshine State; New Jerseyites could greet the "New Idea" men as emancipators from the grip of the utility corporations. Reformers in those states, though seeking only the same objectives, the same social values, as men like Curtis Guild in Massachusetts, worked for what constituted a substantially new departure from existing social policy. In Massachusetts, however, while problems remained and special interests had to be kept continually in check, for the most part the state had such matters under control: its reforms tended to be in the form of *amendments* to measures already taken; its reformers more often played the role of conservatives than of insurgents.

In Massachusetts, the truly "insurgent" groups — that is, those who sought to break through the deep crust of tradition

— did not derive from the middle-class businessmen and professionals whom George Mowry, Richard Hofstadter, and other historians have identified as the vital elements at the core of the progressive movement. They came instead primarily from the large Irish-American segment of the population, who purported to represent the newer Americans generally; and, to a lesser extent, from the growing class of labor unionists. These people were not progressives, but in fact they represented two different kinds of challenge to the social order which the typical progressive sought to preserve through reform (just as his conservative opponent did by standing pat). The first was an ethnic challenge, which in race-conscious America meant only barely less than a challenge to civilization itself. The second represented partly a bid for power (through unionization) by a segment of society (wage-earners) which was traditionally held subordinate to the business and professional classes and partly a challenge to the deep-rooted American myth of rugged individualism — specifically, the right of employers to hire whom they chose and of individual workers to determine the conditions of their own labor. Both the immigrants and the unionists met fierce hostility from progressives in San Francisco, Los Angeles, St. Louis, Topeka, Des Moines, Trenton, and Washington, D. C. But paradoxically, when they were defeated in Massachusetts, the news went out that the Brahmin "interests" had rejected enlightenment — the Bay State had stood pat.

The appearance was not the reality. The state's achievements won no blue ribbons from the country's enlightened elite, but they were achievements all the same. The years 1905 through 1908 in Massachusetts were good years for reform within an old tradition. They were, in addition, years in which political forces that were to grow to power soon after the waning of the Progressive Era began to show signs of strength. While Bay State reformers made advances against the stand-patters, they also beat off the early thrusts toward ascendancy of the immigrant and working classes.

I

The reforms which touched the lives of private citizens most significantly did not concern tariffs and great railroads, but rather such lackluster affairs as park administration, charity organization, and garbage disposal, as well as civil service requirements and local election procedures. It was to such matters that the scores of municipal leagues, civic federations, voter groups, and good government associations devoted themselves throughout the nation. In these affairs, Massachusetts did at least as well as, if not a bit better than, the rest of the country.

As early as 1884, for example, the Bay State had pioneered (with New York) in establishing a civil service system for all its major cities.[5] The state's adoption of the Australian ballot in 1888 for the first time in the country gave legal standing to political parties by placing their candidates for public office under minimal government regulations. Six years later, the state extended protection to voters in party nominating caucuses by printing the ballots, requiring that such caucuses or primaries be held on one of two consecutive days, and prohibiting a party from barring voters who had supported an independent candidate.[6] Although Massachusetts had no statewide mandatory direct primary system until 1911, caucus elections were open and served essentially the same purpose.[7]

In Nathan Matthews, Jr., Edwin U. Curtis, Jr., and Josiah Quincy, the state's one metropolis had had its own unspectacular but comparable versions of the Ben Lindsays, Hazen Pingrees, and Tom Johnsons.[8] The reform mayors governed Bos-

[5] Arthur M. Schlesinger, *The Rise of the City, 1878–1898* (New York, 1933), p. 398.

[6] C. E. Merriam and Louise Overacker, *Primary Elections* (Chicago, 1928), pp. 24–31.

[7] In 1902, for example, when A. P. Gardner and E. N. Foss bid for Republican nominations for Congress in their respective districts, more voters participated in the nominating caucuses than in any election in the state's history.

[8] Cf. Frank Mann Stewart, *A Half Century of Municipal Reform: The History of the National Municipal League* (Berkeley, 1950), pp. 8, 199.

ton throughout the 1890's and apparently provided it with a sufficiently competent administration to bolster its reputation as a "clean" city. At least one early muckraker whom *McClure's* sent there felt impelled to remark on how careful the grafters had to be in such a city of "amateur reformers"; the "dirt" he found amounted to only the inevitable reports of graft at City Hall, a little wild poker, and rather open flouting of an eleven P.M. curfew on the sale and serving of liquor.[9] In a left-handed compliment, the Boston radical, Frank Parsons, grudgingly conceded that his home town was "better governed than some other cities," [10] and it is equally significant that the progressive, Frederic C. Howe, in his scholarly study of city governments, did not once mention a Massachusetts city in any of his accounts of municipal corruption. Howe did note that Boston, "through its Metropolitan Commissions," had developed "one of the finest park, water, and sewage systems in the world." [11] In general, there seems little reason to dispute the National Municipal League's conclusion in 1902 that Boston was "the best governed of any of our larger cities," "best ordered," "most settled," and "least corrupt." [12]

Boston, nevertheless, had much the same kind of troubles as other cities. Not only did it face the challenge to traditional standards which the mere growth of the industrial metropolis presented everywhere, it also had to cope with the ascendancy of cultural subgroups — largely the product of massive immigration — which pointedly denied the virtue of those standards.[13] Religious differences increased the distance between the

[9] Josiah Flynt, "Boston, A Plain-Clothes Man's Town," *McClure's,* 17: 115–121 (June 1901).

[10] Frank Parsons, *"The City for the People,* rev. ed. (New York, 1901), p. 266.

[11] Frederic C. Howe, *The City: The Hope of Democracy* (Madison, 1905), p. 58.

[12] National Municipal League, *Proceedings,* 1902 (Washington, D. C., 1903), pp. 3, 63, 7, and 5, in that order. I should like to thank Mr. Roger Lane, whose honors thesis, "Municipal Reform in Boston, 1902–1910" (Yale College, 1955) first called my attention to the National Municipal League report.

[13] Most American cities had to cope with the second problem as well as the first. The general subject has been covered rather abundantly. I have

newcomers and the dominant classes of the Hub. Civic leaders consequently found it increasingly difficult to appeal to common criteria of good and bad when social conflicts erupted or men transgressed upon the old principles of public behavior.

For most immigrants, survival was more important than abstractions like "clean" politics and honest government. As Robert A. Woods, head of Boston's famed South End House, put it, when the immigrant voted, he wished "to see some new, divisible fruitage produced toward the enlargement of his meagre life." This consideration was "so pervasive that the fulfilment of . . . [his] insistent need" became "the decisive test of political and public service." On the other hand, such measures as civil service reform meant only "administration in the hands of a class that may be honest in an arid sort of way, but not [to him] serviceable or responsible." That one could understand the reasons for the newcomers' different political standards made those standards no less primitive. If industrial conditions had provoked as fierce a struggle for existence "as the barbarians had against wild nature," then the "barbaric outlook" which that struggle produced had to be altered in order to "impart truly civilized conceptions of politics or of life in general." [14]

Boston reformers did as well as any in their efforts to overcome these difficulties. Activity to improve the city reached an intensity probably unequaled anywhere in the country during the years 1905 to 1909. The candidacy and election of Democratic ward boss John F. Fitzgerald as mayor in 1905 presented a direct challenge to traditional standards and provoked massive efforts by the city's numerous "good government" groups. Business associations led the good government drive,

found the following books especially useful: Oscar Handlin, *Boston's Immigrants, 1790–1865* (Cambridge, 1941), and *The Uprooted;* John Higham, *Strangers in the Land* (New Brunswick, N. J., 1955); Marcus L. Hansen, *The Immigrant in American History* (Cambridge, 1940), esp. chaps. iv–vi; and Edward G. Hartmann, *The Movement to Americanize the Immigrant* (New York, 1948). Richard Hofstadter's *Age of Reform,* pp. 173–184, is also especially pertinent.

[14] Woods, *Americans in Process,* pp. 147–150.

which culminated in a new city charter and a finance commission to oversee municipal expenditures.

The city was even treated to a visit from the muckraker extraordinary, Lincoln Steffens. Merchant-philanthropist E. A. Filene invited the journalist in 1908 to do for Boston what he had done for Philadelphia, St. Louis, and Minneapolis.[15] The coming of Steffens was to have been a big event for the good government elements. They passed around the hat to help pay Steffens' salary for the year and to buy all rights to the book he was to produce. Steffens, however, had wearied of writing about political corruption, and he sought a more significant angle. Moreover, he could not find in Boston the sensational stuff he had found elsewhere: "There was less scandal in Boston," he wrote in his *Autobiography,* "few exposures . . . This made Boston look better than Philadelphia; this made it harder to muckrake." [16] Steffens did very little investigating. He talked a good deal with Filene. He apparently had a nice chat with Martin Lomasney, whom he liked (he devoted an entire chapter to him in the *Autobiography*) because the boss of Ward 8 frankly defended the collusion he found necessary to obtain for his constituents what they needed. And he read the Finance Commission reports. From this, he wrote his book.

Little that was fruitful came of his efforts. Steffens' published letters and his autobiography suggest that his manuscript on Boston contained a presentation of his theory — which later led him to admire the Soviet system — that what was wrong with Boston (and American) society was American ideals ("not our bad conduct but our virtue");[17] Americans should not — could not under the circumstances of modern industrialism — abandon their econo-political behavior, but should rather adjust their ideals to it. The Boston reformers, however, were not prepared to surrender old values or even

[15] Gerald Johnson, *A Liberal's Progress* (New York, 1948), pp. 95–96; Lincoln Steffens, *Autobiography* (New York, 1931), pp. 598ff.
[16] Steffens, p. 606.
[17] *Ibid.,* p. 604.

reconsider seriously the basic premises of individual private enterprise, much less replace them with a kind of Machiavellian pragmatism. The book never saw print, and the manuscript has disappeared. Except for stimulating the founding of a city improvement club with a nebulous Six-Year Plan ("Boston 1915"), the Steffens visitation ended a dud.

Louis Brandeis' reform meanwhile had proved more congenial to the spirit of progressivism in Massachusetts. In 1905, Brandeis returned to battle with public service corporations when a newly authorized consolidation uniting nearly all the gas companies serving Boston sought to capitalize at what the Public Franchise League considered an excessive amount. The Company's investors, led by Henry Whitney, lobbied boldly for their bill in the General Court. Neither Brandeis nor the League objected to the consolidation, but they attacked the Company's estimate of its assets, and especially its "illicit interference" with the judicious deliberations of the legislature. Like Steffens, Brandeis saw that much of the intrusion of corporate power into the legislature came from the corporations' need to protect themselves against "strike" bills — that is, legislative blackmail. Steffens, however, saw this as part of the give and take of politics, and recommended in effect a candid acknowledgment of the practice and perhaps a merger of the government with the "offending" business, since the arrangements between the politicians and the corporations amounted to a business-government merger anyway. Some reformers pursued something of this argument in their program of municipal ownership of all utility corporations. But Brandeis rejected municipal ownership. He worked instead to turn corporate gains to public advantage by linking profits to gas rates, while at the same time preserving the traditional separation of business and government.

As in the Boston Elevated Railway contest five years earlier, Brandeis first forced the Company to abandon its intention of capitalizing its entire surplus. In conceding the right of the

Company to capitalize 4 to 5 per cent of the surplus, Brandeis made an obeisance to modern finance for which his friends in the Public Franchise League never quite forgave him.[18] They were with him, however, on the more daring part of his plan. Copying a similar arrangement effective in London, the plan tied corporate dividends to the price of gas, so that the Company could raise its dividends by a fixed amount only when it had first reduced prices by a specific amount.[19]

To get his bill through the General Court, Brandeis enlisted the influence of the Company's own president, James L. Richards. He accomplished this feat by threatening to continue harassment of the Company before the legislature and the gas commission, and by offering, as an alternative, his and the P.F.L.'s services to do the work of the company's legislative agents in ferreting out and defeating all strike bills.[20] In addition, he exploited the *Springfield Republican's* exposure of a clumsy effort by the gas interests to fill the newspapers with propaganda represented as news. It was probably ungracious of Brandeis to forge this issue into a major weapon against the Company in order to force it to submit.[21] He and the P.F.L. did not hesitate to make use of the *Boston Traveller,* the *Boston Evening Transcript,* and the *Springfield Republican,* through editors Fahey, Clement, and Bowles, each of whom had served with the League in diverse capacities.[22] Moreover, Brandeis himself secretly wrote the ultimately prevailing "minority re-

[18] Mason, *Free Man's Life,* pp. 131–132.

[19] For the details of the Boston sliding-scale arrangement, see Irvin Bussing, *Public Utility Regulation.*

[20] See Brandeis, "Gas Problem," p. 595; *Boston Herald,* May 20, 1905, and May 16, 17, 1906. See also J. L. Richards, "The Boston Consolidated Gas Company: Its Relation to the Public, Its Employees, and Investors," *Annals of the American Academy of Political and Social Science,* XXXI (January–June 1908), 593–599.

[21] See *Springfield Republican,* April 18, 1905; *Arena,* 34:93–95 (July, 1905); and Brandeis to Mark Sullivan, July 19, 1906 (Brandeis MSS).

[22] See Chapter Three, pp. 62, 67. On May 16, 1906, in the heat of the battle, Robert L. O'Brien, chief editor for the *Transcript,* solicited from Brandeis a "judicial editorial," which was printed three days later. Mason, *Free Man's Life,* p. 137, and *Boston Evening Transcript,* May 19, 1906.

port" for the commission which the legislature had established
to investigate the London "sliding scale" system.[23]

Brandeis made double use of the contemporary agitation for
radical reform: first, to bolster his own proposals with the generalized demands for change; second, to intimidate the businessmen and conservatives who opposed innovations. Like
Theodore Roosevelt, who was opportunely scolding the railroads for not understanding that his railroad control bill would
save them from government ownership or other radical de-
signs, Brandeis warned: "It is certain that among a free people
every excess of capital must in time be repaid by the excessive
demands of those who have not the capital . . . If the capitalists are wise, they will aid us in the effort to prevent injustice." [24] When the Hearst press and many Democratic leaders
opposed Brandeis' bill because it precluded municipal ownership, he denounced them as "fanatics . . . as ready to do
injustice to capital as the capitalists have been ready to do
injustice to the people." [25]

Brandeis' idea of reform did not challenge the traditional
organization of society. He concentrated rather on making the
social order work with greater justice and efficiency, as he and
his colleagues understood these conceptions. His program for
savings bank annuities and life insurance illustrated this most
clearly.[26] As Brandeis took some care to explain, the program
was a legitimate child of the Massachusetts savings bank system. Dating back to 1816, Massachusetts savings banks were
the oldest in the country. They were operated as a "quasi-
public trust," as a "beneficent not a money-making institu-

[23] Mason, *Free Man's Life,* p. 137. Mason cites Brandeis to McClennen,
March 14, 1916 (Brandeis MSS).
[24] Quoted in Mason, *Free Man's Life,* p. 130.
[25] *Ibid.,* p. 138.
[26] Alpheus T. Mason's *The Brandeis Way* (Princeton, 1938) is a long,
detailed history of Brandeis' insurance program, with good descriptive coverage of the political activities which carried the bill through to passage. I see
no reason to repeat that coverage here. See also Louis Brandeis, "Wage
Earners Life Insurance: A Great Wrong and a Remedy," *Collier's,* September 15, 1906, and "Massachusetts' Substitute for Old Age Pensions," *Independent,* 65:125–128 (July 16, 1908).

tion," solely for the benefit of depositors. There were no stockholders — only unsalaried trustees who administered the
collection and investment of small savings. What Brandeis proposed was to permit savings banks to sell annuities and life
insurance to low-income groups who could only afford a
maximum of $200 for annuities and $500 for life insurance,
and weekly and monthly premiums of less than a dollar.

Brandeis began to work on his idea shortly before Charles
Evans Hughes launched his investigation of New York life
insurance companies, but after the shenanigans of the New
York Equitable's directors had already aroused the Massachusetts holders of $1 million worth of insurance in that Com-
pany. What struck Brandeis most forcefully was not so much
the directors' arrogant irresponsibility as the inefficiency of
private insurance companies which required low-paid workingmen to pay high premiums for sometimes uncertain protection. Brandeis claimed that the savings bank plan, by eliminating paid sales agents, stockholders, and dividends, all of
which bloated the fixed costs of private insurance, would reduce the workers' premiums by almost half.

But Brandeis' most telling argument was that advantages
would fall to the "general community" as well. First, "perhaps
the greatest of its ultimate advantages [Brandeis contended]
would be in localizing in Massachusetts, and distributing
throughout the state the management and control of our insurance reserve." [27] Here he gave expression to the resentment of
the financial community toward the contemporary flight of
capital from the state, and also to the vague but important
sentiment that Massachusetts could handle its own affairs well
enough if the federal system would permit it to control the
affairs it called its own.[28] Second, the voluntary annuities pro-

[27] Quoted in Mason, *Brandeis Way*, p. 142.
[28] Brandeis' provincialism extended even to resisting, in this case, a proposal to establish uniform controls over the country's insurance business by
federal incorporation. "Federal supervision," he objected, "would serve only
to centralize even further the power of our government and perhaps to
increase still further the power of the corporations." Quoted in Mason,
Free Man's Life, p. 154.

vision would serve to allay "the rising demand for old-age pensions supported by general taxation"; it would provide wage earners with "an opportunity of making provision for themselves for their old age," without increasing the tax burden borne by much of the rest of the community.[29]

Using very much the same techniques as in the gas company contest, Brandeis mobilized practically the entire Massachusetts community behind his bill — from Bishop William Lawrence to Martin Lomasney. The *Transcript,* the *Republican,* the *Boston Post,* and other newspapers printed Brandeis' "judicious editorials," and the People's Attorney even secured assistance from *Collier's* and the *New York Evening Post.* He turned churchmen, unions, and business associations into such effective pressure groups that a legislator could oppose the bill only at the risk of becoming a pariah. As the bill approached passage in 1907, Brandeis' insurance program became the veritable test of a citizen's honesty and good will. Governor Guild signed the bill that June.

Lincoln Steffens might have admired the skill with which Brandeis employed power against power; but Brandeis used that skill without conceding either that traditional values were outmoded or that the competing interests in modern society were irreconcilable within a common system of values. Brandeis thus gave expression to the implicit creed of the great majority of Massachusetts reformers. These men held to the ideal of a "common interest" against which they could accurately measure most political, economic, and social behavior. In retrospect, their image of the "common interest" may appear to have been influenced by what was peculiarly suited to their particular tastes and welfare. But if they acknowledged this at all — and there is little evidence that they did — they would have insisted that their conception of a "truly civilized" polity included their particular image of the "common inter-

[29] Louis Brandeis, "Savings Banks' Life Insurance," *American Federationist,* 14:779, 777 (October 1907).

est." More usually they simply condemned as either ignorance
or evil anything which challenged their view of perfection.

II

As elsewhere in the country, the "reform element" in Massachusetts came mostly from the business and professional
classes, especially from among the older families. Its members
derived directly from the Mugwumps, and many who worked
for civil service reform with the Massachusetts Reform Club
— the original Mugwump organization — also served with the
Public School Association, the Municipal League, the Good
Government Association, and the Public Franchise League. As
the work of the P.F.L. indicated, there were many problems
native to the growing urban economy which required scrutiny;
but the almost complete exclusion of immigrant names and
labor organizations from the reform groups' membership lists
may suggest what elements of society the reformers considered
most in need of checking. A few of the reformers had worked
with the notorious American Protective Association, while
many more had taken part in the activities of the Immigration
Restriction League which was founded in Boston in 1894 —
the Reform Club's Charles Warren among the three principal
founders. As one civic leader frankly saw it, there was "an
undoubted relation between chromosomes and politics"; the
various watchdog groups had to see to it that the right chromosomes remained dominant.[30]

Characteristically, the reform groups neglected, when they
did not oppose, the aspirations of labor. Their view of helping
the wage-earning classes often extended little further than
Brandeis' self-help pension plan or the vaunted public baths
program of Mayor Quincy's administration. "If . . . all
bathed regularly," Quincy argued, ". . . filthy tenement
houses would disappear . . . Crime and drunkenness would

[30] William B. Munro, *The Government of American Cities* (New York,
1912), p. 52.

decrease . . . Even the death rate would drop." One wonders, indeed, whom the baths were really intended to benefit:
as Quincy remarked, the Great Unwashed were "a menace to
their fellow citizens whom they come in contact with on the
cars and in the streets and who unknowingly buy the products
of their labor." [31] When Louis Brandeis and others organized
the Good Government Association in 1903, one professional
and six business groups contributed three members each to the
board of directors, but no labor man was invited to join. The
G.G.A. spent its time and money exposing unnecessary expenditures, protecting park lawns, and endorsing candidates for
aldermanic and public school boards.[32] Preoccupied with what
it called "waste," the G.G.A. attacked such innovations as a
twelve-hour day for city firemen and a pension plan for city
workers over sixty-two, because they would tend to raise taxes.
The members' detached and often naïve view of civic responsibility incurred the label "goo goo" from their enemies, and
even those with whom they had no quarrel tended to regard
them as "tax-dodging, holier-than-thou Pharisees, without political experience or judgment." [33]

When Boston's Mayor Patrick A. Collins died in 1905, the
G.G.A. made its most determined show of strength. Collins
had been only the second Irish-American to become chief
executive of the Hub City, but he had had the general confidence of the "good government" elements in the city. He had
already shown great ability as Consul General in London during the second Cleveland administration and as Permanent
Chairman of the Democratic National Convention in 1892;
1902, moreover, he had cooperated with the Public Franchise

---

[31] Josiah Quincy, "Municipal Progress in Boston," *Independent*, 52:
424–426 (February 1900).

[32] A manuscript history of the G.G.A., written in the 1930's by George
R. Nutter, one of its members, is in the Good Government Association
Collection at the Massachusetts Historical Society, Boston. Though incom-
plete, the manuscript does cover the progressive years, and it summarizes
most of the material in the scrapbooks of news clippings which comprise
the rest of the collection.

[33] *Boston Herald*, February 12, 1904.

League's fight against the Boston Elevated Railway Company. The G.G.A. and kindred groups probably would have accepted another Irishman, such as Back Bay Congressman John A. Sullivan, but John F. Fitzgerald, ward boss of Boston's immigrant-jammed North End, was a bit too much for them.

The man who was to become grandfather of the country's thirty-fifth President pleased few of the "better element" early in the century. Born in Boston near the Old North Church, the third oldest of nine children, Fitzgerald was orphaned at sixteen. Like many a son of Irish-immigrant parents, he chose politics as the way up in society — the *only* way up readily available to those of his background. He made that background his pride, and slowly climbed through the ranks from city councilman to alderman to state legislator, and then, in 1896, United States Representative. Characteristically, political issues played little part in his success; he made assets, instead, of his cheery ebullience and his voice (they called him "Honey Fitz"). Some time after his election to Congress he moved out of the "dear old" North End but kept a legal residence there. That was unusual for a ward "boss" in those times, but Fitzgerald's constituents valued his many important political connections and his seemingly limitless energy. For some reason — it was certainly not personal affection — Fitzgerald was able to touch important Republican leaders for favors.[34] Republicans recognized his great local popularity and probably wished to accommodate him to avoid making him a militant opponent. He built close ties, moreover, with several of the public service corporations in the city, and worked openly for the political and economic interests of Henry M. Whitney and William Gaston. In 1901, Fitzgerald quit Con-

[34] See, for example, the May 1900 correspondence between Fitzgerald and Henry Cabot Lodge and between Lodge and other Republicans, in which Lodge tried to help Fitzgerald obtain a liquor license for his brother. See also Secretary of the Navy John D. Long to Lodge, September 22, 1900, in which Long explained how Fitzgerald obtained jobs for workers at the Boston Navy Yard. (All in Lodge MSS.)

gress and thereafter devoted himself to his campaign for mayor. Collins' death removed his principal obstacle.

In anticipation of Fitzgerald's nomination, the G.G.A. and several unaffiliated business associations persuaded the thirty-seven year old Louis A. Frothingham, Republican Speaker of the state's lower house, to run for the G.O.P. nomination. Frothingham was an extreme conservative on labor and other contemporary issues, but that raised no objection from the "good government" people. Frothingham encountered opposition, however, from the Republican City Committee, which resented the intrusion of a man who had worked previously only with the State Committee in quest of high state office. The City Committee would not officially advance a candidate of its own, but one Henry S. Dewey, a previously unknown eccentric and demagogue, ran on his own hook in protest against the state "machine" and the "goo goo." Frothingham beat Dewey in the party caucuses by only 200 votes out of 20,000; his disappointed opponent howled "fraud" and decided to make the race for mayor anyway. In the Democratic caucuses, meanwhile, Fitzgerald polled a majority of votes despite opposition from the Collins faction, Josiah Quincy, and rival ward leaders such as Martin Lomasney.[35] After the primaries the Democrats, with the exception of Lomasney, closed ranks behind their nominee. In the record December balloting, "Honey Fitz" eked out an edge over the "good government" candidate by somewhat less than Dewey's 11,000 votes. "Old Boston," lamented the G.G.A.'s historian, "became a thing of the past."[36]

The reform groups wasted no time getting something on the new mayor. Even during the campaign, the G.G.A. had busied itself with rumors of Fitzgerald's alleged dishonesty and venal-

[35] *Boston Herald,* November 17, 1905.

[36] "Hitherto, we in Boston had rather thought that our affairs were different. Like the Philistine of old, we thanked God that we were not like other men. There seemed to our minds to flourish a different kind of human nature on the banks of Massachusetts Bay . . . But now opened an era which showed that although we might come late into the troubles, we were in them." Nutter's manuscript history of the G.G.A., chap. iii, pp. 2–3.

ity; it had failed, however, to substantiate any of them. ("I *know* such things as these about him," the exasperated executive secretary wrote to Brandeis, "although as yet I am not able to prove them.")[37] The Good Government leaders now left no corner unexplored for evidence of graft, collusion, and payroll-padding. Fitzgerald meanwhile needled the genteel muckrakers with puckish contempt. Holding them up as more concerned with thrift and aesthetics than with public welfare, the Mayor teasingly proposed building a row of houses on the river side of the fashionable Beacon Street residences, and a new City Hall on the site of the Botanic Gardens. He also took little care to conceal his maneuvers to create a personal city-wide political machine. Apparently assuming that he had more to gain from the friends he would make than lose from spurring the already quick tempers of the cultured economizers, Fitzgerald multiplied government offices, evaded civil service regulations by appointing "specialists" and "provisional" workers, and gave out city contracts to favorite bidders.

All this added up to the inevitable intervention of the General Court. The last time there had been an Irishman at City Hall who tweaked the Brahmin nose, the state Republicans rewrote the city charter and expropriated the Boston Police Commission. This time, the Republicans merely threatened an investigation of the Fitzgerald administration. But before the legislature could interfere again with Boston "home rule," Fitzgerald moved suddenly in January 1907 in favor of an investigating commission of seven members named by himself on the recommendation of the leading business and civic organizations.

What Fitzgerald intended is something of a mystery. Perhaps he was bidding for wider support to compensate for the loss

[37] Edmund Billings to Brandeis, November 21, 1905 (Brandeis MSS). (Italics in the original.) "Such things" included reports that Fitzgerald had blackmailed banks to run advertisements in his weekly *The Republic* by threatening to influence the city government to redeposit its funds elsewhere, reports of his scandalous "social life," and allegations that he padded his aides' payrolls with government moneys. Brandeis told Billings to "gather some facts." Brandeis to Billings, November 23, 1905 (*ibid.*).

of ward leaders whom he had antagonized by superseding them with his city machine. Perhaps he was just overconfident that nothing the "good government" people could do would damage his seemingly unbeatable coalition of city workers, public service corporations, and government contractors. In any case, his action deprived him of the opportunity to attack the Republicans for violating the principle of "home rule," a popular issue even with most of the civic reform groups, and he handed to his enemies a valuable instrument for publicizing his admittedly irregular activities at City Hall. He did gain the power to select the investigators, but this proved no advantage. Four of the participating groups belonged to the G.G.A.[38] None of the four Democrats selected, including chairman Nathan Matthews and John A. Sullivan, had supported him during his nomination fight. And one of the civic organizations was dominated by a radical independent who had mayoralty aspirations of his own.[39] Only the representative from the Central Labor Union — this was the first time organized labor had been invited to participate semi-officially in city affairs — could be regarded as "friendly." By the time the Finance Commission issued its final report, the Bostonians had placed Fitzgerald in involuntary retirement; a Republican hack politician, whose chief asset seemed to be (or so many argued) the G.G.A.'s nonendorsement, beat Fitzgerald by a small majority in 1907.

The Finance Commission did not issue its final report until January 1909, but it issued many interim reports (ultimately totaling 127, and filling four large volumes) as it proceeded with its investigations. What impressed the investigators most was the unbusinesslike way in which the city was run. (The

[38] The participants were the Associated Board of Trade, the Merchant's Association, the Real Estate Exchange, the Boston Chamber of Commerce, the Clearing-House Committee, the United Improvement Association (composed of the presidents of neighborhood improvement clubs), and the Central Labor Union. See Elisabeth M. Herlihy, ed., *Fifty Years of Boston* (Boston, 1932). The first four associations belonged to the G.G.A.

[39] John A. Coulthurst of the United Improvement Association ran for mayor in 1907 with Hearst backing.

vague concept of "business efficiency" was a common measure against which reformers throughout the country tested "progress.") The 75-man city council, of course, was an abomination, a carry-over from colonial democracy which required representation of each small district as it came to be included within the greater metropolis. The councilmen, moreover, appeared to work primarily to increase the appropriations estimates which the Mayor and the Board of Aldermen presented for public improvements. In addition, between 1895 and 1907, the number of city workers had increased more than two and a half times faster than the city's population growth, and expenditures and debts had mounted at a similarly anomalous rate. As for the more scandalous improprieties, the commissioners denounced the mayor's practice of letting contracts without competitive bidding, upbraided both the city legislators and private businessmen for justifying collusive logrolling in the distribution of municipal projects "as a part of . . . regular business methods," and charged that the labor employed by the city had decreased its per capita efficiency by about half since 1895. Summing it up, the Commission concluded that the political system had produced leaders who were "intellectually and morally incapable of action in the interest of the citizens at large," and a mayor who sought "not merely to use or perfect the political machine then in existence but to become the machine itself." [40]

Although the reform body had observed that "dishonesty was not confined to any one class in the community," critics saw in the report a definite class orientation. Not a single line commended existing social services or suggested the necessity of additional services to meet problems occasioned by the growth of the city. The Commission proposed two alternative city charters — one of which the public ratified in 1909 — which sharply reduced the number of government workers at all levels and established a continuing Finance Commission

[40] Boston Finance Commission, *Final Report* (Boston, 1909), pp. 22–27, and *passim*.

to systematize and publicize city expenditures. It made no recommendation, however, for an agency to accommodate the city's thousands of immigrants, or to investigate housing and labor conditions, even as it criticized ward politicians for their greater attention to getting jobs for their constituents than to "the interest of the citizens at large." Significantly, the labor union representative alone dissented from the report. He made no effort to dispute the others' findings, but he rebuked them, first, for neglecting to credit Fitzgerald with creating the commission while attacking him personally; second, for criticizing the practice of providing the needy with jobs through political patronage; third, for suggesting that city workers' wages be reduced; and fourth, for recommending the award of contracts to non-union contractors when they offered lower bids on city projects.[41]

The dissenting opinion suggested how far apart were the interests of the "good government" groups from those of the city's working classes. They differed fundamentally on the issues of political morality and social policy. While the civic guardians strove with some success to maintain traditional standards,[42] the insurgent immigrant and working classes had to look elsewhere for representation.

III

In 1906, it appeared that the state Democratic party would throw off its dependence on particular corporate and other business interests for funds and candidates and, in the process, would become the truly radical party of the state. That year the state organization fell into the hands of a young group of predominantly Irish-American leaders who united behind a radical program and Boston's sensational new district attorney,

[41] *Ibid.*, pp. 69–75. See also Harvey N. Shepard, "The Boston Finance Commission," *Cincinnati Conference on Good Government, Proceedings,* 1909.

[42] This is not the place to discuss the contemporary American consensus on social values and standards or the progressives' conception of the Good. See, however, May, *End of Innocence;* Hofstadter, *Age of Reform;* and Mowry, *Era of Roosevelt,* esp. chap. v, "The Progressive Profile."

John B. Moran. Moran and his followers effected an alliance with the Prohibitionists and William Randolph Hearst's freshly organized Independence League. For a time they gave the Commonwealth's old guard its most uncomfortable moments since the days of Hideous Ben Butler.

The son of Irish immigrants, District Attorney John B. Moran played a lone hand in most of the things he did. He never married, he renounced Catholicism, and he posed throughout his political career as an independent. His independence, however, did not always place him on the side of "reform" — at least so far as reformers of the era understood that appellative. In 1893 he opposed Boston's reform mayor Nathan Matthews, and two years later he fought with equal vigor the Republican reform mayor Edwin U. Curtis. In each campaign he spent large sums of his own money though he himself held no nomination. Moran soon turned bitterly against Josiah Quincy, who had beaten Curtis in 1895, and who meanwhile had built his own reputation as a reformer. Moran completed his wrong-sided independence during the following years by opposing Mayor Patrick Collins. In each case, he appeared to be motivated by very personal reasons.

Moran's behavior suggested severe paranoid tendencies which his failure in politics reinforced. In 1902 he received the most unkind snub of all when the Democratic State Convention withdrew his nomination for attorney general because (according to Moran) Gaston and others protested against "too damn much Irish" on the slate.[43] (Actually, the objection to Moran as stated by the very Irish David I. Walsh, the future Senator and Governor, was that there were "too many Bostonians" on the slate.)[44] Moran supported Bates against Gaston that year.

In 1905, Moran's fortunes turned upward when he secured the support of a fellow eccentric, the Boston financier Thomas

---

[43] The quotation is from Moran's own advertisement in the *Boston Traveller*, October 29, 1902.

[44] *Boston Evening Transcript*, September 17, 1902.

W. Lawson. With Lawson's money, he ran for district attorney that year as "The Man Who Dares," championing, in magnificent soap-opera fashion, the cause of a young widow whose elderly and socially elevated husband had bequeathed her a large fortune but whose snobbish stepson had broken the will after lengthy and somewhat questionable litigation.[45] Moran defeated the incumbent, who had received both the Democratic and the Republican nominations.

To some reformers and most dissidents, Moran appeared as a gallant knight in the fight for damsel Clean Government. Buoyed up by the prevalent spirit of reform, he charged out seeking malefactors of great and small wealth. He quickly became the paladin of the temperance movement by pressing the enforcement of liquor laws (with the enthusiastic cooperation of the notorious police commissioner of Governor Bates's administration). He even demanded that drug stores and hotels remove their window curtains so that diners and imbibers could be seen from the street. He kept his name conspicuous in the newspapers with a sensation a day — storming into hotels after hours in search of illicit drinking, boldly announcing future investigations of graft and corruption, and demanding that the Governor or the President or somebody commute the death sentence of a singularly popular murderer of the day.[46] His investigations rarely came off, but he did send a probing lance into the General Court and pulled it out with a confessed suborner dangling on the end. This sensation captivated the public's attention for about a month, and the indignant legislature expelled the culprit for having tempted

[45] For a summary of the Urial H. Crocker will case, see *Boston American,* September 23, 1906.

[46] The murderer was one Charles L. Tucker, who had killed his girl friend in a lover's quarrel. Tucker's lawyers presented to Governor Guild a petition with 115,000 signatures calling for commutation of the death sentence. See the *Springfield Republican* of June 16, 1906, for Guild's refusal. Moran was not the only politician to make capital of the case. One of Tucker's lawyers was James Vahey, who used the publicity he gained to win election to the legislature and, in 1908 and 1909, the Democratic nomination for governor. See Chapter Seven.

its virtue.[47] But nothing was done about the bribetakers, and Moran did not press the issue. He quickly rode off in another direction with perjury proceedings against Republicans who had testified for Senator Lodge's private secretary (a convicted embezzler of campaign moneys). He subpoenaed the Senator to Boston to testify, and even threatened to extend his investigation to the Treasury Department. The threat won another headline, but that was all.[48]

Inevitably, the man thrilled some and exasperated others. "The honest desire of people for reform," wrote one, "has afflicted us with a certain number of freaks . . . [like] one Moran." [49] President Roosevelt, who knew of Moran only through his correspondence with Lodge, compared him to New York's crusading district attorney William Travers Jerome — and condemned both to oblivion in the world's nether parts.[50] Louis Brandeis, who admired Jerome, refused to place Moran on the same high shelf, but he believed Moran might ultimately contribute some good.[51] The radical journal, *Arena,* however, saw in Moran a "progressive democrat" who was carrying forward in Massachusetts the impartial fight of Wisconsin's La-Follette and Missouri's Joseph Folk against both rich and poor lawbreakers.[52]

It is clear that for a time, at least, many agreed with that image. Certainly Moran struck a responsive chord among all who deplored the way in which private business often evaded the law with impunity. He pointed out that the General Court had hastened to legalize the sale of liquor in hotels past eleven

[47] For the expulsion of Frank J. Gethro, see *Boston Herald,* June 22, 1906. Moran carried on his investigations during April and May.

[48] For Robert G. Proctor's conviction, and Moran's announcement of further investigations, see *Boston Post,* June 30, 1906; see also Roosevelt-Lodge correspondence, July 2, 6, 9, 1906, in *Correspondence,* II, 219ff.

[49] Judge Francis Lowell to George Meyer, January 22, 1906 (Meyer MSS).

[50] Roosevelt to Lodge, July 4, 1906, in *Correspondence,* II, 220.

[51] Brandeis to L. Veiller, November 15, 1905 (Brandeis MSS).

[52] "Leaders of True Democracy" and "The Battle Between The Plutocracy and The Democracy in The Democratic Party in Massachusetts," *Arena,* 36:406, 418–419 (October 1906).

P.M., after he had closed the fashionable Touraine for violating the curfew; yet the legislature had denied him the assistants and additional funds he had requested to carry on his work. "The criminal petitions and you grant all asked for," he protested. "The county law enforcing officer petitions and you ignore him." [53] It was, of course, an old story, but people were becoming more sensitive about it.

Moran's avowed objective was the governorship. His admirers, the Prohibitionists, early supplied him with the lever with which to pry loose a nomination from a more important group. They nominated him that June.[54] Inevitably he attracted the attention of his spiritual cousin, William Randolph Hearst, who that year sought New York's governorship and a bridge-head to the Presidency in 1908. Hearst founded an Independence League in Massachusetts on July 31, 1906, and seven weeks later Moran had another nomination. It does not appear, however, that Moran personally solicited either nomination. He sought rather the control of the Democratic party.

Democratic leaders, meanwhile, began maneuvers to head off a Moran boom. Moran had been boasting that he would force John F. Fitzgerald, Boston's new mayor, to support him for the nomination despite his strong opposition to "Honey Fitz" during the campaign, and the *bête noire* of the civic reformers indicated that the District Attorney could indeed intimidate him. In the spring, about forty Democrats met quietly in Boston to sound out party sentiment.[55] The organization, however, was so entangled in personal squabbles and factional feuds that the leaders could not agree on a man to oppose Moran. Ex-Governor Douglas urged Charles Hamlin to seek the nomination, but Hamlin still nursed wounds which Colonel Gaston had recently inflicted; he begged off to accept a retainer from the Boston & Maine Railroad. Douglas really wished the nomination himself but could not *appear* to wish it.[56] The

[53] *Boston Evening Transcript,* May 2, 1906.
[54] *Boston Post,* June 30, 1906.
[55] *Boston Post,* May 20, 1906.
[56] Hamlin Diary, entries for July 1906 (Hamlin MSS).

problem seemed solved when Henry Whitney agreed to accept the nomination, but he made it clear that he would not like campaigning against Curtis Guild.

The difficulty came to a dramatic climax on August 22 when Whitney suddenly withdrew his candidacy in favor of Douglas, who, Whitney said, had indicated his own availability. (A spokesman for Douglas had in fact merely said to a reporter that he would not comment on a rumor that Douglas would accept a nomination by draft.) That night, Fitzgerald precipitated a rush to Moran by announcing that he would support the District Attorney because there was no one else in the field to oppose him. This "argument" appeared unanswerable, and the major ward leaders of Boston, including Fitzgerald's old enemies Martin Lomasney and James Curley, climbed on the bandwagon. So did the long-suffering supporters of sulking Charles Hamlin.[57] So did George Fred Williams, who was supporting Bryan again for 1908 and had earlier suspected Moran to be Hearst's "tool."

State Chairman Josiah Quincy fought on almost alone. Quincy may have been on firm ground when he argued that Moran was another party's nominee who sought to use the Democratic organization for his own purposes and would oppose the Democrats if he failed to get their nomination. "This position," Quincy observed, "strikes at the very basis of party organization." [58] But Quincy himself demonstrated all that was wrong with the existing Democratic organization by insisting that the one important cause of the day was tariff revision, and that Moran would deprive the party of its only winning issue.[59] With a tone of exasperation that probably evoked a hearty "amen" from many a citizen, Hearst's *Boston American* exclaimed: "For nearly 100 years men like Mr. Quincy have used the tariff issue to throw dust in the eyes of the Democratic masses that they might not see and fight for the

[57] *Boston Herald, Boston Globe,* and *Boston Traveller,* August 21–23, 1906.
[58] *Boston Herald,* September 20, 1906.
[59] *Boston Herald,* August 7, 1906. See also *Boston Evening Transcript,* July 28, 1906, for a similar statement by Congressman John A. Sullivan.

real issues of the campaign." Alluding both to the Democrats' stolidity and the service corporations' lien on the party, the *American* insisted: "Mr. Quincy is an issue. Mr. Gaston is an issue . . . The Boston Elevated is an issue. The Consolidated Gas Company is an issue . . . Tariff revision nonsense will not obscure them." [60]

Apparently the majority of state Democrats agreed. Moran clinched the Democratic nomination by sweeping the party caucus elections for convention delegates; the Man Who Dared won 516 delegates to the opposition's 127.[61] Two weeks before the convention, Chairman Quincy conceded: "The returns from the caucuses are now sufficiently full to show beyond a doubt that a considerable majority of the delegation is in favor of the nomination of Mr. Moran . . . The responsibility of the coming campaign now belongs wholly to the democrats who have advocated or acquiesced in the nomination of Mr. Moran, and we leave the field entirely to them." [62] The old-line Democrats withdrew, and Moran emerged on top.

But the confusion had only begun. On October 4, the delegates met at Boston (where they had some trouble obtaining a hotel because the proprietors feared a brawl) and endorsed the Independence League's slate of John B. Moran and old bewhiskered Elbridge Gerry Brown, the state's Populist candidate for governor more than a decade before. The convention went on to pass essentially the entire Independence League platform, which covered nearly every economic and moral issue of the day — from the abolition of capital punishment and the strengthening of the laws against divorce and abortion (for "the prevention of child murder") to government ownership of public utilities, an eight-hour day for all workers, and mandatory imprisonment for violators of the antitrust laws.[63] ("Such crazy violence," exclaimed Cabot Lodge; "it reads like

[60] *Boston American,* August 9, 1906.
[61] *Boston Herald,* September 26 and 27, 1906.
[62] *Boston Herald,* September 28, 1906.
[63] There is a complete copy of the platform in the Bridgman Scrapbooks.

a manifesto of a Jacobin Club.")[64] These proceedings went peaceably enough, but George Fred Williams threw the convention into an uproar when he proposed endorsing William Jennings Bryan for President in 1908. The Hearst men protested vigorously, arguing that Moran — who was absent — opposed all endorsements.[65] They agreed, however, to a "compromise" by which Hearst, too, received an endorsement — for governor of New York.

The injection of national politics into the convention profoundly displeased Moran. Shortly before the convention he had already startled his followers by vehemently repudiating a state-wide newspaper advertisement, signed by his own manager, which jointly endorsed Hearst and Moran for governor in their respective states; the advertisement also proclaimed: "In the next Democratic presidential convention there will be nothing and nobody but Hearst and Moran."[66] Now the Prohibitionist, Independence League, and Democratic nominee went into seclusion without even announcing whether he accepted his latest nomination. Moran apparently resented the strings that Hearst was tying to him; it is possible that the man may even have had some grandiose ambitions of his own. In addition, Moran was ill; within thirty months he would be dead of tuberculosis of the throat, though no one at the time knew the nature of his illness. Moran only knew that he was tired and sick, and that the convention had double-crossed him. The public knew only that Moran had disappeared. For six days he remained in hiding amidst wild rumors, protests, and lamentations. ("Even his closest friends," commented one newspaper, "declare his actions are not those of a sane

[64] Lodge to Roosevelt, October 6, 1906, in *Correspondence,* I, 242. Lodge used the same words to George Meyer, October 6, 1906 (Meyer MSS).

[65] In a letter allegedly written October 2, but made public only after the convention, Moran urged "no endorsement of a presidential candidate" and warned: "No friend of mine will attempt to force such." *Boston Journal,* October 10, 1906.

[66] See almost any important Massachusetts newspaper for Sunday, September 30, 1906.

man.")[67] He flitted briefly into view at Hearst's house in New York, but he evaded the reporters and did not emerge again until October 11 when he attended a rally at Faneuil Hall and again rebuffed all reporters. Finally, on October 12, he announced his acceptance of the Democratic nomination, said he had been ill, and refused to comment on Bryan or Hearst. Two days later he dismissed all his various campaign managers with the declaration that he would conduct his campaign himself.[68]

The campaign that followed was almost ludicrous. Moran refused to cooperate with the leaders of any of the parties which had nominated him. Nor can it be said that they cooperated with him; the Hearst men even reprinted the same advertisement which he had specifically repudiated.[69] The issue of the Presidency came to plague him; in speech after speech he labored the theme that he was no one's man, that he cared "nothing about either Hearst or Bryan," and that he would take his stand in 1908 "not as a follower of either, but as an equal." [70] The press, including much of the Democratic press, deliberately interpreted such statements to mean that he was declaring himself a candidate for the Presidency.[71] Ridicule, which was not confined to the Bay State, did not stop him from pursuing the issue. He became the victim of daily editorial and letter-column jibes. ("I note you quote a Mr. Moran of Boston as aspiring to the Presidency. Kindly inform me, and others who may be equally in ignorance. Who the hell is Moran?")[72]

---

[67] *Boston Traveller,* October 11, 1906.

[68] *Boston Evening Transcript,* October 13, 15, 1906. Mayor Fitzgerald blamed it all on Williams, who, he charged, was "more anxious to boom Bryan and defeat Hearst, than to elect Moran." Fitzgerald was known to be favoring Hearst (*The Republic,* October 12–19, 1906).

[69] See the Worcester, Springfield, and Boston papers for November 6, 1906.

[70] *Boston Post,* October 19, 1906.

[71] The Democratic *Boston Post's* headline for October 19 read, "Moran's Goal Is the Presidency"; the *Boston Journal* that day announced, "Moran Candidate for President"; the *Boston Globe* ran a sub-head: "Moran Sure He Will Be Elected to Presidency."

[72] *New York Sun,* October 21, 1906.

Moran's defeat was an anticlimax, but Guild's victory left Republican leaders uneasy. Although the incumbent Governor won by more than a 30,000 plurality, polled the largest Republican vote (222,500) since 1900 and the highest percentage of the total vote (53 per cent) since 1901, and regained for the first time in three years a slim margin (2,000 votes) in the cities, he did not do as well as had been expected. Guild's margin amounted to only about half the aggregate Republican plurality in the vote for Congressman, and he lost the two traditionally Republican industrial cities of Brockton and New Bedford. In addition, Moran managed to poll an incredible 192,000 votes — more by far than any Democrat in history except Douglas in 1904 — despite the chaos of the campaign, the instability of the candidate, the poverty of his campaign chest, and the large exodus of traditional supporters from the Democratic party. The fact that 75,000 citizens voted for Moran on the non-Democratic tickets indicated that he had captured a large part of the state's disaffected element, including thousands who usually voted Republican. Moreover, the Man Who Dared cut deeply into Socialist strength in Haverhill, Brockton, and Rockland, which had sent Socialist representatives to the legislature only a few years earlier; the Social Democratic and Socialist Labor parties, in fact, hit their low for the era, their aggregate vote dropping from 4 to 2 per cent despite a popular Social Democratic candidate for governor.[73]

"The results of the election are disheartening," Senator Lodge wrote to President Roosevelt.[74] Against the issues which Moran raised, "protectionism" appeared inadequate to keep the factory operatives loyal. Aside from the partisan problem, moreover, it chilled the hearts of the Republican leaders that so many would vote for a man and a platform which directly challenged the general order of things. "We have got a terrible

[73] James F. Carey, one of the organizers of the Social Democratic party in the state, had served in the General Court for Haverhill for several years; he polled 5000 votes more in his 1905 campaign for governor than in 1906.
[74] Lodge to Roosevelt, November 7, 1906, *Correspondence*, II, 259.

struggle before us," Lodge lamented, "to save the country from a movement which strikes at the very foundations of society and civilization." [75]

IV

Republican fears were premature. While Moran's strong showing suggested the measure of social needs which had gone unrepresented among the traditional leaders of the Commonwealth, his coalition of immigrant, working class, and morally incensed followers quickly disintegrated. Moran was too independent and erratic to maintain the loyalty of local politicos who sought power through him; he was too skeptical for religious leaders and too "dry" for the classes he most depended on. Above all, he was too sick to try to lead the insurgent groups again.

As for the civic reformers — progressives like Brandeis and Eastman — Moran never had their support. They had more in common with the standpat conservatives than they did with the likes of Moran. Their criticism of existing political and economic activities was predicated upon the desire to preserve old institutions, not to overthrow them. It was symbolic that they had united behind a Frothingham in their attempt to beat a Fitzgerald. In rejecting Moran and Fitzgerald the reformers strove to maintain an ideal of public service which was fast dying. It perhaps had never been a wholly or adequately realized ideal, but it represented an agreed-upon standard against which to measure men and their acts.

Still, some argued that, in concentrating on upholding noble purposes, the civic reformers neglected basic needs. So long as the insurgent classes remained excluded from the rewards which the Commonwealth had to offer, they would find little enchantment with its vaunted ideals. In that respect the reformers proved their failure to meet the most fundamental of moral issues. With this in mind, one commentator, in the midst

[75] *Ibid.* See also Lodge to George Meyer, December 6, 1906 (Lodge MSS).

of America's heralded moral renascence, remarked sourly: "That there is a moral awakening is not true, and if there is a semblance of it, the appearance in fact is merely one class of property trying to get even with another class." [76]

[76] Raymond L. Bridgman, "Legislative Review," *Springfield Republican,* June 18, 1909.

CHAPTER SEVEN

BOURBONISM IN THE AGE OF PROGRESSIVISM

Our laws and customs recognize no noble titles; but men can
forego the husk of a title who possess the fat ears of power.

Josiah Strong (1885) *

IT was with ironic but commonplace arrogance that the leaders of the Massachusetts polity denounced radicals like Moran
as "fomenters of class hatred." [1] The only distinct class sentiment within the state, outside of certain small and extreme
segments of the socialist movement, emanated from the dominant classes themselves. In no way confined to the Bay State,
upper-class sensibilities were manifest on many levels, sometimes in expressions against immigrants and Catholics, sometimes in the shunning of politicians from non-genteel families
— as in the case of John L. Bates. Those ascendant in the
business world in particular laid claim to privileged status,
and the claim received the most extravagant deference from
society at large. That deference helped define the dominant
"in" class of the age, and affirmed the self-made myth of the
Businessman as paragon. So accepted was the Businessman's
claim to dominance that it rarely evoked note except in extreme cases — as when George F. Baer opined that American
workingmen would be cared for by the "Christian men" to
whom God had given control of the property interests of the
country.

Members of the dominant classes, perceiving the danger in
the expression of such candid contempt for "the peepul," were
quick to repudiate and denounce the Baers. This reaction

* Quoted in Arthur M. Schlesinger, *New Viewpoints in American History* (New York, 1923), p. 94.
[1] Senator Lodge used the phrase in his address to the Republican State
Convention in 1906, and similar statements occurred frequently during the
campaign.

came typically from the social elements which claimed status on the basis of old wealth and family descent — the so-called Brahmins. Such elements, self-conscious shadows of the English gentry, wielded great influence in Massachusetts and other communities all over the country. Their devotion to the tradition of disinterested public service contributed immeasurably to the reputation for good government which the old Commonwealth maintained. Their ostensible disdain for the overt pursuit of money helped to check crass materialism and to keep alive standards of excellence that were unrelated to wealth. It may also have served as a defense against the challenge of new wealth to their own status claims. Nevertheless, more often than they were willing to admit, the patrician classes tended to identify with wealth and power of all vintages. This attitude frequently blurred their standards and induced the most blatant forms of hypocrisy on important public issues.

Many who expressed hostility to class discrimination on one day, on the next practiced what they had earlier found objectionable. On one Monday, for example, the *Boston Herald* denounced labor's demand for an eight-hour bill as unconstitutional and un-American because it amounted to granting special privileges to a particular class; on Tuesday, the same columns argued that a man of such obvious integrity as Charles W. Morse should not be sent to jail even though the courts had found him guilty ("technically," said the *Herald*) of stock frauds in his (also illegal) attempt to monopolize coastwise shipping on the Atlantic.[2] When the Boston police jailed one Morrison I. Swift, a harmless agitator-eccentric who had livened the public scene for many years, because without a license he had distributed handbills criticizing widespread unemployment, most of the newspapers agreed that Mr. Swift "should not expect to be treated except as everyone else is treated under law in a democracy"; but, in the same month, the same newspapers saw no point in punishing the Speaker of the Massachusetts House ("so distinguished a person") who admitted

[2] *Boston Herald,* September 1 and 2, 1909.

soliciting and receiving railroad passes in direct violation of the law, and they all applauded his acquittal after a brief trial as "a good thing for the honor of the state." [3]

"Most of the men of our little world," President Roosevelt complained privately, "do not see beyond their own circle . . . They do not realize the fervor of intensity with which [insurgent groups] are demanding a change in the old order of things in politics and in the world of great business." [4] Roosevelt, playing the role of patrician, thought little of the alleged wisdom and good will of the American Businessman. At times he grew caustic about the Businessman's propensity for aggravating social unrest. ("The idiotic folly of the high financiers and of their organs"; "the dull purblind folly of the very rich men, their greed and their arrogance.") [5] "I am continually brought in contact with very wealthy people," he wrote to one confidant. "They are socially the friends of my family . . . I think they mean well on the whole, but the more I see of them the more profoundly convinced I am of their entire unfitness to govern the country . . . [and of their] rancorous stupidity . . . Moreover, usually entirely without meaning it, they are singularly callous to the needs, sufferings, and feelings of the great mass of the people who work with their hands." [6]

During moments of reflection, men of responsibility within the old order found occasion for such criticisms of the wealthy and business classes. When Boston financier-philanthropist Henry Lee Higginson published a broadside against critics of businessmen, Cabot Lodge objected that "the fact that the great mass of our business men are both able and honest does not seem to me quite to cover the whole ground." The recent aggregations of wealth, he pointed out, had "led to unques-

[3] The quotations are from the *Boston Evening Transcript,* February 8, 1908, *Boston Globe,* February 10, 1908, and *Boston Herald,* February 16, 1908. See also *Springfield Republican,* February 12 and 16, 1908.

[4] Roosevelt to G. D. Cushing (then President of the Massachusetts Republican Club), February 17, 1908, in Morison, VI, 954.

[5] Roosevelt to Lodge, October 2, 1906, in *Correspondence,* II, 240; Roosevelt to W. H. Taft, March 1906, quoted in Pringle, Roosevelt, p. 290.

[6] Roosevelt to W. H. Moody, September 21, 1907, in Morison, V, 901.

tionable abuses . . . and to indifference to law which are . . .
perilous to a free State." Lodge concluded: "The mistake that
I think is made by business men is in their refusal, as a class,
to condemn [the dishonest men among them]. So long as they
keep the money in their pockets they command the support of
the business world . . . because they have succeeded, without
regard to their methods." [7] As President, William Howard
Taft, too, found it appropriate (privately) to brand "Wall
Street" as "the biggest ass I have ever run across," and (also
privately) to condemn the "sort of feeling on the part of businessmen who violate the law that their prosecution for doing
this calls for some explanation." [8]

But when the chips were down, men like Roosevelt, Lodge,
and Taft hastened to close ranks to preserve their "little world."
When revelations about insurance company scandals, food-
processing crimes, and oppressive business practices by Standard Oil and the Harriman railroad interests had stirred up great
public agitation, Lodge remonstrated with his friend Roosevelt
that the time had come to cease attacking the great aggregations of wealth and to concentrate on the agitators: "We ought
to be careful," he urged, ". . . not to alarm and confuse the
great body of American people who are hard working and
thrifty and have some little property." [9] Taft's affinity for "the
classes" is an oft-told story. Even when planning to carry out
the Rooseveltian corporation reform program, he could think
only of the leading corporation lawyers as "the best fitted to
do this without injury to the business interests of the country." [10] And when he became afraid of criticism if Charles
Morse should die in prison, he gave the convicted fraud a

---

[7] Lodge to Higginson, January 7, 1908 (Lodge MSS). For Higginson's
article, see "Justice to the Corporations," *Atlantic Monthly,* 101:9–16
(January 1908). Lodge seems to have resented Higginson's portrayal of
politicians as generally inept and corrupt.

[8] W. H. Taft to Henry Taft, February 21, 1910, and W. H. Taft to A. R.
Kimble, November 21, 1911, quoted in Henry F. Pringle, *The Life and
Times of William Howard Taft* (New York, 1939), pp. 655, 656.

[9] Lodge to Roosevelt, October 13, 1906, in Roosevelt MSS (LC).

[10] Taft, quoted in Mowry, *Era of Roosevelt,* p. 237.

presidential pardon.[11] As a federal judge he had shown no such sensitivity to public criticism when it was directed against the slaying of strikers by federal troops. ("They have only killed six of the mob as yet. This is hardly enough to make an impression.")[12]

A respectable nonpartisanship governed the deference to upper class prerogatives. In 1912, for example, after Democratic leader Josiah Quincy had been indicted for using the mails to perpetrate stock frauds, Murray Crane pleaded with the President to intervene: "It would have a very bad effect [he wrote] to have a man of Josiah Quincy's standing sentenced to prison, and no good would result from it." [13] To his credit, Taft did not prevent the Justice Department from pressing the case, though he made repeated inquiries of his Attorney General, and wrote solicitously to another eminent Republican who had made a plea for Quincy that nothing gave him greater concern "than this prosecution of Josiah Quincy, a scion of a noble ancestor." [14]

Indeed, one must view with considerable skepticism, the occasional outbursts against businessmen and other men of wealth by political leaders like Roosevelt, Taft, and Lodge. Businessmen's criticism of their politics and the economic tangles which jeopardized their power usually preceded their verbal assaults. Lodge, for example, found "the businessman . . . worse . . . than men of any other class" only after Roosevelt had to force settlement of the coal strike which Lodge had feared would cost the Republicans the 1902 elections.[15] And it was only when the banking community and much of the press charged Roosevelt with plunging the country into the

---

[11] Morse outlived his emancipator. See Pringle, *Taft*, pp. 627–637.

[12] *Ibid.*, p. 128.

[13] Crane to Taft, August 29, 1912 (Taft MSS).

[14] Taft to ex-Congressman Samuel L. Powers of Massachusetts, February 29, 1912 (Taft MSS). See also District Attorney Wise to Attorney General G. W. Wickersham, April 23, 1912, R. Forster (Taft's secretary) to Wickersham, September 2, 1912, and Wickersham to Taft, September 5, 1912 (Taft MSS).

[15] Lodge to Roosevelt, October 20, 1902, in Roosevelt MSS (LC).

financial crisis of 1907 that he lashed out publicly at the "male-factors of great wealth." He raised a great public hurrah when he demanded enactment of what was essentially a major part of the old Populist program for government control of the financial community. But the only action he took was to bestow special immunities from the law upon men of the class he had just publicly belabored, and to trust to them the safety of the nation's economy.[16] As for his legislative demands, friend Lodge reassured banker Higginson: "Congress will not take any action in those directions so that nobody need be disturbed." [17]

It was conditions such as these which encouraged what Norman Hapgood called "the easy defiance by the strong." [18] What the less fortunate attempted at their peril, those among the dominant classes accomplished with impunity. Upper-class solidarity was perhaps not the only reason for this, but it was a major reason. It explains, for example, why the New Haven Railroad's Charles S. Mellen could violate laws which regulated railroad corporations and proscribed monopoly, and yet reply with a smile to a delegation of protesting businessmen: "Paternalism must be exercised by those who have power, and I think we have that power." [19] The "condition of excitement and irritation in the public mind" that Roosevelt and others had perceived during the latter years of the decade continued to inspire political and social reforms, and helped induce politicians to challenge party leadership by championing popular issues of the day. But in many ways the central story of politics, at least in Massachusetts, was the tenacity of the state of

[16] Roosevelt gave immunity from the Sherman Antitrust Act to a syndicate headed by J. P. Morgan so that the United States Steel Corporation could absorb the Tennessee Coal and Iron Company and thus bail out an important New York investment house which was near bankruptcy. This was only one of several "accommodations" that Roosevelt arrived at with the leading businessmen of his time. See Robert H. Wiebe, "The House of Morgan and the Executive, 1905–1913," *American Historical Review,* 65: 49–60 (October 1959).

[17] Lodge to Higginson, November 22, 1907 (Lodge MSS).

[18] From *The Advancing Hour* (New York, 1920), p. 77.

[19] *Boston Herald,* March 7, 1907.

mind which committed the traditional social leaders to men of their own class more than to avowed ethical standards. The persistence of that mentality, a variety of bourbonism, even among men of ingenuous good will, made the task of social reform that much more formidable.

I

When John B. Moran withdrew from state politics to nurse his health after the 1906 elections, the diverse groups which had joined behind him for their own particular reasons returned to their separate corners. Men like Mayor Fitzgerald, who had never had much interest in Moran's program, had taken hold of the district attorney's coat tails merely in the hope of overthrowing the genteel, anti-Irish leadership of the Democratic party. Similarly, George Fred Williams and his allies, as well as the erstwhile supporters of Charles S. Hamlin, had supported Moran in order to oust the Whitneys and Gastons from party power. The Hearst men, led by Gerry Brown, retired to the exclusive task of building the Independence League, particularly with an eye to the presidential election of 1908. Williams, the Bryanite, was disinclined to work with them any longer, nor could gold-bug Hamlin work well with Williams — while an alliance of either or both with Fitzgerald, particularly in view of the Boston scandals, was out of the question.

The following year, there was a free-for-all for control of the Democratic party. Henry Whitney once more entered the fray — he had a vital interest in the pending merger of the New Haven and Boston & Maine railroads, and consequently no longer deferred to Governor Guild, his reciprocity ally. Guild had indicated his unfriendliness toward the New Haven, and Whitney expected to draw the support of the important financial interests who were promoting the merger. Although it was unlikely that he could unseat Guild, by heading the Democratic ticket he might at least aid in the return of men to the General Court who would not obstruct the New Haven's controversial activities. Once more Whitney's money and his corporate interests attracted the support of Fitzgerald and many urban bosses like him. But the large group of young Irish politicians who, like State Chairman John P. Feeney of Boston, had achieved party eminence only in 1906 through their support of Moran, held tenaciously to their newly won power. Their chief strength lay in control of the state committee. As Whitney's candidacy gained momentum, the Williams group joined them; Martin Lomasney, too, lined up with them, hoping to beat his Boston nemesis, Fitzgerald. The Stop-Whitney forces united behind "General" Charles W. Bartlett, the Democrats' nominee in 1905. Except for Williams, Lomasney, and Bartlett himself, not a single man among them had had any standing at all in state politics before 1906.

The contending factions met in Springfield during the first week of October. It was a long time before the city recovered from the blow. The party caucuses in the districts throughout the state had apparently given the Whitney forces an edge. Curiously, even Moran had given the Whitney cause a boost by withdrawing his support from another candidate because, as Moran put it, Whitney already had most of the state "in the bag." [20] But on the trains converging upon Springfield, reporters sensed trouble when they noticed among the delegates a large number of individuals not usually found at state party gatherings. The Whitney men had known that they would have to contend with a state committee loaded against them, and that the state committee would control the organization of the convention; but they had remained confident in the belief that they had the necessary votes. Now it appeared that they would have to contend with roughhouse tactics as well.

On the evening of October 3, the delegates and pseudo-delegates piled into a city equipped to accommodate only about half their number. Throughout the night the seat of western Massachusetts reverberated with sounds of revelry and explod-

[20] *Springfield Republican,* July 20, 1907.

ing firecrackers. Several brawls erupted. In a hotel suite, the state committee met and, by a majority of only two, selected George Fred Williams to be chairman of the convention, and Martin Lomasney's lieutenant, Daniel J. Kiley, to be temporary or organizing chairman. At the same time, Bartlett men circulated among the crowds in the streets below and distributed to their supporters the pink tickets from which the convention later got its name.

The doors of the Court-Square Theatre, the convention hall, opened at nine A.M. the next day. Toughs stationed at the entrances, evidently under orders from the state committee, admitted pink-ticket holders, while the majority of the Whitney men holding certified credentials as delegates were kept waiting in line for two hours. Inside the theater at last, the Whitney delegates discovered the entire orchestra occupied by the Bartlett men. Amidst considerable confusion, State Chairman Feeney secured approval, by voice vote, of Kiley and Williams as chairmen. In the rear and balcony of the theater, the Whitney men protested futilely. Williams read a long indictment of the New Haven Railroad for attempting to monopolize New England's transportation system, and indirectly assailed Whitney for supporting the merger of the New Haven and Boston & Maine; Williams' "platform" was "adopted by acclamation." At one-thirty in the afternoon, before any candidate had been placed in nomination, the Whitney forces filed out of the theater, and met again at a small hotel down the street. There they nominated Whitney for governor and adopted a platform which attempted to resuscitate the tariff issue. Josiah Quincy and Charles Hamlin wrote in provisions calling for a public service commission which would place within a single agency the responsibility for regulating all the public utilities, and they even persuaded Whitney to accept a plank which criticized the New Haven's purchase of Boston & Maine stock without legislative consent.[21]

[21] This account of the Democratic convention(s) is taken from reports in the *Springfield Republican* and *Boston Herald,* from the Bridgman Scrapbooks, and from the Hamlin Diary entries for 1907 (Hamlin MSS).

When the rump convention in the Court-Square Theatre meanwhile named Bartlett and John A. Thayer of Worcester as standard bearers, the state faced the prospect of two candidates who claimed to head the Democratic ticket. Although the Whitney group hauled the state committee and Charles Bartlett into court and secured a ruling that only Whitney had the right to campaign as a Democrat, on the grounds that most of the accredited delegates had been excluded from the Court-Square Theatre, the Bartlett men refused to give up. They entered the campaign as an Anti-Merger party.

The rump party, however, was soon isolated. Bartlett's own running mate renounced him and what he called the Feeney-Williams-Lomasney cabal. As a "party," the Anti-Merger group had little to recommend it besides its opposition to the New Haven, and on this issue it failed to obtain even the support of the leading opponents within the business community, or of the arch-opponent himself — Louis Brandeis. Judging from the names of its leaders, it attracted principally Irish-American politicians who sought a place in the state political sun. In the end, the Anti-Merger party ran a sad fourth.

The Independence League, meanwhile, offered a platform which appealed to those with a more general grievance against the "corporate interests," and a slate of candidates more acceptable to the non- or anti-Irish elements in the population. (The only Irishman to gain a position of eminence on either the state committee or the party slate was the candidate for state auditor.) In addition to opposing the New Haven merger, the Independence League's platform favored public ownership of public utilities, and a law to prevent price discrimination by large corporations. Going it alone this year, the party nominated one Thomas L. Hisgen of West Springfield for governor, and E. Gerry Brown again for lieutenant governor. Hisgen was a petroleum oil dealer whose appearance on the public scene coincided with Standard Oil's invasion of his market area in western Massachusetts. Beginning in 1906, Hisgen strove to have the General Court pass an "antimonopoly" or "price discrimination" bill which would outlaw the typical Standard Oil practices of charging lower prices (even below cost) where necessary to undercut competition, and higher prices where no competition existed. (No less an individual than Calvin Coolidge, then a representative from Northampton, sponsored Hisgen's bill in the legislature.)[22]

The election attracted the smallest turnout since 1901. Governor Guild coasted in with 188,000 votes, though he carried only 50 per cent of the total vote. Hisgen made a remarkable showing, polling more than 75,000 votes. This was 5000 more than Whitney polled on the Democratic ticket, though two other ticket entries, made for Whitney in advance of the court ruling in order to guarantee that he would appear on the ballot, gave him a total of 80,000 votes. Bartlett managed only 11,000 votes. That was only about 1,000 more than the combined Socialist vote, which for the second straight year totaled only 10,000.

It is difficult to assess the relative importance of the many elements involved in the election results. Hisgen's high total may represent nothing more than the disgust of Democrats with their party's squabbling. It may represent the impact of the banking panic during the year, though employment figures show no serious distress among workers before November. There is no evidence that the New Haven merger controversy had any effect at all on the results. There appeared to be considerable anti-Republican sentiment in the state, but there was little indication as yet that the diverse elements which expressed that sentiment were politically reconcilable. The 1907 election campaign indicated only that the Democratic party was still paralyzed by factionalism and special-interest financing, and that the insurgent groups had failed to demonstrate any capacity for responsible leadership.

[22] Coolidge continued to sponsor the Hisgen bill through 1909. It passed the House but met defeat in the Senate in 1908. See *Springfield Republican,* April 22, 1908; Claude M. Fuess, *Calvin Coolidge: The Man from Vermont* (Boston, 1940), p. 103.

II

Meanwhile, Theodore Roosevelt's experience with the financiers during the panic year of 1907, especially with their effort to blame him for the crisis, led him into increasingly radical assaults upon the business world. Since he had ruled out a third term for himself, by the end of that year he was something of a lame-duck president; no doubt the resulting diminution in his power intensified his feelings. Partly in self-defense, he struck his favorite pose as champion of justice and righteousness. ("If your soul does not rise up against corruption in politics and in business, why, then, naturally you are not in sympathy with me," he retorted to a class-conscious friend who deplored his "undignified" criticism of business methods.)[23] Throughout 1908 his relations with party leaders worsened. Nevertheless, since the public exercised greater control over the selection of presidents than it did over legislation and judicial decisions, Roosevelt wielded decisive power in determining his own successor; for the standpat Republicans to defy the President on this would have been to invite defeat.

To secure control of the Massachusetts delegation for the nomination of William Howard Taft at the National Convention, Roosevelt depended on the influence of Senator Lodge and Congressman A. P. Gardner. That they were not entirely successful testified to Lodge's reduced power within the state, and to a quiet anti-organization revolt among the rank and file which, ironically, focused on Lodge as the popularly imagined Republican "boss." Roosevelt had made his preference for Taft known to party leaders some time in 1906. In December of that year, a discerning newspaper reporter correctly interpreted Senator Murray Crane's favorable comments about Taft as indicating the President's own inclination.[24] By January 1908,

[23] Roosevelt to N. M. Butler, February 1908, quoted in Pringle, *Roosevelt*, p. 338.
[24] *Cleveland Leader*, December 6, 1906, in Bridgman Scrapbooks.

however, much to Lodge's bewilderment and discomfort, Crane had changed his mind, and he took with him into the opposition the chairman of the state committee and ex-Governors John D. Long and John L. Bates.[25] Though Crane worked (characteristically) behind the scenes, the newspapers soon were filled with reports of his opposition to Taft and also noted his clash with Lodge. They pointed out, in addition, that many secondary party figures, long hoping to take a crack at the senior senator, would line up behind Crane.[26] Crane was careful not to oppose Taft directly — that would have jeopardized the government jobs held by potential supporters. He took a stand instead against instructing the state delegation to the National Convention for Taft or anyone else, but he let it be known that he thought Taft's candidacy contained "elements of weakness." [27] An "anti-instruction" slate was drawn up quickly in several of the eastern congressional districts, and it was clear that many of the men behind the movement opposed Lodge more than they opposed Taft or supported Crane.[28]

Crane's position rattled his Senate colleague. Lodge knew he could not afford an open break, and he urged Gardner in particular not to antagonize Crane or "stir up any fights" in

[25] P. M. Longan to George Meyer, January 11, 1908, and Lodge to Meyer, January 21, 1908 (Meyer MSS). There is evidence that Crane had begun to defect early in 1907. See James O. Lyford to Jacob H. Gallinger, July 23, 1907 (Gallinger MSS); and Lodge to Roosevelt, April 13, 1907, *Correspondence*, 266–267. Lodge wrote that he could not credit reports that Crane might be lining up with Foraker of Ohio; Lyford wrote: "There does not seem to be much doubt that there is a break between the administration and Crane."

[26] See *Springfield Republican*, February 12, 1908, and Bridgman Scrapbooks for January and February 1908 containing clippings from Massachusetts, Connecticut, and New York newspapers on Crane's opposition to Taft, and the tendency of important party members to sympathize with Crane's view in order to slap at Lodge. The clippings indicate Crane's support of New York's Charles Evans Hughes, though George Mowry, citing the Joseph B. Foraker papers, suggests that, at least in January 1908, Crane supported Senator Foraker: *Theodore Roosevelt and the Progressive Movement* (New York, paperback edition, 1960), p. 30.

[27] *Fitchburg Sentinel*, February 12, 1908.

[28] See J. J. McCarthy to Lodge, March 9, 1908 (Lodge MSS); Bridgman Scrapbooks for January and February 1908; P. M. Longan to George Meyer, March 10, 1908, and ex-Congressman Samuel Powers to Meyer, March 28, 1908 (Meyer MSS).

the campaign for the election of convention delegates.[29] To his ally, Robert Lincoln O'Brien of the *Transcript,* he complained, "Does political liberty consist in giving absolute freedom of action to thirty-two delegates and denying to all the Republican voters of Massachusetts the right to express any opinion? . . . Have [not] constituencies the right before voting to know the opinion at the moment of voting of the man for whom they vote?"[30] It was curious to find Lodge championing the cause of popular government, but then his opponents were equally inconsistent. As they professed to see it, their support of Crane the Standpatter and of uninstructed delegates made them "independents" and "progressives" in the fight for the public weal.[31] It illustrated how, in the political shuffling of the day, some "out" groups made use of reform rhetoric.

Lodge publicly announced for Taft late in March, but Crane's opposition forced the senior senator out of the fight for instructed delegates. ("You understand the difficulties of my own position," Lodge wrote to O'Brien on the day of the caucus elections. "I have kept out of the fight because I don't want to hurt the Party in the State by needless division and because of my personal attachment to some of the men who differ with me, especially for my colleague.")[32] Lodge's regard for his colleague's feelings ultimately betrayed the fight to commit the state to Taft. The balloting on March 31 resulted in a victory for the Taft-instructed delegates in the sixth, ninth, and eleventh congressional districts where "pledged to Taft" appeared on the ballots; elsewhere, the pundits estimated a Taft victory as a result of the election of men known publicly to favor Taft.[33] But Murray Crane, in typical fashion, wrested

[29] Lodge to George Meyer, January 21, 1908 (Meyer MSS).
[30] Lodge to O'Brien, March 7, 1908 (Lodge MSS). It is possible that Lodge hoped O'Brien would print this letter as an unsigned editorial. In his "Reminiscences," O'Brien confessed that he frequently printed Lodge's missives as editorials, at least before 1913. See "Reminiscences of Robert Lincoln O'Brien," Columbia University Oral History Office, p. 93.
[31] See, e.g., *Fitchburg Sentinel,* February 12, 1908; *Springfield Republican,* February 15, 1908.
[32] Lodge to O'Brien, March 31, 1908 (Lodge MSS).
[33] *Boston Herald,* April 1 and 5, 1908.

the decision from the Taft forces without even an open test of strength; he bypassed the opposition by simply mastering the negotiations with the politicians at the top. He achieved this by persuading Lodge to accept what the two senators chose to call a "compromise." Lodge agreed to oppose a pro-Taft resolution at the state convention in April, as well as specific instructions to the delegates. Meanwhile, Crane persuaded his supporter John L. Bates to withdraw his candidacy for delegate at large so that ex-Governor Long could attend the National Convention; a pro-Taft man had defeated Long in the caucus fight for a convention seat.

A. P. Gardner and ex-Congressman Samuel L. Powers, Taft's managers in New England, continued to fight up to the last moment for instructed delegates and a favorable resolution. But Lodge now worked for the opposition, while Crane retired to the shadows. With a series of telegrams and telephone calls to the White House, Lodge secured Roosevelt's support for the Crane position by advising that the convention would defeat a pro-Taft resolution if it were introduced. Gardner wired the President that that was not so, but Roosevelt counseled Gardner to give up. In the end, the convention resolved simply that the majority of delegates favored Taft's nomination, but neither pledged the delegates to support him at the National Convention nor expressed enthusiasm over his candidacy.[34] As one news commentator put it: "Taft wasn't endorsed. He was mentioned." [35]

III

The Bay State, meanwhile, also prepared to undergo a change of executive leadership. Governor Curtis Guild's third

[34] The telegrams and memoranda of the telephone conversations appear in the Roosevelt MSS (LC). The crucial passages are printed in Morison, VI, 997–998. According to the editor, "The Taft men . . . won a decisive victory." But, although the Massachusetts delegation ultimately went into the Taft column at the National Convention, the action at the Boston convention represented no victory for the men who had fought for Taft. See Boston Herald, April 9 and 10, 1908.

[35] Boston Herald, April 11, 1908.

term expired in 1908, and with Eben Draper "scheduled" by the party organization to ascend to the governorship, the G.O.P. treated the state to its triennial contest for a new lieutenant governor. Draper's candidacy had essentially been decided on three years before when he had won the lieutenant governorship. The fact that he had served as acting governor during much of 1908, while Guild fought off pneumonia and appendicitis, gave him added claim to top place on the state ticket.

As in 1905, three men vied for the second step on the escalator and, presumably, for the "succession" in another three years. Characteristically, all the candidates claimed the right to the nomination on the grounds of partisan services rendered, and at least on the surface they made no effort to identify themselves with a point of view or administrative program. ("But what are the issues . . . involved in the rival candidacies?" inquired the *Boston Herald,* which was prissy enough to believe that political leaders ought to stand for something. "Is the campaign . . . merely a matter of personal rivalry between ambitious men?") [36] It was by sidetracking specific issues in intraparty maneuvers that the Republicans had managed to maintain their coalition of Back Bay gentility, industrial-ward politicians, small town and rural businessmen, and civic-minded public servants. Yet the candidates did represent three of the major segments of the Republican party.

The leading contender for the nomination was Louis A. Frothingham of Boston, who intimated that he believed he deserved the nomination for his "sacrifice" in 1905 when he had given up the House speakership to run against Fitzgerald for mayor of Boston; in fact, Frothingham hinted that the party leaders had promised him the nomination.[37] It was generally acknowledged that he did have the support of the state committee as well as the "Better Element" among the Repub-

---

[36] *Ibid.,* August 10, 1908.
[37] *Boston Evening Transcript,* January 21, 1908. See also J. J. McCarthy to Lodge, January 31, 1908 (Lodge MSS).

lican regulars throughout the state. His legislative record was conservative and pro-business; he had opposed municipal ownership of utilities, the initiative and referendum, innovations in election procedures, graduated inheritance and income taxes, and tariff revision; he had shown little resistance to the newer methods of business, and had supported the Boston Elevated's tainted franchise bill in 1901 until Governor Crane made known his opposition; he had opposed legislation to improve the bargaining power of unions and the labor conditions even of women and children. Those were important qualities for a Republican gubernatorial candidate. Still, if that kind of record had stood as a criterion of good Republicanism in the state, the party could not have held the support of labor centers such as Worcester, Lowell, and New Bedford, and the state could not have achieved its advanced position on so much of the progressive program. The party had many men, like Curtis Guild, who opposed Frothingham's political philosophy but who were equally acceptable as leaders. Other qualities more decisively identified Frothingham with the established party leaders: he was of good family and was well-to-do; he was quiet and colorless; he loyally supported organization candidates regardless of their ideals or lack of them. He was, in fine, a man after Murray Crane's own heart. When in 1903 he received the unofficial but effective support of Senators Lodge and Crane for the House speakership,[38] it was already rumored that the organization had selected him for the governorship after Draper.

It was exactly on the issue of Frothingham's dependence on the "machine" that Speaker John N. Cole of Andover attacked his candidacy and claimed for himself the support of the party rank and file. Cole's legislative record, which was slightly more enlightened than Frothingham's, was as inconsequential to his supporters as Frothingham's was to the organization leaders. He had been a small town editor and publisher before he decided to seek power and eminence through

[38] Lodge to A. P. Gardner, July 11, 1903 (Lodge MSS).

state politics. In 1908, he sought to exploit a rebellious sentiment deep within the party similar to that which had boomed
John L. Bates' fortunes a decade earlier. Its target was what
Bay Staters commonly called the "Back Bay set," a phrase
which covered all the self-conscious "classes" from Boston to
the Berkshires. "For many years," one newspaper remarked,
"this class of men has contrived to hold the governorship as if
it were a prize for them." [39] ("Because of that certain and
immovable gulf between you and many of my associates,"
Cole once wrote to Cabot Lodge, "we shall probably be frequently on opposite sides in our selection of candidates.")[40]
Cole was of the Bates class, a representative of men of small
(or at least unacknowledged) qualities in quest of power within
the party — in sum, a representative of the "outs" wanting
"in."

Robert Luce of Somerville, the third and most interesting
contender, could claim the support of neither the party organization nor the rank and file. He was, rather, a typical example
of that small phalanx of Massachusetts reformers whose presence in the General Court throughout the Commonwealth's
history had helped create its advanced position on so many
social and political matters. An editor who also ran a news
clipping service, Luce won election to the General Court in
1898. There he stood for what the "Back Bay set" liked to
believe it stood for when partisan and personal exigencies did
not confound its conscience. Many of his colleagues resented
him because he continually injected "moral considerations"
into legislative deliberations, and because he insisted on working for what he regarded as "right" even when it sometimes
appeared to handicap the party at election time.[41]

Luce's candidacy did have the support of diverse reform
and "moral" elements in Massachusetts, including anti-saloon
leagues, the Sabbath observance associations, the good gov-

[39] *Brockton Enterprise,* February 6, 1908.
[40] Cole to Lodge, March 8, 1909 (Lodge MSS).
[41] Interviews in 1957 with former Governor Channing Cox and former
editor of the *Boston Herald,* Frank W. Buxton.

ernment forces, and the genteel reformers generally.[42] He had cooperated with Louis Brandeis on several occasions in the fight for traditional standards of business techniques and clean legislative practices. He had helped fight against the Boston Elevated franchise and for savings bank insurance. Each year after the Elevated battle he had introduced "corrupt practices" bills to ban corporations from hiring employees on the recommendation of a legislator and from making contributions to political campaigns. He succeeded in both objectives — the first, early in 1903 with the aid of Governor Bates, and the second in 1906 and 1908 with the aid of Governor Guild.[43]

Luce's chief interest, however, was in enlarging the influence of the public on governmental processes ("predicated on the assumption that the democratic process is successful, and ought to be extended").[44] From 1901 on he fought for state-wide direct primaries (he achieved his objective ultimately in 1911). Beginning in 1905, he worked for a "public opinion" law in order to give voters an opportunity to express their views on current issues without either permitting them to vote directly on pending legislation or legally requiring state legislators to follow those views ("advisory initiative and referendum" became law in 1913). In both causes Luce ran into direct opposition from the party leaders, including the state committee and both United States senators. Cabot Lodge, who liked to pretend that he never interfered in state legislative matters,[45] subverted Luce's efforts for the direct primary by

[42] See Bridgman Scrapbooks, XXVII, 78.

[43] Robert Luce, *Legislative Assemblies* (Boston, 1924), p. 390, and *Legislative Principles* (Boston, 1930), pp. 405ff; *MHRJ,* May 14, 1906, pp. 1032–34; *MSJ,* June 13, 1906, p. 1027; *Boston Herald,* January 3, 1908.

[44] Robert Luce, "The Primary Election," unbound pamphlet, Massachusetts State House Library, Boston.

[45] See, e.g., Lodge to Crane, May 17, 1900 (Crane MSS), and Lodge to H. L. Higginson, March 8, 1909 (Lodge MSS). Lodge went so far as to state on the floor of the United States Senate: "I do not attempt to interfere in any way with legislation pending in the Legislature of Massachusetts. I think that is something wholly beyond the province of the representatives of the state in Congress" (*Boston Herald,* April 13, 1910).

letters to the State House, and went so far as to address the General Court personally in order to defeat the public opinion bill in 1907.[46]

Yet Robert Luce had other qualities which maintained his standing not only as a good Republican, but as a Republican with leadership potentialities. Although the party leadership distrusted him because of his unorthodox political views, he was not an "outsider." Early in his legislative career, Luce secured appointment as chairman of the committee on elections, and throughout the era he also held a seat on the important committees on ways and means and on railroads. He owed his place partly to the premium which the party put on "harmony" and on smoothing over differences, and partly to the tradition of independence and respect for ability among the legislators which the security of the party in the nearly one-party state had permitted. In addition, for all his unorthodoxy, Luce never broke party regularity at election time. Insisting on "party government," he liked to emphasize that his primaries system would help eliminate the independents and Democrats from Republican nomination contests. Finally, Luce came from a good family background, and his particular district — mostly residential and well-to-do — enabled him to stay in the General Court without having to resort to the more sordid compromises of ward politics.

It surprised no one, therefore, that early in the 1908 nomination contest Luce made it clear that if he did not win more delegates than Frothingham on the first ballot at the convention he would throw his support to him, and it was understood that the ex-Speaker would so support Luce. Luce made this choice despite the fact that he had always drawn greater support for his legislative measures from the ranks behind Cole

[46] Lodge to Crane, February 17, 1902, J. J. McCarthy to Lodge, April 24, 1907, Lodge to McCarthy, April 27, 1907 and McCarthy to Lodge, May 3, 1909 [sic] (all in Lodge MSS). Lodge to Roosevelt, April 7, 1907, in *Correspondence*, II, 264. Lodge called the public opinion bill "one of the most dangerous measures I have ever seen" (Lodge to Roosevelt, *ibid.*).

than he ever could expect from those behind Frothingham. But the point was to beat the "outsider," John Cole.[47]

One vital party element remained outside the struggle for power in the party councils. That was the large body of "labor representatives" — Republicans with primarily wage-worker constituencies — who regularly voted for bills to improve working conditions and to facilitate the organization of trade unions, and frequently also for popular-government measures such as the initiative and referendum. Party leaders, who almost always viewed politics through the eyes of the employers, sometimes regarded these men as little better than the Democrats with whom they were so frequently aligned. Yet the labor legislators found a comfortable niche within the G.O.P. In the first place, the Democracy's inflationary program of the 1890's and its more longstanding opposition to protective tariffs held no charms for the mass of wageworkers; on those two crucial issues, the labor representatives proved highly "regular." In addition, their support of labor measures did not preclude their support of other bills in which corporations (especially public service corporations) had an interest; thus during the Boston Elevated, Consolidated Gas, and New Haven merger contests, for example, the labor representatives almost unanimously supported the company position.

It was not strange, then, that a Republican legislator like Samuel Ross, head of the New Bedford Spinners union and a high official in the Massachusetts branch of the American Federation of Labor, held the chairmanship of the important state House Labor Committee for a decade; when he moved up into the state Senate in 1908, his colleague Andrew Doyle, also of New Bedford, assumed the leadership of the labor representatives in the lower house. The General Court also received labor men from Haverhill, Taunton, Fall River, Lynn, and Lawrence, though they rarely stayed long enough to make their mark as Doyle and Ross had. On the other hand, while the

[47] Bridgman Scrapbooks, XXVIII, 8, and editorial in *Brockton Enterprise*, September 24, 1908.

G.O.P. made room for these men, held them largely by virtue of its stand for protectionism, and depended on them for its continued hegemony in the state, it never let them into the high party councils, nor did it let them represent Republicanism on a state ticket. They took no part in the fight for the lieutenant governorship in 1908.

In the end, the party machinery operated as programed. Luce's stand probably served only to assure his own defeat as well as Cole's; he could not be the compromise candidate for those who had hoped to challenge the incumbent party leadership. The fence-sitters found it safer to back the organization candidate. On the first ballot, Frothingham polled 734 delegate votes to Cole's 453 and Luce's 331 — or about 50 short of the necessary majority. Cole anticipated Luce's swing to Frothingham, and leaped to the convention platform to concede the nomination.[48] In this manner he preserved the façade of unity in the party, and kept intact his chances of future preferment.

Massachusetts Republicans thus committed the party in 1908 — and apparently for the next six years — to the conservative "business" leadership of Draper and Frothingham. The escalator system had operated to elevate two men far removed from the spirit of the times. For those heated by the fires of reform, it was a chilling prospect. The condition of politics in the state offered them no real alternative. They could not go to the Independence League, which promised to substitute only demagogic impudence for cavalier arrogance. And the Democratic party was a shambles, reduced again to the mere shadow of a political organization.

Despite the absence of an effective partisan opposition, it would seem that the G.O.P. was courting trouble — not immediately perhaps, but in the not too distant future. The party had been in power a long time. A new generation of potential leaders had not yet been given a chance to realize its natural ambitions. (Frothingham was, to be sure, a young man, but

[48] Hennessy, *Twenty-five Years,* p. 202.

he was still the old guard's young man.) By overlooking the popular mood, the party's old guard made available a source of strength to potential rebels within its ranks.

IV

In the elections of 1908, the Democrats once more offered the Republicans little opposition. The 1907 campaign had all but completely demoralized the Gaston-Whitney wing. In an effort to stem the tide toward the renomination of William Jennings Bryan for President, that faction put in an appearance in May at Faneuil Hall, Boston, for the State Convention — where disorder once again became a feature of the proceedings. But on the whole, as one reporter noted, "Most of the former leaders were conspicuous by their absence," leaving the party "wholly in the hands of its radical element." [49] George Fred Williams and his Irish allies had full control. By almost a three to one majority, they carried the vote for a delegation committed to Bryan at the National Convention. They adopted a platform which denounced predatory wealth and favored a tariff for revenue only, graduated income and inheritance taxes, federal bank deposit guarantees, parcel post, postal savings, an eight-hour day, anti-injunction laws, and limited railroad profits calculated on a basis of "fair valuation"; the platform also demanded federal laws against stock watering, and (paradoxically) the subjugation of all corporations to the jurisdiction of state courts and an end to the "invasion of state rights by national authority." [50] In addition to Williams, John B. Moran and two other Irish Democrats were named delegates at large — the traditional leaders of the delegation; it was suggestive of an ethnic as well as a political shift within the party.

At Faneuil Hall again in October, Democrats chose young James H. Vahey of Watertown to lead the state ticket; it was

[49] *Springfield Republican,* May 7, 1908.
[50] *Boston Herald,* May 8, 1908.

only the second time they had picked an Irish-American for that place. Vahey had announced early in the year that he wanted the nomination. He had no opposition; no one else had an interest in running a losing race. Only thirty-six years old, Vahey had developed a prosperous criminal law practice and had gained state-wide popularity in 1906 for his defense of Charles L. Tucker, the murderer whose cause District Attorney Moran had also exploited. That fall he won election to the state senate from a traditionally Republican district. In the General Court he fought energetically for popular causes, including abrogation of the New York Central Railroad's lease of the Boston & Albany, against which shippers had begun to make serious complaints because of poor service, and the abolition of capital punishment, which came within one vote of passing in 1907. In his freshman year in the legislature, he helped more than any other man to push through a bill outlawing bucket shops, a measure Governor Guild had been urging for two years. But he was known mostly for his attacks against the United Shoe Machinery Company. Each year he had introduced legislation against the tie-in clauses contained in the Company's leases to the manufacturers, and charged the Company with undermining the New England shoe industry by spreading the manufacturers' trade secrets to other parts of the country.[51] Throughout his brief political career, he had the financial support of Richard H. Long, a Framingham shoe manufacturer.[52]

The campaign which followed was listless. Neither of the major presidential candidates entered the state at any time. Even Thomas L. Hisgen, Hearst's candidate for President,

---

[51] *Boston Herald,* December 31, 1906. See also *Boston Globe* for March 9, 1907, May 5, 1907, and June 2, 1907, and *Boston American,* June 2, 1907.

[52] Long deserted Vahey in 1909 because Vahey attacked the Payne-Aldrich tariff, which Long believed deserved a "trial." Long became a major figure in the Democratic party after 1915, and ran against Calvin Coolidge for governor in 1919. See Lodge to L. A. Coolidge, January 1, 1919 (Lodge MSS); Fuess, *Coolidge,* pp. 167–169, 234–237. Fuess says Long was a lifelong Democrat, but the newspapers in 1906 referred to him as a Republican.

failed to enliven the Massachusetts campaign; in his home state
he ran 3,000 votes behind his party's gubernatorial candidate,
who polled only 5 per cent of the vote — a sharp drop from
Hisgen's 22 per cent the year before. Bryan was a bad candidate to lead any ticket in the Bay State, especially against
someone like Taft, who had earned the good will of Roman
Catholic voters by the settlement he had arranged as Commissioner of the Philippines for lands belonging to the Church.
Although the Democratic platform had failed to endorse
Bryan's stand for public ownership of railroads, his well-adver-
tised views were sufficient to frighten away the conservative
Democrats, to whom even a protégé of Terrible Teddy seemed
good by comparison. At the same time, his fundamentalist
proclivities tended to alienate many of the Catholics among
the Democrats. In addition, the probability that George Fred
Williams would become top man in the Massachusetts Democracy if Bryan won led a major faction of the party to sit on its
hands during the campaign. Bryan ran 100,000 votes behind
Taft in Massachusetts, 13,000 behind his party's gubernatorial
candidate, and carried the Democratic stronghold of Boston
by only 200 votes. Taft's plurality was more than 10,000 larger
than Roosevelt's had been in 1904.

The gubernatorial campaign meanwhile showed that Vahey
had failed to draw together the feuding factions of the party.
The young Irishman lost to Draper by 60,000, which represented the largest Republican plurality since the days of Murray Crane. By passing over nearly all Bostonians in his selection of state committee officers, Vahey had alienated the Boston Democracy. His 45,000 votes in Boston compared poorly
with Moran's 52,000 there in 1906.[53] His Irish background
and his attacks on "the corporations" contributed to his loss
of the support of many old-line Democrats. Most of the regular party contributors ducked the election altogether or contributed only token amounts. The Democrats reported only

[53] *Springfield Republican* and *Boston Herald* for November 4, 1908.

$2,632 collected for campaign purposes, against the Republicans' $51,000.[54]

Despite the Democrats' shortcomings, the size of Draper's victory was astonishing in view of both his much narrower margins as a second-place candidate earlier and the fact that he represented the kind of leader which the American public seemed to have been tiring of. In opening his campaign against Draper, Vahey had attacked the Republican leader as a representative of "the power of money in politics." [55] That was a little unfair. Draper was indeed a wealthy man, and his financial contributions had had more than a little to do with his eminence in the party councils; but he did not use his money illicitly — as Whitney, for example, admittedly did. It might have been more accurate to say that Draper symbolized a somewhat dated type of the American business mind in politics — the kind of mind which both Roosevelt and Lodge had agreed had little place in government or politics and which most hopeful men of the era had rejected.

Long before his election as governor, Draper had given ample evidence of what that mentality meant. With his older brother, arch-protectionist General William F. Draper, Eben Draper had been patriarch of the company town of Hopedale, Massachusetts — once the site of one of the many experimental communities which had dotted New England during the "American Renaissance" some sixty years before. There the family textile machinery factories were located. Hopedale had once won a prize for model workmen's housing, but the Drapers had since earned the hostility of the labor unions for maintaining a non-union shop, paying wages which averaged less than $9.00 per week, and moving a few of their mills to the South where lower wages prevailed.[56] In 1903,

[54] *Springfield Republican*, December 3, 1908. Gaston's $550 topped the list, and Vahey's own $500 came next. Gaston was Vahey's personal friend, though he never shared Vahey's political views.

[55] *Boston Herald*, May 24, 1908.

[56] See *New Review*, 1:985 (December 1913); Harold U. Faulkner, "Eben S. Draper," *Dictionary of American Biography*, V (1930), 435.

Eben Draper had blamed "the exorbitant demands of the labor unions" for the financial crisis that year, though most observers thought reckless stock speculation was chiefly to blame.[57] As lieutenant governor and chairman of the governor's council — among whose antiquated functions remained the power to reject a governor's appointments — Draper had successfully vetoed Governor Guild's reappointment of the state commissioner of statistics, primarily because the man had proved *persona non grata* to the protectionist interests of the state; Mr. William Pidgin had achieved this status, it seems, by protesting the United States Census definitions of invested capital which made it appear that certain industries, notably the woolens industry, were not prospering as well as in fact they were.[58]

A man of limited intellectual powers (his chief political aide once complained privately of his almost childish manners and his uneducated and uncultivated way of expressing himself),[59] Draper sometimes embarrassed his friends by his awkwardness. As acting governor during Guild's illnesses in 1908, he discomfited his supporters by denouncing certain Democrats for "playing to the grandstand" because they had sent him a confidential letter urging him to throw his influence behind a bill to reduce the maximum weekly hours of labor for women and children. He compounded his silliness by charging that the Democrats had in effect asked him to violate the constitution by "interfering" in a legislative matter.[60] Only a babe could have believed that governors abstained from influencing legislation.

As governor, Draper in fact frequently and overtly intervened in legislative matters. The most important piece of legis-

[57] Draper to G. Meyer, November 13, 1903 (Meyer MSS). Cf. Meyer to Lodge, August 12, 1903 (*ibid.*).

[58] *Boston Evening Transcript,* June 17 and 20, 1907. Certain antitariff newspapers were quick to observe that S. N. D. North, the director of the Census, had also served as Secretary for the National Association of Woolen Manufacturers (*Boston Herald,* April 3, 1907). See also Arthur H. Cole, *The American Wool Manufacture* (Cambridge, 1926), II, 29–30.

[59] W. D. Sohier to S. P. O'Meara, December 21, 1905 (O'Meara MSS).

[60] *Boston Herald,* June 1, 1908.

lation of his two-year administration was popularly referred to as the "Draper Act," which testified to the extent to which he bore responsibility for it. The Boston Railroad Holding Company Act, as it was officially called, legalized and endorsed the already (and illegally) achieved merger of the region's two major railroad systems, the Boston & Maine and the New Haven. The act obviated the likelihood of federal antitrust action, and, as many people saw it, gave the state's sanction not only to the principle of regulated monopoly in the railroad business, but to the rule that He Who Has Money and Violates the Law May Go Unmolested Unless and Until He Becomes a Public Nuisance.

V

Draper's victory in 1908 may appear an oddity for those times of high social criticism. ("Give the radicalism in this state a decently respectable leader," wrote one political commentator, "and the Republican party would be unhorsed so quickly that the leaders would not know what hit them.")[61] His election did suggest more about the ineptness of the opposition than about his own qualities. But then, perhaps the journalists and politicians-without-power — who had something of a special interest in the "moral awakening" — also failed to account for the force of solidarity among the dominant classes. For Draper to have achieved the plurality he did meant that thousands of independent, well-intentioned citizens of Yankeedom, fully aware of Draper's dim-sighted attitude toward social problems, had shelved their social criticisms and voted for him as a "man of integrity" — rather than countenance the bushy-haired son of Erin who had taken the lead of the Democracy.

[61] *Lewiston Sun,* datelined "Boston, December 19, 1908," in Bridgman Scrapbooks, XXVIII, 34.

CHAPTER EIGHT

DECLINE OF AN ETHIC: THE NEW HAVEN– BOSTON & MAINE MERGER BATTLE

When the New Haven reduces its dividends and Mellen resigns, the "Decline of New Haven and Fall of Mellen" will make a dramatic story of human interest with a moral — or two — including the evils of private monopoly . . . Anticipating the future a little, I suggest the following as an epitaph or obituary notice: "Mellen was a masterful man, resourceful, courageous . . . He fired the imagination of New England; but being oblique of vision, merely distorted its judgment and silenced its conscience. For a while he trampled with impunity on laws human and divine; but as he was obsessed with the delusion that two and two make five, he fell at last, a victim to the relentless rules of humble arithmetic."

Louis D. Brandeis

No doubt the most marked tendency . . . among [railroad] incorporation laws has been the extension of the power of railroad corporations to consolidate or merge with other railroads; to lease, purchase, or operate other railroads, or to hold the securities of other corporations. A study of the statutes discloses a decided movement in this direction.

Interstate Commerce Commission*

IN August 1903, J. P. Morgan selected Charles Sanger Mellen to head the New York, New Haven & Hartford Railroad Company. As president of the Northern Pacific Railroad — also part of Morgan's empire — Mellen had won the respect of responsible public leaders throughout the country; no less a person than President Roosevelt had consulted with him

* The first quotation is from a letter (1911) from Brandeis to Norman Hapgood. The second is from the 16th Annual Report of the Interstate Commerce Commission, December 15, 1902.

on important political decisions.[1] ("Mellen is a first class fellow," the President wrote to his Attorney General in 1905,
"and what he asks is almost always right.")[2] Within six years
of his appointment to the New Haven, Mellen had supervised
its consolidation with all the important interurban street railways in southern New England, the region's intercoastal
steamship lines, and finally the great Boston & Maine Railroad.
These activities stirred up a storm of opposition. The Massachusetts Supreme Court found the New Haven's activities contrary to state law on the ground that it had not obtained legislative permission for its consolidation. Louis Brandeis and
others evoked the specter of monopoly, and the United States
Justice Department began antitrust proceedings. But Mellen
succeeded in subduing both legalistic and antitrust sensibilities.
In 1907 he secured assurances from President Roosevelt that
his administration would not attempt to force the New Haven
to relinquish its steamship acquisitions.[3] He proceeded with the
Boston & Maine merger a few months later, similarly assured.[4]
In 1909 he persuaded the Massachusetts government to ratify
his avowed objective of consolidating New England's transportation system under a single management.

But the New Haven's ascendancy was short-lived. In 1913,
I.C.C. Commissioner Charles A. Prouty came to Boston to
investigate complaints about railroad service. His findings indicated that the New Haven's books had been deliberately dis-
ordered so as to conceal the company's poor financial condition. Meanwhile a succession of serious accidents on the road
suggested that the directors had been sacrificing maintenance

[1] In 1903, Roosevelt sought Mellen's advice before deciding to challenge
Mark Hanna to declare openly if he was going to oppose him for the Presidency in 1904. Roosevelt to Lodge, May 27, 1903, in Morison, II, 19–20.

[2] Roosevelt to W. H. Moody, November 20, 1905 (RMA MSS).

[3] Mellen's testimony before I.C.C. in *New York Times*, November 11,
1915. Roosevelt later regretted his assent (Roosevelt to Lodge, May 28,
1908, in Morison, VI, 1040).

[4] Mellen to H. M. Whitney, May 22, 1907, cited in H. L. Staples and
A. T. Mason, *The Fall of a Railroad Empire: Brandeis and the New Haven
Merger Battle* (Syracuse, 1947), pp. 172–173.

to continued dividends. That July, a rebellious group of stockholders forced Mellen's resignation. The following year a full-
scale I.C.C. investigation into company affairs disclosed
"loose, extravagant, and improvident" [5] — to say nothing of
illicit — practices, as Louis Brandeis had perceived earlier. At
the year's end, the company by-passed its dividend for the first
time in its history, and six months later went into receivership.
The debacle fulfilled Brandeis' prophesies, and heavy judgment fell upon the entire consolidation effort.

If one had followed the course of the controversy through
the publications and statements of Louis Brandeis from 1906
on, the disaster could have come as no surprise. The "revelations" of the I.C.C. hearings in 1913 and 1914 only confirmed
most of the longstanding charges against the New Haven. That
corporation *had* absorbed too many unprofitable railway companies, and *had* paid too much, even for many of the profitable ones. The railroad *had,* as charged, paid exorbitant commissions to investment bankers — specifically to J. P. Morgan
and Company, which dominated the New Haven's own board
of directors — for underwriting each successive stock issue in
the course of constructing the vast railroad "empire" in New
England. The New Haven *had* made enormous payments to
newspapers and in some cases to news reporters (in order to
"popularize" its cause, New Haven spokesmen maintained).
And the New Haven *had,* at an early date, begun paying dividends out of capital rather than from earnings. In short, it
appeared that the New Haven's escapades had provided only
another illustration of the inept, illicit, and sullying character
of monopoly and banker-management; the public's conven-
ience had been sacrificed to the profits of "inside financiers,"
and a great Commonwealth's traditions had been corrupted
against the public will.[6]

[5] "Evidence taken before the Interstate Commerce Commission relative to
the financial transactions of the New York, New Haven & Hartford Railroad
Company, together with a report of the Commission thereon" (I.C.C.
Hearings), Senate Document 543, 63 Cong., 2 Sess., 1914, p. 2.

[6] For a comprehensive statement of the Brandeisian view, see Staples and
Mason.

The ignominious demise of the New Haven venture, the death of J. P. Morgan, and the enduring humiliation of Charles Mellen left the Brandeis version after 1913 unrebutted and seemingly irrefutable. It has also left obscured the really complex nature of the argument before disaster seemingly settled it. Actually, the issues were so entangled that the antagonists rarely even agreed on what was at stake in the New Haven's activities. The Brandeisians stressed primarily the intrinsic evils of monopoly and the economic perils for the state implicit in "banker-management," particularly New York management; later, they stressed the dishonor which the state would bring upon itself for acquiescing in the powerhouse tactics of great corporate wealth; finally, they contended that the New Haven's overextended financial condition would pull down the ostensibly healthy companies that it absorbed — most importantly, the Boston & Maine Railroad. On the other hand, those who supported the New Haven's consolidations — and they were not by any means all predatory corporate spokesmen — argued that (1) steam railroads could no longer withstand the competition of the street railways and would have to buy into them or succumb to them; (2) the B. & M. was in fact up for sale anyway, and if the New Haven did not buy it, some syndicate more alien to Massachusetts would do so; (3) railroad consolidations elsewhere in the country had already isolated Massachusetts shippers and reduced their bargaining power for adequate service and rates, so that only consolidation of the New England transportation system could restore some of the power that the region had once enjoyed. The Brandeisians never directed themselves to any of those three points, while the New Haven's partisans usually chose to overlook, or to deny the relevance of, the points which their opponents raised.

There were other reasons for confusion in the controversy. It was quite possible, for example, to oppose some of the New Haven's activities, such as its acquisition of street railways, while supporting the New Haven in its most important act, namely, its merger with the Boston & Maine. But the most obfuscating complication derived from the behavior of the New Haven management in general, and of Charles Mellen in particular. In a display of arrogance which ranged from simple disregard for state officials and public sensibilities to outright violation of the law, they injected into the controversy the question whether — regardless of the merits of the consolidations — the state could afford to permit the New Haven and its directors to get away with their transgressions.

Ultimately the state answered that question in the affirmative. Its plea of justification was economic expediency. The state's acquiescence, in the face of commercial pressures, symbolized, as it contributed toward, the decline of a venerated tradition of government-business relations in Massachusetts.

I

Railroad consolidation was not at all new to Massachusetts. As late as 1890, eight independent railroads had supplied the state with nearly all its steam rail transportation. By the end of the decade there were only three, one of which was actually a spur of the giant New York Central.[7] The state had formally approved each merger, and businessmen and economists generally favored the developments. The Board of Railroad Commissioners noted that between 1872 and 1898 the process of consolidation had been accompanied "by a voluntary reduction of the average passenger fare from 2.43 to 1.78 cents per mile, and of the average freight rate from 2.81 to 1.22 cents per ton mile"; moreover, there had been "in the meantime a marked improvement in the quality of the railroad service rendered." [8] Freight and passenger rates continued to decline

[7] The eight were: the New York, Providence & Boston, the Old Colony, the New York & New England, the Fitchburg, the Massachusetts Central, the Boston & Albany, the Boston & Maine, and the New Haven. The New Haven later absorbed the first three; the B. & M. consolidated with the next two; and the New York Central leased the B. & A.

[8] Mass. Board R.R. Commissioners, *30th Annual Report* (Boston, 1899), p. 15.

through 1909, despite the general rise in the cost of living. In an earlier report, the Board had found that the extension of the New Haven system into Boston had provided "the benefits of continuous transportation at through rates," as well as the added advantages of the New Haven's connections with trunk lines to the West.[9] The consolidation of street railway companies, too, had produced "lower fares and larger transfer privileges" and had "brought to more than one weak system the advantages of financial strength and able management." [10] The commissioners did have some misgivings. "There can be no question," they warned, "that there is also a limit beyond which consolidation ought not to go." But they made no effort to define a limit.[11]

After the turn of the century, the commissioners began to urge consolidation of the scores of interurban street railway companies with the major steam railroads. "The laws of neighboring states," they noted, "encourage this evolution in transportation enterprise." Remarking on the exuberance of electric railway promotion which followed the conversion from horse-drawn railways in the 1890's, the commissioners pointed out that too many companies had inflated expectations of financial returns, and had failed to allow adequately for depreciation and for costly safety devices which the public inevitably came to demand. By 1904, only 10 out of 74 trolley companies operating showed a 5 per cent earning on capital for the previous five years; dividends had dropped sharply, and net indebtedness had climbed. More experienced steam railroad management, the Board contended, would bring stability to New England transportation through greater financial strength and

[9] Id., 27th Annual Report (Boston 1895) pp. 31–32.
[10] Id., 33rd Annual Report (Boston, 1902), p. 55. Cf. Edward S. Mason, The Street Railway in Massachusetts: The Rise and Decline of an Industry (Cambridge, 1932), pp. 12–14. Mason points out that consolidation of street railways produced the effects desired by the Railroad Commission, but ultimately (after 1910) overburdened the stronger companies with too many "weak sisters" and led to their collapse.
[11] Mass. Board R.R. Commissioners, 30th Annual Report, p. 15.

sounder business practices. In any event, the commissioners concluded, "the competition between the steam railroad and the street railway must eventually end." [12]

State legislation nevertheless continued to favor street railways over steam railroads. Special laws granted railways choice routes, the right to carry freight, and permission to maintain grade crossings even while steam roads were compelled to eliminate theirs.[13] The growth of the interurban network presented increasingly serious competition for the steam railroads. Trolley lines extended right to the back doors of factories, thus depriving steam roads of considerable commuter business, as well as much of the highly profitable less-than-carload freight. The railroads were soon left with the prospect of handling only low-grade bulk shipments.[14]

Consequently, beginning in 1902, railroad interests petitioned the General Court each year for permission to enter the electric railway business.[15] ("The railroads know well," wrote one interurban railway promoter, "that the crucial moment has arrived in maintaining their monopoly. The prospect of interurban roads which has been fully demonstrated in the West has now reached Massachusetts, and if these roads are allowed to be built they give the prospect of developing into a new set of trunk lines for high speed passenger service, and this, of course, will make the railroad monopoly much less valuable.")[16] In Massachusetts, unlike smaller states like New

[12] *Id., 34th Annual Report* (Boston, 1903), p. 52, and *36th Annual Report* (Boston, 1905), p. xxxvi.

[13] See Walter S. Allen, "Street Railway Franchises in Massachusetts," pp. 91–110 (esp. p. 108).

[14] See Ripley, *Railroads,* pp. 465–466.

[15] See Mass. Board R.R. Commissioners, *41st Annual Report* (Boston, 1910), p. 112.

[16] H. C. Forbes to A. E. Adler, August 26, 1905 (Eastman MSS). Forbes headed a company which sought a charter to construct a railway from Boston to Providence and eventually to New York; he ran into opposition from the New Haven Railroad, with which the projected railway would have competed directly. He and his associates received some "unofficial" advice from Joseph B. Eastman, Secretary of the Public Franchise League, on how to beat the big financiers behind the railroads. See Eastman to David Whitcomb, November 19 and December 7, 1906 (Eastman MSS).

Hampshire or newer states like California, the multiplicity of rail and financial interests presented formidable obstacles to any single railroad that appeared before the legislature. In addition to the time, money, and energy necessary to overcome the opposition of diverse economic interests and to persuade the legislators favorably, railroad managements had to surmount after 1900 the widespread suspicion of large-scale corporate enterprise which the muckrakers and reformers had aroused. But, of course, this was the method which republican institutions required.

II

Charles Mellen chose a different method. In 1905, without consulting the Massachusetts government, and under the cloak of the Consolidated Railroad Company, a holding company chartered by Connecticut, the New Haven Railroad began extending its purchases of interurbans into the western part of the state. ("But I don't want to deceive anybody," President Mellen told a legislative committee the next year. "I am president of the [New Haven] Railroad Company. I am president of the Consolidated Company. I am president of the boards of trustees. I am the president of your street railway companies.")[17] The Boston & Maine Railroad countered with an urgent request for legislative permission to make similar purchases, and the Railroad Commission itself drafted the bill presented in the General Court.[18] Representative Joseph Walker of Brookline introduced a different bill which served the same purpose but strengthened commission control over such mergers. Both moves met with the vehement opposition of Representative Robert Luce. Citing the law which forbade a railway corporation from selling its stock to any other corporation, foreign or domestic, without explicit permission from the General Court, Luce asserted that the solution to the Boston & Maine's problem lay not in legalizing the New Haven's

[17] *Boston Herald,* June 27, 1906.
[18] *Ibid.,* March 9, 1905.

usurpations but in enforcing the law as it stood.[19] Caught in the cross fire between reformers like Luce who saw only the New Haven's violation of the law, and the New Haven interests which sought to keep the Boston & Maine out of the market for Massachusetts railways, neither bill passed the General Court that year.

Public discussion meanwhile centered on the economic and political, rather than the strictly legal, issues which Luce had raised. The Massachusetts Board of Trade voted in the spring, after lengthy discussions, in favor of postponement of legislation pending further exposition of the issues.[20] In the fall, Secretary Joseph B. Eastman of the Public Franchise League reported that after several debates the members of the League were "unable to agree as yet whether . . . to favor a bill allowing such consolidations subject to approval of the Railroad Commissioners in all respects."[21] The consensus appeared to be that if consolidations were desirable the legislature could change the law if necessary.

If debate had continued to center on the economic and political merits of railroad ownership of interurban street railways, and later of the B. & M. merger, the controversy might have contributed to the solution of a major problem of the American private enterprise system. But neither side permitted that. The New Haven's directors persisted in behaving as if the state was maliciously meddling with their manifest destiny to bring the millennium to New England's economy. In response to that attitude, the opposition effectively shaped the debate into an ethical issue concerning good government versus corporate truculence.

In 1906, Governor Curtis Guild entered the contest. In a

[19] *Ibid.*, April 15 and May 4, 1905.
[20] *Boston Globe*, April 19, 1905.
[21] J. B. Eastman to G. B. Upham, October 20, 1905 (Eastman MSS). As late as 1907, Eastman reported, the League was uncertain as to whether the merger of the Berkshire Trolley system with the New Haven could be in the public interest, and recommended only that the legislature postpone action on enabling legislation for another year. See Eastman's Annual Report for 1907 (Brandeis MSS).

special message to the legislature, Guild declared that a railroad corporation (the New Haven), "controlled by men who are not citizens of Massachusetts," had "throttled healthy competition in western Massachusetts." "Slowly, surely," he continued, "the control of our railroads, the control of the passage to market of every Massachusetts product, the control of the transportation to and from his work of every Massachusetts citizen, is passing from our hands to those of aliens." He demanded that the legislature do something to correct "this grave injustice" and insure that transportation within the state "be controlled by the people of Massachusetts, and not by men beyond the reach of her law and the inspiration of her ideals." [22]

Despite Guild's message, Mellen persuaded the General Court to postpone action against his company, promising, in a letter to Representative Walker, that he would purchase no more railway lines until the courts could pass upon the legality issue.[23] But the New Haven president evidently made this promise in bad faith. That summer he set up the New England Security & Investment Company, a voluntary association which lay beyond the laws regulating corporations,[24] and transferred to it the New Haven's street railway stock.[25] All of the new company's directors, including Mellen, were also New Haven directors. The N.E.S. & I. soon began buying up stock in four other railway companies, and in the face of mounting protests the New Haven president blandly denied that there was any relationship at all between the railroad and the in-

[22] *Boston Globe,* June 23, 1906.

[23] *Boston Herald,* June 29, June 30, 1906; *Boston Post,* June 29, 1906. The letter, which was signed by Charles F. Choate, Jr., the New Haven's attorney, was reprinted in full in the *Boston Herald,* June 13, 1907. The General Court did re-enact the earlier state law which prohibited direct or indirect acquisition of a railway company by a railroad corporation, and called for a test case to decide whether this applied to the New Haven and its affiliated holding company, the Consolidated. The Railroad Commission in 1909 observed that this amounted to "a declaration of the common law, and, as such, a statement of the policy of the Commonwealth itself" (*41st Annual Report,* p. 111).

[24] I.C.C. Hearings, pp. 24–25.

[25] *Boston Post,* August 17, 1906.

vestment company.[26] This was one of the many Mellen subter-
fuges that exasperated his opponents and embarrassed his
friends.

Public agitation arising from corporate abuses in general
caused Mellen many uneasy moments, especially in view of
his long-range plans. In February 1907, Mellen wrote to William Rockefeller, a New Haven director:

The general condition is rather unsatisfactory . . . The agitation
against corporations and railroads in particular at Washington is
making itself more or less manifest in local legislatures, and causing
us considerable trouble.

He expressed confidence, however, that he could control Rhode
Island and Connecticut, and he believed that attention in the
Massachusetts legislature was "directed more toward other
corporations than our own this year, and we are looking to
escape . . . any serious trouble." [27] (James Vahey and
Thomas Hisgen had launched their campaigns that winter
against the United Shoe Machinery Company and Standard
Oil.) A week later, Mellen made his first trip to Washington
to secure assurances from "our great and good friend in Washington." [28]

In March, Mellen entered negotiations for a controlling
block of Boston & Maine securities, a move already rumored
for months by the *Boston News Bureau,* which had begun serving Mellen as something of a press agency. The Boston &
Maine merger quickly overshadowed all other New Haven
issues, and remained thereafter the focal point of the controversy. Once again Mellen was less than candid with the public.
He bluntly denied considering the purchase of B. & M. stock,
even while he engaged in negotiations for it and consulted with
the President about whether such an acquisition would bring

[26] *Boston Herald,* January 11, 1907.
[27] Mellen to Rockefeller, February 4, 1907, in *New York Times,* November 12, 1915.
[28] *Ibid.*

a federal antitrust suit against the New Haven.[29] By the middle of May, he had concluded arrangements for the transfer of 109,948 shares of B. & M. stock to the New England Navigation Company, another New Haven subsidiary. Still no comment came from the New Haven's office, though rumors of the transfer were now widespread. Henry Whitney, a director of the B. & M. who favored the merger, wrote to Mellen urging him to set the issue squarely before the public: "I think it meets approval among our business men as a whole, but there is still a large problem to be reckoned with, and a few words now outlining in general your policy . . . would go far to allay excitement and hostile criticism, and might save you considerable annoyance later on." [30] But Mellen rejoined that the principal directors had come to the decision to let the public have only as much information "as is absolutely necessary." [31]

Apparently the New Haven strategists were counting on slipping the affair past a drowsy public and an inattentive legislature. It was symbolic of their condescending regard for both. But the new-style businessmen did not quite count on the old-fashioned pride of family ownership still strong in the old Puritan Commonwealth. Samuel and William B. Lawrence, whose family had long held a major share of Boston & Maine stock, refused to surrender their influence in the Company's affairs without a fight. They had allies in Robert Luce, Louis Brandeis, and Governor Guild, among others. Brandeis presented a bill in the General Court which forbade the acquisition of control in the Boston & Maine directly or indirectly, required the disposal of stock already acquired by April 1, 1908, and provided criminal penalties for defiance. Attorney General Dana Malone presented a similar bill. And the battle was on.

Many state leaders, including Senator Lodge, were deeply

---

[29] Mellen to William Loeb, Jr. (Presidential Secretary), April 19, 1907, and Loeb to Mellen, April 20, 1907 (Mellen MSS). Mellen had an appointment to see President Roosevelt on this matter on May 1, 1907.

[30] Whitney to Mellen, May 21, 1907, quoted in Staples and Mason, p. 172.

[31] Mellen to Whitney, May 22, 1907, *ibid.*

disturbed by the possibility that the stock would land in the hands of a railroad system with terminals at other ports, thus making the New England railroads mere adjuncts of greater trunk lines. The New York Central's control of the Boston & Albany had already given them a taste of what that would mean. Between 1902 and 1907, six large cargo ships had ceased docking at Boston, and the Ledyard Line was threatening to leave because of failure to fill their holds. During this period the New York Central apparently had diverted grain and other shipments to merchants in New York City because, it claimed, demand was heavy and it had to satisfy first those merchants nearer the sources of supply.[32] Lodge had reacted to the news of the B. & M.–New Haven merger in 1907 by writing to one confidant that it would not be good "for New England, for Massachusetts, and above all, for the City of Boston to have the entire railroad system put under the control of a Connecticut corporation which is owned in New York." [33] While Governor Guild again asked the legislature to reaffirm the state's determination "to control the operation of the railroads within her border," Lodge issued a press release which more specifically warned Boston's commercial leaders that they might suffer disaster if the B. & M. should become another B. & A., and he urged the legislature "to prevent the diversion from Boston of grain and other through freight which constitute the exports of the port." [34]

Lodge's interest in the merger was not wholly economic. Mellen's B. & M. maneuvers in 1907 had caught the Republican leaders by surprise, presenting serious political difficulties.

[32] *Boston Herald,* January 31, 1907. One crisis in grain shipments occurred in January 1907 when the Central imposed a "grain embargo" on Boston, and only partially lifted it thereafter. *Boston Herald,* February 3, 1907.

[33] Lodge to R. L. O'Brien, May 16, 1907 (Lodge MSS). See also Lodge to O'Brien, May 20, 1907. Contrary to the statement by Elting Morison and John Blum that Lodge was "the persistent advocate of the New Haven" (Morison, VI, 1040n), Lodge opposed the B. & M. merger until at least the end of 1908, and he never gave up his opposition to New Haven consolidation with interurban railways.

[34] *Boston Evening Transcript,* June 6, 1907. See also Lodge to Crane, June 7, 1907 (Lodge MSS).

It was not simply that leading members of the party like Governor Guild, Attorney General Malone, Congressman John W. Weeks (later Senator and Secretary of War), and Eben Draper differed sharply on the issue; but by May 1907, it was almost certain that Henry Whitney, who had publicly identified himself with the merger, would be the Democratic candidate for governor. No Republican (except perhaps Guild and Luce) had cared to fight Whitney on the merger issue and risk antagonizing the railroad magnates, on whom the party had usually counted for support. At the same time, as Senator Lodge wrote confidentially to the *Transcript's* Robert Lincoln O'Brien: "One thing, politically speaking, is perfectly clear to me, and that is that the Republican party must avoid, with the utmost care, doing anything that would make it appear as a champion of these corporation schemes" — especially schemes, one might add, with which Whitney was identified.[35] Murray Crane, characteristically, ducked the issue. ("Some very troublesome business matters . . . are now taking up nearly all my time and thought," he wrote to Lodge, who had asked his assistance.)[36] But with the aid of Guild and Speaker Cole, Lodge deftly guided a bill through the legislature which deprived the New Haven of the power to vote its B. & M. stock for a year, and postponed decisive action on the problem in the meantime. Although Brandeis and others protested that

[35] Lodge to O'Brien, May 20, 1907 (Lodge MSS). Since Lodge was already looking ahead not only to the 1907 elections but to the 1908 presidential campaign and to the problems of his own re-election to the Senate by the legislature to be elected in 1910, he was considerably agitated by the troubles the railroads might cause him. "The whole thing is a stock speculation backed by Harriman and the Standard Oil — of which Mellen is a tool, I am afraid," he wrote to Roosevelt. ". . . When one comes up against these stock movements in railroads it is not easy to keep one's temper." Lodge to Roosevelt, June 20, 1907, in *Correspondence*, II, 271–272. Lodge was wrong about Harriman; in fact the New Haven soon after used Harriman as a foil, threatening the state with the possibility that that current bogeyman of finance might take over the B. & M. if the state did not permit J. P. Morgan and the New Haven to do so.

[36] Crane to Lodge, June 5, 1907 (Lodge MSS). "The position of Senator Crane," O'Brien commented with a touch of irony, "is subject to some inquiry and controversy in Boston" (O'Brien to Lodge, May 24, 1907, *ibid.*).

the Cole bill implicitly recognized the New Haven's acquisition as an accomplished fact and would give it the state's sanction upon the expiration of the bill in June 1908,[37] the Republicans had achieved their purpose of taking the issue out of politics for the year. ("You did excellent work about that merger," Roosevelt wrote exultantly to Lodge, noting that Whitney "would be pretty well knocked out as a candidate.")[38]

Mellen reacted to state interference with his plan with ill-disguised contempt — a reflection of his supreme confidence in the rightness of both his objectives and his legal position, as well as his belief that all "right-headed men" were with him. He was an articulate man, with a sharp sense of humor and a facility with words. Before the Joint Committee on Railroads, which summoned him for a statement, Mellen created a sensation. ("Mellen was very funny, yesterday," reported the sympathetic *Boston Herald*. "He had the hearings room in a continual uproar.") To meet objections that the merger would expunge the name "Boston" from all railroads serving the city, Mellen promised to paint the word on top, bottom, and each end of all railroad cars in order to be accommodating. When Senator Vahey said that he believed there was a law against the merger and that the attorney general ought to enforce it, Mellen retorted: "Perhaps that is why you are not attorney general." Mellen suggested that the Brandeis and Malone bills were not strong enough; he would prohibit anyone from buying New Haven stock, the New Haven from selling its stock, and punish any discussion of the subject by jail sentences. Finally, when the Committee recognized Brandeis for some questions, Mellen abruptly rose from the hearings table and walked out, saying: "I'll read the gentleman's remarks in the newspapers." [39]

The state supreme court soon upset Mellen's legal position.

---

[37] See *Boston Globe*, June 17, June 18, and especially June 19, 1907; Mason, *Free Man's Life*, p. 181.

[38] Roosevelt to Lodge, July 4, 1907, in *Correspondence*, II, 274. See also Lodge to W. E. Chandler, October 19, 1907 (Lodge MSS).

[39] *Boston Herald*, June 12, 1907.

On May 8, 1908, it found that the New Haven had acquired its interurban railway properties illegally, and that the holding company or "voluntary association" device was too transparent an effort to evade the law. The ruling also applied clearly to the railroad's B. & M. holdings.[40] But Mellen's confidence in his objectives remained unbowed. When Attorney General Malone reported to the legislature that the street railway companies which had sold out to the New Haven should have their charters revoked, Mellen commented: "I certainly am not disturbed by the opinion of the attorney general." [41] Meanwhile, he "sold" the New Haven's 109,948 shares of B. & M. to one John A. Billard. The move fooled absolutely no one,[42] but he got away with it. (Later, when Eben Draper's Boston Railroad Holding Company Act effectively legalized the merger, Mellen explained to the New Haven board of directors about the $2 million which dummy Billard had received from the company: "For his services in securing to the New Haven Company immunity from attack by the Massachusetts authorities because of the holding by the New Haven of Boston & Maine stock . . . Mr. Billard's compensation was modest and moderate, and he might well exclaim, as did Warren Hastings at his celebrated trial, 'My God, when I consider my opportunities, I wonder at my moderation.' ")[43] He also transferred the New Haven's holdings of interurban railway properties to a dummy corporation, and in a letter to a fellow director he justified the high costs of this maneuver with a complete sense of righteousness: "While this seems a large sum [he wrote], it is not . . . an unreasonable compensation for the service performed . . . for it thus leaves in friendly hands the control of the trolley

[40] Mass. Board R.R. Commissioners, *41st Annual Report,* p. 115; I.C.C. Hearings, pp. 24–25. Cf. *Boston Herald* editorial, May 11, 1908.

[41] *Boston Herald,* January 21, 1909.

[42] No one, that is, except perhaps the aged abolitionist and banker Henry Lee Higginson: "Brandeis and [Representative Norman] White . . . do not believe that Mellen sold the Boston & Maine shares, which to my mind shows that they probably are themselves in the habit of lying." Higginson to Lodge, May 25, 1909 (Lodge MSS). Higginson was in a position to have known better. Cf. Lucius Tuttle to Mellen, June 3, 1908 (Mellen MSS).

[43] I.C.C. Hearings, p. 30.

system . . . in . . . Massachusetts, until such time as will eventually arrive when good sense will prevail and the policy of the Commonwealth be changed so far as railroads controlling railways is concerned." [44]

Mellen's deliberate evasion of the law appears to have had considerable support throughout the state. While Brandeis and others strove to shift attention to Mellen's deceptions and bad faith — indeed, to invoke the Commonwealth's ideals to which Governor Guild had alluded — some of Mellen's supporters in the business community considered the issue of legality entirely irrelevant. "The union could be made in no other way," wrote Henry Lee Higginson, "and if it is worth making, the end justifies the means." [45] "The owner of a peanut stand," remarked the *Boston Herald,* "has certain recognized property rights in his business, but if he insists on planting himself in the pathway of a rushing city crowd . . . he sees his peanuts tipped over while the crowd goes by on the shortest and most direct route to its goal. That is the rule in every progressive community . . . The plan of railroad development promised . . . the shortest and most direct route to industrial and commercial achievement . . . but the peanut men . . . have held up progress." [46]

With the stout aid of Republican representatives Luce, Robert Washburn, and Norman White in the General Court, Brandeis and Guild continued to oppose "the crowd." Guild's opposition was decisive as long as he remained governor. But he did not present the strongest possible case against the New Haven interests. His chauvinistic attack on "alien control" did not begin to grapple with the true nature of the problem. Given the interstate character of modern business enterprise — a fact which Guild himself had apparently accepted in advancing the cause of national incorporation and child labor laws — his plea for an insulated state economy seemed hope-

[44] Mellen to B. W. Warren, July 28, 1908, *ibid.,* p. 25.
[45] Higginson to Lodge, April 27, 1909 (Lodge MSS).
[46] *Boston Herald,* June 14, 1910.

lessly inappropriate. Yet one can understand his agitation. The Mellen-Morgan invaders had employed techniques, such as the foreign-chartered holding company, which challenged the traditional business structure within which the conservative part of the Massachusetts business community had felt comfortable.[47] In addition, they threatened the state with monopoly. Finally, by ignoring the state government, they threw in its face the mounting evidence of its superfluity in the large economic matters of the day. A Rooseveltian progressive, Curtis Guild felt keenly the sting of condescension from members of the business community, just as Roosevelt did. It is not surprising, then, that the weight of his supporters' attack on the New Haven in the legislature fell on the company's attempt to render state power impotent.

With an arrogance which may have passed for cleverness in other parts of the country, and did well enough in the Bay State, Mellen continued to do everything he could to chafe the opened wounds. He might have made the envelopment of the state in the web of corporate capitalism less painful if he had not been so thoroughly convinced of his right to "exercise paternalism." His maneuvers even got under Lodge's skin. "They took great pains," the Senator wrote to O'Brien in December 1907, "to let me know, from various quarters, that there is danger of selling the stock to the New York Central or Canadian Pacific . . . I think there is a desire to force our hands under the threat, and I hope the Legislature will be very careful in anything it does." [48] The threat of selling the stock

[47] The unfamiliarity of many Massachusetts leaders with the holding company device is suggested by Joseph Eastman's letter to Charles L. Underhill, Majority Leader of the House, June 2, 1909, in which he undertook to explain the technique. Cf. Underhill to Eastman, May 31, 1909, and Eastman to Samuel Bowles, June 14, 1909 (Eastman MSS).

[48] Lodge to O'Brien, December 18, 1907 (Lodge MSS). Lodge probably was referring to a letter to him dated December 11, 1907, from Gardiner M. Lane of Lee, Higginson & Co., reputedly the man who personally managed the sale of the B. & M. holdings to the New Haven. (See I.C.C. Hearings, p. 16.) The letter may be found in the Meyer MSS, together with a similar letter of the same date to George Meyer, and with a clipping of an interview in the *Boston News Bureau,* also dated December 11, in which Mellen announced that he might sell.

to one of the large trunk-line railroads always served the New Haven well with the state's sensitive merchants, just as ultimately it helped to persuade Lodge to support the New Haven's objectives. But Mellen's power-play tactics tended, as the *Springfield Republican* complained, to "derogate from the dignity of the Commonwealth." The *Republican* — which supported the B. & M. merger — regretted that Mellen had come before the legislature in 1907 only after he had achieved consolidation with the B. & M. "He would like the State's sanction," the paper observed; "it will be for our advantage to give it," it continued, "but the merger has been made a fact, whether or no — in other words, what are we going to do about it?" [49] Similarly, while rejecting an attack on the company's financial condition by Louis Brandeis,[50] the *Republican* blamed the company for incurring such criticism by hiding the facts; the New Haven had thus "aroused a hostile public sentiment which would not otherwise have existed." All these antics, as the *Republican* put it, constituted "something like an obstacle to confidence." [51]

III

When Curtis Guild left the governorship, the issue remained unresolved. But in Eben Draper the New Haven interests found a man in the State House who fully concurred with the modern business spirit. The Boston Railroad Holding Company Act of 1909 consummated the New Haven–B. & M. merger by using the same business techniques that traditionalists like Brandeis and Guild rebelled against. The inclusion of the word "Boston" in the title of the new holding company served only to highlight the cynicism of the measure. On the

[49] *Springfield Republican,* June 5, 1907. Cf. *Boston Evening Transcript,* June 6, 1907.

[50] See "The Financial Condition of the New York, New Haven, & Hartford Railroad and the Boston & Maine," a pamphlet (c. January 1908) in the Brandeis MSS, summarized in Mason, *Free Man's Life,* pp. 184–185, and in Staples and Mason, pp. 29–34.

[51] *Springfield Republican,* January 8, 1908. Cf. *Boston Journal,* January 8, 1908.

pretext of affirming the law which prohibited railroad mergers without legislative consent, the Act set up a new company to purchase and hold the B. & M. shares which Mr. John Billard still possessed. Although the New Haven was forbidden to own B. & M. stock, it could — and would — control the holding company. Draper jammed the bill through the legislature, with the active assistance of Senators Lodge and Crane,[52] declaring that the state was in peril of losing control of the railroads within its borders. The Governor bluntly refused to consider any amendments, and the New Haven interests pretended that they would not accept the bill except as introduced.

Despite the highhanded manner in which the Governor forced it through, the Draper Act seems to have expressed the judgment of a majority of the interested leaders of the Commonwealth that railroad consolidation might bolster the state's economic position against the challenge from without. The Boston Railroad Holding Company had the virtue at least of preventing the B. & M. stock from going further than the New Haven. By 1909 that seemed to have become the best of the alternatives which most men in Massachusetts allowed themselves. Several Democratic leaders and the state federation of labor had come out in favor of state ownership of the stock, but the idea had never got a hearing either from the Republicans or from Brandeis and the anti-merger trade associations. Nothing in the election returns during any of the years of the controversy can be used to indicate that the electorate had any serious objection to the Draper administration's handling of the railroad problem. As the New Haven began to run into financial difficulties in 1910 and 1911, moreover, the state followed up its commitment to the enterprise with further aid — for example, by making the Holding Company's stock legal investments for savings banks, and by permitting the company to issue preferred stock. In the end, its help proved unavailing. The New Haven had overextended itself, apparently in the over-optimistic expectation of a revival of boom conditions

[52] See Lodge to Higginson, April 28 and May 19, 1909 (Lodge MSS).

such as existed before 1907. An I.C.C. arbitration settlement
(1912) of westward rate differentials, which aggravated the
New Haven's problems by placing the products manufactured
in New England and imported through Boston at a severe disadvantage in western markets, may have been the final blow
to those expectations.[53]

There was undoubtedly some substance to the Brandeisians'
contention that the merger could not have been achieved without deliberate misrepresentation and coercion. It is clear,
nevertheless, that the B. & M.–New Haven consolidation did
have the independent support of a very impressive group of
public-spirited men (or at least men who were frequently engaged in progressive activities). They included Eugene Foss,
the anti-Lodge Republican; John T. Moors, an original member of the Boston reformers' Finance Commission and an early
associate of Brandeis in the Good Government Association and
the Public Franchise League; Charles Sumner Bird, the Wal-
pole paper manufacturer, an old-line Democrat who ultimately
became the leader of the state's Progressive party in 1912;
Joseph Walker, a leader of reform causes in the General Court
who quit the Republicans for the Progressives in 1913; James
L. Richards, the civic-minded president of the Boston Consolidated Gas Company whom Brandeis admired so much; Samuel
Bowles of the *Springfield Republican,* long a supporter of
Brandeisian causes; and E. A. Filene, founder of "Boston
1915," financier of the Public Franchise League and the
G.G.A., and social dreamer extraordinary.

The *Springfield Republican,* which usually spoke out against
the consolidating tendencies in private enterprise, found the
Brandeisian position against railroad monopoly contrary to
the established, traditional state policy on railroads. "This
policy," it contended, "rests broadly upon the proposition that
the steam roads are essentially monopolies to be regulated by
the state and not by competition, which can play only a small
part as a regulative force." What Brandeis and his allies ap-

[53] See Clapp, pp. 98–100.

peared to be attacking was not simply consolidation but the idea that regulation could be effective. But the alternative was either public ownership — which at least until 1912 Brandeis explicitly rejected — or a "return" to competition, which, the *Republican* asserted, "never has had and never can have an adequate existence in railroading." [54] In 1908, the report of a special Commission on Commerce and Industry, signed by (among others) Charles Francis Adams, Jr., the venerable pioneer of railroad regulation, affirmed the same position and added what many businessmen throughout the state had been arguing in defense of the merger: that consolidation might be the answer to (1) the railroad traffic snarls that had been plaguing Massachusetts industry in recent years, (2) the rate differential disputes, and (3) the periodic "boycott" of New England distribution centers by the continental trunk lines and their eastern connections when eastern demand for western products grew heavy.[55] "New England needs to count for more in the railroad scheme of the country," the report declared, "and the way to accomplish this is to add to her importance by unifying her interests." [56] In brief, a very great deal of the support for Mellen and the New Haven came from those who simply believed that they would solve New England's transportation difficulties.

There were, in addition, many important weaknesses in the opposition's case. The anti-merger forces appeared to be struggling to maintain a *status quo* for the Boston & Maine that did not exist even before the New Haven gained control in the spring of 1907. A large segment of the block of securities

[54] *Springfield Republican,* February 15, 1908. Cf. *Brockton Enterprise,* February 17, 1908.

[55] One of the most serious "boycotts" (Boston merchants used that word to describe what the railroads preferred to call an overload of their facilities) developed at the end of 1906, when Boston merchants could not obtain shipments of grain for export although the railroads were filling the orders of merchants in New York. For a summary of the situation at the point when it was resolved temporarily, see the *Boston Herald,* January 31 and February 3, 1907.

[56] *Report of the Massachusetts Commission on Commerce and Industry* (Boston, 1908), p. 21, and *passim*.

which the New Haven picked up had not for a long time been controlled by "Massachusetts interests"; the American Express Company, a New York corporation, had held it. This was well known, but no one had ever questioned the propriety of an express company owning so large a share of a railroad with which it had major contracts. Apparently, the Express Company had moved on its own to get out of the B. & M., possibly for more profitable investments, and had engaged Lee, Higginson & Company as its broker.[57] The B. & M., moreover, had not been in good financial condition, despite Brandeis' contention.[58] The B. & M. in fact had long needed money for improvements which it could not raise at that time, at least partly because its weak condition was well known in important places, and partly because industrial securities by then were yielding much higher returns. Its failure to sell $6 million worth of new stock in 1906 persuaded the state the next year to liberalize the laws governing the issuance of stock by public service corporations, a change which had the approval of the Public Franchise League.[59] By that time the Express Company

[57] See *Springfield Republican,* January 20, 1908. The I.C.C. hearings confirmed these facts: Hearings, pp. 16–17.

[58] See especially Louis Brandeis to Alfred Brandeis, October 19, 1907 (Brandeis MSS); and Staples and Mason, pp. 26, 34, Cf. Francis B. C. Bradlee, *The Boston and Maine Railroad: A History of the Main Road with its Tributary Lines* (Salem, 1921), p. 73; and Robert L. Masson, *New Shares for Old: The Boston & Maine Stock Modification* (Boston, 1958), pp. 28–29. According to Masson, the New Haven's management of the B. & M. only "completed the disorganization of the railroad's finances" that had begun with "the shortsighted policies of the preceding management" (p. 30). Much the same story was true, incidentally, of the street railway companies which the New Haven absorbed (Mason, *Street Railway,* pp. 39–40).

[59] Grosvenor Calkins, "The Massachusetts Anti-Stock Watering Law," *Quarterly Journal of Economics,* 22:640–645 (1908); James C. Bonbright, *Railroad Capitalization: A Study of the Principles of Regulation of Railroad Securities* (New York, 1920), pp. 138–139. See also Secretary J. B. Eastman's Annual Report of the Public Franchise League for 1907 (Brandeis MSS). The P.F.L. appeared before the General Court to argue that the charges against the old law had been exaggerated, but, Eastman reported, "the League did not oppose a change in the law which would make it more flexible and somewhat less stringent . . . In this way the law was relaxed without abandoning public supervision." These words are symbolic of the old-line civic reformers' strategic withdrawal before the advances of modern corporate finance.

interests had already pulled out. Finally, while opposing the New Haven's possession of the disposed stock, Brandeis and his supporters failed to present an alternative purchaser — as they had done in the Boston Elevated contest. If the anti-merger forces wished to be taken seriously, that was some-thing they should have considered. They rejected government ownership of the stock, and it never appears to have occurred to anyone that the government might force the Express Com-pany to take back its part of it — if that was in fact desirable.

On the other hand — and most essential for our purposes here — Charles Mellen and his allies had committed enough highhanded acts to have made rejection of the corporation's program imperative in the interest of all that the state had held valuable in a Commonwealth. For example, both the governor and the railroad people had made it appear that the company had done everyone a great favor by accepting the Draper Act. Yet, at the time, the New Haven faced an antitrust suit in which the federal government had made it clear that it doubted the authenticity of the "sale" of stock to Billard. If the Draper bill had failed, the New Haven might well have lost its control of the B. & M. as a result of the suit. Thus, it appeared to many that the New Haven needed state action more than the state did.[60] In effect, the Draper Act represented an attempt to legalize what the United States Justice Department was in process of proving was a violation of federal law. In withdraw-ing the Department's proceedings against the New Haven, U. S. Attorney General George W. Wickersham stated that the Draper Act had indicated that the people most concerned with the issue had given sanction to acts which the Department had presumed were illegal and injurious to those people; he implied that he saw no reason to protect a people against itself.[61]

[60] See Eastman to C. L. Underhill, June 12, 1909 (Eastman MSS).
[61] See full statement in Staples and Mason, pp. 81–82. Cf. Wickersham to U. S. Senate, June 25, 1909, Norman White to W. H. Taft, April 3, 1912, Wickersham to C. D. Hilles, April 4 and April 10, 1912 (all in Taft MSS). The U. S. District Attorney for Massachusetts regretted Wickersham's order

In addition, the Draper Act placed an official stamp of endorsement upon the holding company device, long suspect in Massachusetts business circles and only recently denounced by the state's attorney general.[62] Even some who favored the merger, like E. N. Foss, could not swallow the holding company. The state had thus admitted through the back door, without direct public consideration, a form of business enterprise which contradicted the studied traditions of its political economy.

But most important, the state had thoroughly degraded itself by legalizing transactions which the New Haven corporation had made in bad faith and in clear contempt of public authority. In giving itself up to Mellen's devious maneuvers, Massachusetts had not simply joined in the mainstream of modern American capitalism, but had compromised principles more vital to the Commonwealth than traditional principles of business methods: namely, its principles of government under law and the supremacy of the state over its corporate creatures. The sacrifice was made by the same leaders who, on other days of the week, lamented the decline of old New England standards under the burden of unionism and mass immigration.

When in 1910 the General Court passed a law validating all the New Haven's acquisitions which had been made dubious by court decisions and investigations, many Bay Staters were impelled to recall a controversy during 1901 in which the owners of a building in Boston had been forced to remove an expensive cornice because it added to the height of the building beyond the maximum permitted by a city ordinance. In vetoing a bill to exempt the owners from the ordinance because the violation amounted to only a few feet, Governor Crane had declared that the moral principle of obedience to

---

to drop the case: "I hated to do it," he wrote some years later; "I had spent nearly two years in working up our case and believed there was ample ground for criminal prosecution, but orders were orders." Quoted in Mason, *Free Man's Life*, p. 198.

[62] See Attorney General Dana Malone's statement in the *Boston Evening Transcript*, October 1; 1907.

law was at stake, however trivial the transgression appeared to be. But, as the *Springfield Republican's* State House reporter observed, "in the case of the New Haven road, the urgency of business issues has forced into the background the ethical issue, which should have been settled first." [63] Anxiety in the Massachusetts business community that it was becoming isolated by recent economic developments led businessmen to trust in the unorthodox and to overlook ethical transgressions. The view of the independent *Boston Post* was typical. After a series of articles on the financial condition of the New Haven in 1909 which bore out Brandeis' contention that the New Haven was insolvent, the *Post's* financial editor concluded: "This . . . is the essence of the whole situation; the present capitalization is certainly too big for any earning power so far shown; but when men like Mellen and Morgan believe in the future of the road under the present policy the stockholders should rest easy." [64]

Senator Lodge's conversion to the merger may serve as a final illustration of the nub of the problem. He appears to have had a genuine interest in protecting the commercial welfare of the state. But by 1909, the senior senator had already begun lining up support among the legislators who were likely to be in the General Court in January 1911 to vote on his re-election. Characteristically self-complacent that the purity of his motives could never be impugned, Lodge solicited aid from the railroad managers, including Mellen himself, for those purposes,[65] even while he participated in the deliberations toward a feasible solution of the railroad problem.

It was the arrogance of that kind of self-complacency which

[63] *Springfield Republican,* June 16, 1910.

[64] *Boston Post,* November 3, 1909. Cf. William E. Soule (*Boston Post* financial editor) to Mellen, October 29, 1913 (Mellen MSS).

[65] See especially C. S. Mellen to Lodge, February 25 and 28, 1908, Lodge to Mellen, February 26, 1908, T. E. Byrnes to Lodge, September 28 and 30, 1909, and F. C. Dumaine to Lodge, November 1, 1909; see also Lodge to Harry White, January 12, 1909, White to Lodge, February 14 and March 10, 1909, Lodge to Byrnes, June 5, 1911, and Lodge to J. O. Wardwell, May 19, 1909. The foregoing are all in the Lodge MSS; the Lodge-Mellen correspondence appears also in the Mellen MSS.

deserved the hostility of contemporaries even more than the economics and politics of railroad consolidation or modern corporate finance. It was that which presented, to use the *Republican's* delightful understatement once more, "something like an obstacle to confidence" in *anything* that leaders of American society such as Mellen and Lodge did. The New Haven's ultimate financial collapse probably proved only the managers' abominable business judgment — certainly nothing conclusive about railroad consolidations in general or the New Haven–B. & M. consolidation in particular. But Representative Washburn trenchantly summed up the whole episode when he declared it "poor business, poor law, poor politics, poor ethics." [66]

[66] Unidentified clipping dated June 2, 1909, in the Washburn Scrapbooks.

CHAPTER NINE

POLITICAL INSURGENCY COMES
TO MASSACHUSETTS

While there is apparently no organized movement among those republicans who believe in progressive policies . . . I think you will find, if you talk with the 'men in the street', that there is a very widespread and deep feeling of dissatisfaction with the old-line leadership, and that much of the very severe burden of high living expense at the present time is ascribed, whether rightly or wrongly, to the fact that, apparently, an undue proportion of the profits, resulting in part from a high tariff and in part from . . . consolidation, is going into the pockets of the few.

A Republican party worker, 1910

To support the Ins when things are going well; to support the Outs when they seem to be going badly, this, in spite of all that has been said about tweedledum and tweedledee, is the essence of popular government.

Walter Lippmann*

WILLIAM HOWARD TAFT came into the Presidency in 1909 as heir to Theodore Roosevelt's reform policies, and in his own way he went on to promote at least as many important reforms during his four years in the White House as his militant-sounding predecessor had done in seven. Taft's administration also fell heir to the cross pressures of (1) the long neglected popular urge for a more equitable distribution of the rewards which modern society had to offer, (2) the deeply rooted but outmoded notions of justice which governed the outlook of the traditional leaders of American society, and (3) a fierce sectional partisanship which grew out of the long

* The first quotation is from a letter to Henry Cabot Lodge, August 18, 1910 (Lodge MSS); the second is from Walter Lippmann, *The Phantom Public* (New York, 1925), p. 126.

dominance of the East in the nation's affairs. Consequently, in spite of its real contributions to reform, the Taft administration was marked for destruction by forces which most observers agreed represented enlightened progressivism.

Taft waged a successful fight for many Rooseveltian reforms while at the same time he resisted the ascendancy of the reformers. His administration's contributions to a progressive political economy included the first federal corporation tax and the federal income tax amendment. The Taft administration inaugurated a system of postal savings for people of small means who were hurt the most by savings bank disasters. Taft brought suit against more than twice as many corporations for violations of the antitrust laws as had Roosevelt, the reputed trust-buster, and he carried a greater number through to a successful conclusion. He aided the passage of a railroad control bill which conformed more satisfactorily to progressive standards than Roosevelt's Hepburn Act. He retrieved from Congress the power (which Roosevelt had lost) to remove from entry by executive decree any public-domain lands, and his use of that power reserved more lands for conservation than Roosevelt had done in the same period of time. He plunged earnestly into the long-agitated reform of the Dingley tariff, did his best to obtain substantial reductions, and set up a tariff board as a prototype of a commission which he hoped would eliminate legislative logrolling from periodic tariff revisions. Finally, he rammed through a Canadian reciprocity treaty which at least certain reform elements in the country regarded as a big step toward international trade amity, lower tariff rates in general, and possibly lower consumer prices. In addition, he fought unsuccessfully for a national incorporation act, and a permanent tariff commission.

On the other hand, sometimes in spite of himself, Taft aided and abetted the rule of the arrogant old guard. He refused assistance, for example, to a year-old movement among Democrats and about thirty Republicans of diverse social persuasions to deprive Speaker Joseph Cannon of the power to appoint

House committees. Although he personally detested the "dirty and vulgar" man from Illinois and before his inauguration had told several Republican leaders including President Roosevelt that the Speaker would "have to go," [1] Taft deferred to T. R.'s advice that any effort to shackle Cannon would jeopardize the reform program. In any case, Taft thought it foolish to side with a small fluid group of anti-Cannon Republicans who appeared to have in common little more than strong resentment against a man whose use of power had made their own role in Congress seem superfluous. Kansas' Victor Murdock confessed, for instance, that he saw nothing wrong with Cannon's political philosophy; but the Speaker had not permitted Congressmen "free expression," so Uncle Joe had to go. Senator Lodge's son-in-law, Augustus P. Gardner, one of the three original ringleaders against Cannon, like Taft resented Cannon personally and believed that his autocracy tended to undermine party unity — as Gardner set about to prove by example. For reasons of their own, other conservatives, like Massachusetts' William C. Lovering and Butler Ames, helped make up the insurgent ranks.[2] As the House controversy dragged into January 1910, Taft found it necessary to use his patronage to support Cannon when the Democrats and some of the insurgents sought the power to select the House members of a joint committee to investigate the Pinchot-Ballinger affair. As for that business, Taft probably cannot be said to have supported the cause of conservation in the Rooseveltian sense, though in his own way he was prepared to lend aid to the movement — as his eventual replacement of Ballinger with Pinchot's associate, Walter Fisher, suggests.[3] On the other hand, Taft's

[1] Quoted in Mowry, *Era of Roosevelt,* p. 239.

[2] See Kenneth W. Hechler, *Insurgency: Personalities and Politics of the Taft Era* (New York, 1940), pp. 37–38, 41–42. Hechler does not mention Ames or Lovering but discusses others of the same category, such as Charles Fowler of New Jersey.

[3] George Mowry believes Taft's appointment of Fisher shows that the President was really not opposed to the Roosevelt program (*Era of Roosevelt,* pp. 256–257). Compare, however, Samuel P. Hays, *Conservation and the Gospel of Efficiency: The Progressive Conservation Movement, 1890–1920* (Cambridge, 1959), esp. pp. 122, 148–149, 152, 171–172.

detractors were not in the mood to make subtle distinctions. Certain groups of conservationists saw in Louis Glavis and Gifford Pinchot the image of Rooseveltian progressivism, and zealous partisans of T.R. regarded the dismissal of the two men as a betrayal of the ex-President. Thus, Taft was really no friend of Cannon, and perhaps no foe of conservation; but that was not how the public read the story.

Tariff revision, meanwhile, had turned out less successfully than Taft had hoped, but like most early editorial opinion throughout the country Taft believed the Payne-Aldrich Act better than no revision at all.[4] A small clique of midwestern Republican senators thought otherwise. They resented — very likely in order — (1) the way in which the Senate leaders forced through their tariff proposals, (2) the disproportionate share of the benefits which went to manufacturers as against agricultural interests, and (3) the injustice to consumers which resulted from the high rates of the Aldrich bill. The insurgents lit brush-fires of sectional patriotism by charging that it was an eastern bill written for eastern interests. Although they appear to have voted their special interests as loyally as their antagonists voted theirs,[5] the Senate insurgents successfully made the fight on the Aldrich tariff a "progressive" issue. It

[4] Baker, pp. 109–112. *Outlook,* of which Roosevelt was nominally an editor, called it "the most enlightened protectionist measure ever enacted in the history of the country" (quoted *ibid.,* p. 109). Even after a year of widespread criticism of the bill, Roosevelt published his belief that "the present tariff is better than the last, and considerably better than the one before the last" (*Outlook,* September 17, 1910, quoted *ibid.,* p. 128). Roosevelt, of course, had not even had the virtue of believing there was anything wrong with the Dingley Act.

[5] Baker, pp. 84–85, 98. George Mowry, in support of the insurgents, found that "the numerous roll calls . . . reveal that LaFollette, Clapp, Beveridge, Bristow, Cummins, Dolliver, and Nelson voted oftener against the Aldrich rates than for them" — faint praise indeed. Prof. Mowry added that three other insurgents — W. E. Borah of Idaho, Jonathan Bourne of Oregon, and G. S. Nixon of South Dakota — in supporting Aldrich throughout, "frequently voted against their inclinations." How their vote for, say, high woolens duties in exchange for protection of their states' mineral products differed in principle or motivation from a vote by Senator Lodge for protection of mineral products in exchange for high woolens duties, Prof. Mowry leaves unexplained (see his *Roosevelt and the Progressive Movement,* p. 60).

became the issue on which popular agitation over high prices tended to focus, as well as the issue on which anti-Taft sentiment in Congress first took form.

Taft's verbal ineptitude worsened his condition.[6] His open identification that fall with Nelson Aldrich, truculent Senate leader from the pocket borough of Rhode Island, son-in-law of Standard Oil, and principal architect of the dubious tariff bill, made Taft a ripe target for the ten-year-old nationwide animus toward "Bosses." [7] By calling it "the best tariff bill that the Republican party ever passed," when he already had a bad press because of the Ballinger affair, Taft exposed himself to ridicule.[8] In his first annual message that December, Taft exacerbated press relations by calling for higher postal rates for newspapers and magazines, and by describing existing rates as "an enormous subsidy" to the press. The publishing industry was already militant about the rising costs of newsprint[9] and the failure to obtain adequate reductions on newsprint duties in the Aldrich bill,[10] and it was already filling the

[6] Taft's biographer writes: "At least one unfortunate phrase seems to have been inevitable in every major campaign conducted by Taft" (Pringle, *Taft*, p. 584).

[7] In a speech Taft made in Boston at the beginning of his tour to justify the tariff act, he described Aldrich as "the real leader of the Senate" who had only the country's welfare at heart. See Mowry, *Era of Roosevelt*, p. 249.

[8] From Taft's speech at Winona, Minnesota, September 17, 1909. A year later Taft explained to Roosevelt — to whom he owed no explanation — what he meant by his statement at Winona: "I have, as you have known, always been a low tariff and downward revision man, and the reason why I favored the last tariff bill and praised it as the best one we had ever had was, that the consideration of it on its passage, and the efforts of those who defended it to show that it was a downward revision, were all a concession by the Republican party that downward revision was necessary, and that the rule upheld by [ex-Secretary of the Treasury Leslie M.] Shaw and Cannon and other standpatters of the orthodox type that no tariff could be too high because what you needed was a Chinese wall, had been departed from." Taft to Roosevelt, January 10, 1911 (Taft MSS). Cf. Frank W. Taussig, *The Tariff History of the United States* (New York, 1923), p. 408.

[9] In April 1908, the Associated Press meeting in New York denounced the Census Bureau for supplying Congress and the public with "false reports of newsprint paper prices" and for persisting in its "error" after the Associated Press had publicly contradicted it. See Baker, p. 71.

[10] See L. Ethan Ellis, *Newsprint: Producers, Publishers, Political Pressures* (New Brunswick, New Jersey, 1960), p. 12 and *passim*.

public's appetite for charges against the existing social order. Taft's clumsiness further provoked the press to give its favors to the enemies of his administration.

One of the reasons Taft privately gave for not vetoing the Payne-Aldrich bill, though he reportedly was tempted to do so, perhaps reveals the President's tragic flaw: he said he thought "too highly of Aldrich" to do that, and he did not wish "to be popular on those terms." [11] This personal, in-group loyalty and the behavior to which it committed him was the key to Taft's position. All the reform measures which passed during his administration could not obscure Taft's status as a representative of the undesirable *status quo*. He was an instinctive bourbon, and in his time, the men with whom he consulted and consorted were as much an issue as the reforms they usually opposed.

Before he had resided in the White House a year, Taft was already pegged as an obstacle to progressivism, and a Judas to Theodore Roosevelt. The progressive movement now had something better than a champion in the White House; it had there a central object of opposition.

I

Insurgency was contagious. Although Congressional insurgents often directed their criticism of the *status quo* at the particular position which Massachusetts seemed to enjoy in it, they helped to popularize the idea of *change* in that state as well. The idea was popular enough, of course, among the Democrats. But increasingly after 1908, it had especial appeal also to certain groups within the Republican party in Massachusetts. One group included Republicans from the industrial wards, the labor legislators. By 1909, the cumulative effect of twelve years of rising prices and lagging wages[12] had increased

---

[11] Quoted in Mowry, *Roosevelt and the Progressive Movement*, p. 57.

[12] See Richard Olney II, "The Laboring Man of Today as Compared with 50 Years Ago," *New England Magazine*, 42:81–85 (March 1910); MBSL, "Changes in Rates of Wages and Hours of Labor in 1910," *Labor Bulletin No. 86* (Boston, 1911). Cf. Albert Rees, *Real Wages in Manufacturing, 1890–1914* (Princeton, 1961).

the militancy of their constituents. The wage earners, moreover, had been learning the knack of organization; more than 65 per cent of the labor organizations in existence in Massachusetts in 1909 had been established during the previous nine years.[13] A second group included various individuals who sought a place of eminence within their "Grand Old Party." The generation of party leaders which had come to power in the 1890's was now vulnerable; it had held decision-making and patronage-dispensing places for almost two decades, and the proportion of able, ambitious party men without place had grown. A new generation of "Young Republicans," like those Henry Cabot Lodge had led in 1890, had arisen. Finally, there was a third, very small group of progressive reformers committed in a general way to extensive social reform.

Behind the insurgent impulse within the Republican party lay a vague feeling of discomfort that most people seemed to share. The trusts and the tariff served as objective political symbols for a much more generalized sense that somehow injustice had triumphed. Inflation, the continuing flow of social criticism in the magazines, the impact of more than 5,000,000 immigrants between 1905 and 1910 — more than 350,000 of whom entered Massachusetts — all helped to spread the sentiment of discontent. Labor militancy, itself a product of these pressures, served to agitate the more comfortable segments of society. The appearance in even the most conservative newspapers of editorials which extolled as "progressive" nearly any innovation suggested the almost universal appeal that *change* had at the time.

Indeed, it seemed everyone was a "progressive." "Progressivism" was the language of the day in which men of all political hues conversed and appeared (though perhaps *only* appeared) to understand each other. The *Boston Herald* — between denunciations of Charles Mellen's critics — without the slightest sense of irony joined in the cheers for Robert Bass when the anti-railroad New Hampshire insurgent won the Re-

[13] MBSL, *39th Annual Report* (Boston, 1909), p. 185.

publican nomination for governor in 1910. It was "a progressive victory," the paper declared, an "assertion of the power
of the rank and file of the party, the majority[,] over the domination of the machine." The once Democratic newspaper,
which had been moving close to the Republicans because of
Democratic attacks on the United Shoe Machinery Company
and the New Haven–Boston & Maine merger, went on to compare Bass's achievement with the "progressive victories in Kansas, in California and in other states where the voters have
arisen to assert their rights." [14] Similarly, a leading political
commentator who had never conspicuously championed the
cause of the wage-earning majority in Massachusetts was writing by 1909 like a Marxist polemicist — without, of course,
meaning anything like what Marxists meant when they used
precisely the same words and phrases. "The Legislature," wrote
the *Springfield Republican's* State House reporter, "does not
seem . . . to have shown the force, initiative and originality
which must be shown if the gradual solidification of the upper
classes against the lower . . . is ever to be broken up and the
rights of the exploited masses ever to be asserted against the
aggrandizement of the wealthy and dominating few." [15]

Under the circumstances, it is perhaps not too surprising
that even Senator Lodge had illusions of progressiveness: "I
am aware," he wrote to a troubled supporter, "of the discontent and dissatisfaction that exists . . . I think that I favor
all the policies which are commonly known as progressive and
have supported them in the Senate." [16] In a very broad sense
there *was* some similarity between Lodge's views and the
general objectives of the progressive movement,[17] but it was

[14] *Boston Herald,* September 7, 1910. "No one . . . can deny," the paper
asserted on another day, "that although the formation of the battle line may
vary with the topography of the country . . . the struggle is clearly defined
between the forces of intrenched [*sic*] privilege and the embattled people
fighting for the rights of the individual." *Ibid.,* August 5, 1910. Cf. the
thoroughly anti-insurgent editorial of May 12, 1910.

[15] "Legislative Summary," *Springfield Republican,* June 18, 1909.

[16] Lodge to E. E. Gaylord, August 19, 1910 (Lodge MSS).

[17] See Chapter One, p. 19.

untrue that in 1910 he sympathized with *policies* then "commonly known as progressive." It was in fact the specific proposals of the insurgents which Lodge and the old-line leadership resisted. Indeed, one of the "policies" of the Massachusetts insurgents was to displace the old leaders, with special attention to the senior senator himself.

In Massachusetts, Senator Lodge represented to most Republican insurgents what Cannon did in the House of Representatives. Still more clearly than in the fight against Cannon, the effort to unseat Lodge and "his machine" had little relationship to a fight for social justice — that is, for labor legislation, for example, or action to curb the growth of giant corporations, or even (in most cases) efforts to reduce the protective tariff. Almost to a man the leading Republican insurgents supported Charles Mellen's New Haven schemes, and few ever indicated indignation at the new corporate methods. On the labor issue, which drove a deep wedge into Republican unity during the Draper administration (1909–10), the men who emerged as the leading insurgents took the conservative position even more emphatically; they were quick, however, to exploit for their own purposes the heavy losses which Governor Draper suffered in 1909 in Republican strongholds like New Bedford, Brockton, and Lynn, which were due primarily to the administration's defeat of labor measures. Similarly, as it became evident that the Payne-Aldrich tariff suffered even in Massachusetts from the popular identification of the measure with "Bossism" and high prices, they became "revisionists" though they never backtracked on protectionism. They made their principal claim to "progressiveness," however, in their advocacy of institutional political reforms like direct primaries, popular election of United States senators, and the initiative and referendum. Such institutional reforms, which serve to increase popular participation in government, have been the traditional proposals of "out" groups throughout American history; considering the Massachusetts insurgents' opposition to particular measures usually identified with progressivism, it is evident that they hoped increased popular participation would accomplish little more than their own accession to power. Possibly they were, as a group, with only a few true exceptions, only slightly less guilty than Lodge of misappropriating the language of progressivism.

II

Industrial difficulties in the Bay State gave encouragement to the dissident elements within the G.O.P. By weakening the position of Republican officeholders, economic troubles gave insurgents an opportunity to undermine the old guard's leadership. Disunity among the insurgents, however, foredoomed any direct challenge to the old guard, and in the end the Democrats were the political beneficiaries of the rising social tensions.

Toward the end of 1907 and throughout 1908, in the backlash of the financial panic, wage rates had dropped sharply in most Massachusetts industries. In the generally prosperous year of 1909, only 18,000 workers in Massachusetts received upward adjustments of wage rates, although 95,000 had been cut the previous year. The fact that 95 per cent of the raises followed strong pressures from unions, and that more than 40 per cent came only after strikes, illustrated the employers' resistance to sharing their renewed prosperity.[18] The factory owners claimed that out-of-state competition made it impossible to maintain or raise Massachusetts wage levels.

Massachusetts employers characteristically responded to the pressures on their profit margins from outside competition and rising costs by using cheap immigrant labor where they could. ("Of course, you understand, we cannot run the mills of New England without immigrants," wrote one Massachusetts businessman to a member of Taft's cabinet.)[19] In the three years

[18] MBSL, *40th* Annual Report (Boston, 1911), pp. 3–4, 10, 14.
[19] F. C. Dumaine to George Meyer, June 8, 1909 (Meyer MSS). Dumaine asked Meyer to do what he could to lift restrictions on immigrants, especially French Canadians, whom employers preferred because they rarely sought citizenship and resisted the typically English- and Irish-American labor organizers. See, e.g., MBSL, *43d Annual Report* (Boston, 1913), pp. 48–49.

1907–1909, some 150,000 immigrants arrived at the ports of Charlestown and Boston; although many of these went on to jobs outside the state, at least an equal number entered Massachusetts from other states and from Canada.[20] Only a small proportion of immigrants belonged to labor unions. Anti-union activity by employers was probably the chief cause of that condition. In addition, immigrants themselves tended to resist union organization; they preferred the semiformal associations based on their nationalities. Finally, many types of immigrant workers remained outside unions because the conservative trade unions would not take on the task of organizing them. Some even formally excluded aliens.[21] (After 1910, the International Workers of the World moved into this vacuum and had considerable success with industrial-type organizations.) That immigrant workers were not unionized did not mean that they did not strike or cooperate with unionized strikers. Usually, however, their strikes were defensive — against wage cuts, unfavorable changes in working conditions, or the introduction of immigrants of a different ethnic group into the factories. Such strikes occurred with increasing frequency after 1908.

The presence of large numbers of foreign-speaking laborers milling discontentedly in the streets of industrial cities and towns tended to heighten the concern of the nonindustrial segment of the population with social problems. There seemed to be a rising tendency, moreover, to blame the industrialists for the prevalent social tensions. Even conservatives became cynical about the manufacturers' allegations that they could not afford higher wages, especially as the business journals reported high corporate earnings and bonus dividends.[22] In many

[20] Massachusetts Commission on Immigration, *The Problem of Immigration in Massachusetts,* p. 267.

[21] MBSL, *39th Annual Report,* p. 155.

[22] One Republican "boss" of a traditionally Republican district where the workers were becoming increasingly rebellious wrote sarcastically to Senator Lodge: "Owing to the high price of raw material the mills are not able to increase their price of wages to keep pace with the increased cost of living. The Pepperill mills this last week almost doubled their capital given

cases, their cynicism was well justified; in others, the problem was more complicated.

Toward the end of 1909 a strike of immigrant workers in the town of Ludlow, just outside Springfield, attracted state-wide attention and caused the Draper administration grave anxieties. In September that year, 1500 Polish-speaking opera-tives walked out of the jute mills when the manufacturers re-fused to restore wage rates which had been cut during the recession early in the year. The walkout might have been settled quickly even without a wage boost; but instead, with "the easy defiance of the strong," the employers solidified the strikers' unity by posting an additional 16 per cent wage cut, claiming that they were no longer able to compete with Scot-tish and Indian jute producers at the prevalent Ludlow wage scale. To keep the mills operating, they brought in Greek and Italian strike breakers from New York City. Trade unions from all over the state gave aid to the strikers, and the Spring-field Central Union intervened to assist in the negotiations with the foreign-speaking strikers. It was characteristic of the con-servatism of Massachusetts trade unions that one of the prin-cipal concerns of the Springfield Central was to prevent vio-lence; the Union even ran out of town the single Polish-speak-ing "agitator" who allegedly came from outside to harden the strikers' determination.

Draper ordered the State Board of Conciliation and Arbi-tration to intervene in the strike before violence did occur, and Lieutenant Governor Frothingham took charge of the media-tion. The Board's investigation revealed a common industrial condition in Massachusetts. The workers were so poorly paid that few families could make a living unless more than one in a family worked. The companies provided "model" low-rent housing (*not* a common condition in Massachusetts or any-where else), but the tenants turned their quarters into slums

---

to stockholders, and I clipped the following from today's News Bureau as to another one of the down trodden corporations. 'Boston — The Pacific Mills has declared a regular semi-annual dividend of 6 per cent ($60), and $40 extra.' " J. O. Wardwell to Lodge, November 19, 1909 (Lodge MSS).

because they were forced to take in boarders to help meet the cost of living. On the other hand, the Board pointed out that, even with the wage cuts, the manufacturers were paying higher wages on the average than their chief American competitors in Brooklyn. The tariff on imported jute, moreover, was not high enough to keep out the Scottish and Indian product. The Ludlow employers seemed determined to close rather than restore the wage cuts. In the end, the workers agreed to go back to the mills, 16 per cent cut and all, on condition only that the employers agree to fire the strike breakers.[23]

The Ludlow experience had a counterpart in Brockton, which suffered a rash of strikes during 1909 and 1910. Labor in Brockton was both predominantly native-born and well unionized. The strength of their unions had enabled Brockton shoe workers to appropriate the highest percentage in their industry of the margin between the cost of materials and the selling price of the finished product. In 1909, against the recommendations of the National Boot and Shoe Workers Union, which opposed further increments for Brockton until lower paid shoe workers could bring their wages up, the Brockton workers struck. As a result, several companies pulled out of the city for a more placid environment. Aside from certain peripheral gains, the Brockton workers succeeded only in reducing the number of jobs in the city. Emigration appeared the only alternative to the manufacturers as long as lower wage scales prevailed elsewhere.[24]

The experience of the Fall River cotton textile workers, also well organized, was another case in point. Fall River was particularly vulnerable to southern competition because, unlike New Bedford, its sister manufacturing city, it produced mostly prints and other coarser cotton constructions. During the de-

---

[23] MBSL, *40th Annual Report*, pp. 146–165; *Springfield Republican*, September 1909–January 1910.

[24] Norton, pp. 49–50, 115, 124; *Boston Herald*, June 29, 1909. Trade unionism in the shoe industry went into decline in the succeeding decades. On migration within the shoe industry, see Horace B. Davis, *Shoes: The Workers and the Industry* (New York, 1940), esp. chap. i.

pression of the 1890's and again in the recession of 1903–04, southern competitors had shown what lower production costs could mean in a limited market;[25] after 1903 it had become increasingly evident that southern manufacturers could claim a larger share of the market in good times as well. The great Fall River strike of 1904–05 had followed two successive wage cuts which the companies claimed high cotton prices and southern competition had necessitated. The workers finally agreed to accept Governor William Douglas as arbitrator and returned to the mills. But Douglas' settlement upheld the employers' position; it placed wages approximately where the companies had set them following the second wage cut.[26] Shortly thereafter, the Textile Council, the coordinating committee for the five craft unions in the city, persuaded the manufacturers to establish a sliding-scale wage system. But from the workers' viewpoint the system failed, because print cloth prices, to which wages were tied, remained low through 1906. (The manufacturers, meanwhile, prospered on sales of fancy and odd cloth constructions.)[27] In May 1907 the employers agreed to raise the wage scale substantially, and for a year it worked well as profit margins widened. But by 1908 the margin had dropped sharply, and within another year it fell below the lowest point on the scale. Consequently, the workers found themselves in the awkward position of having to accept the "magnanimity" of the employers who maintained the May 1908 wage rates although the sliding-scale system justified lower rates.[28] There was little the workers could do in the face of the apparent decline of their industry.[29]

[25] MBSL, "Cotton Manufacturing in Massachusetts," *Labor Bulletin No. 5* (January 1898); Sarah S. Whittelsey, "Massachusetts Labor Legislation," in *Trade Unionism and Labor Problems*, ed. J. R. Commons (New York, 1905), esp. p. 496.

[26] MBSL, "The Fall River Sliding Scale of Wages," *Labor Bulletin No. 41* (Boston, 1906), pp. 192–196; also see "Five Years' Strikes in Massachusetts," *ibid.*, pp. 171–192; *Boston Herald*, January 18, 1905; *American Federationist*, 12:138–139 (March 1905).

[27] See "Fall River Sliding Scale of Wages," p. 196.

[28] MBSL, *40th Annual Report*, pp. 13, 44–45.

[29] Smith, *Fall River*, p. 121. According to Smith, "The handwriting was on the wall for those who could read . . . Fall River's dominance of the

It is important to understand that Fall River conditions did not prevail throughout Massachusetts industry. Possibly in most cases, employers' labor policies fully justified workers' agitation. Mills in New Bedford, Lowell, and Holyoke, for example, produced fabrics with which the South still offered only negligible competition. Nor could low paying shoe manufacturers in Haverhill and Lynn claim that their wage scales were already higher than elsewhere. Haverhill and New Bedford were among a few industrial cities which experienced near-boom years after 1907.[30] In such cities, social critics' charges about exploited labor more accurately reflected actual conditions.

After 1908, labor legislators applied increasing pressure for labor measures, and more and more Republicans responded to the pressure out of fear of social upheaval. In the House during 1909 and 1910, labor bills which an average of only 12 per cent of the Republicans had supported during the previous eight years now had the support of an average of 28 per cent.[31] It was significant for the future that the rank and file gave strongly favorable attention to a number of bills which would have facilitated effective labor union action. In 1909, for example, the House voted 106 to 84 for a bill which allowed unions to fine members. Labor union sponsors hoped to obtain a weapon to enforce solidarity during the strikes. Although the bill ultimately failed on later readings, the next year it passed the Senate by a 26 to 9 vote, and finally lost in the House by only a narrow margin.[32] In 1910, the House ap-

market was gone . . . A crisis in the city's major industry was clearly well under way." Only World War I gave the city's industry "a 10-year reprieve." See also analysis of Fall River conditions in a speech made May 26, 1908, by Congressman William Greene of Fall River, *Congressional Record*, 60 Cong., 1 Sess., Appendix, pp. 318–319.

[30] See industrial survey in *Boston Herald*, August 15, 1910; Green, *Holyoke*, pp. 226–231; Maurice B. Dorgan, *Lawrence, Yesterday and Today* (Lawrence, 1918), pp. 45–46; Norton, p. 171; Wolfbein, *New Bedford*, p. 10.

[31] Figures are based on my own calculations from roll calls in the House, 1901 through 1910.

[32] *MHRJ*, April 5, 1909, pp. 780–782, May 25 and 26, 1910, pp. 1302–1304, 1313–1315; *MSJ*, May 20, 1910, p. 900. The House vote for the bill

proved by 113 to 102 the first draft of a bill to limit the use of injunctions in labor disputes and to provide jury trials in contempt cases arising from violations of such injunctions; the bill lost on the final reading by only two votes.[33] Action by the government to provide for the welfare of its laboring citizens had been an established tradition in Massachusetts politics. But these new measures would have encouraged workers to exact better wages and working conditions from employers by their own direct action. It is not surprising that the Republican party leaders united to defeat the exertions of the labor legislators.

It was indicative of the stolid, pro-business prejudices of the Draper administration that it resisted just as stubbornly even the more traditional labor bills for the reduction of the working hours of women, children, public employees, and workers on government contracts. For two successive years the administration thwarted the textile workers' efforts to reduce weekly hours for women and minors from fifty-six to fifty-four despite powerful support from the Republican rank and file. (Since the industry depended so much on women workers, a reduction of hours for them meant essentially a general hourly reduction.) The bill was killed in the Senate in 1909 after the House passed it 121 to 90; in 1910 only a tie vote in the Senate saved the measure from a sure veto after the House had sent it on with an emphatic 162 to 55 majority.[34] The administration was less successful with a bill designed to plug a hole in the Eight-Hour Law of 1907 which had enabled contractors

---

in 1910 was 97 to 109. It must be said, however, that many legislators probably assumed that the fining power might make unions into effective disciplining agencies for workers who tended to "get out of hand" during labor disputes.

[33] *MHRJ,* April 6, May 3, 1910, pp. 867–869, 1103–1106. See also Senate vote on a similar bill in *MSJ,* May 24, 1910, pp. 971–972.

[34] *MHRJ,* May 4, 1909, pp. 1036–1039, April 12, 1910, pp. 924–926; *MSJ,* April 21, 1910, p. 789. See also *Boston Herald,* April 21, 1910. The General Court had passed the 56-hour-per-week bill only in 1908, and it was not until 1910 that it was supposed to take effect. Labor interests, however, had considered the 1908 bill a defeat because they had sought 54 hours then.

to evade the law by securing workers' "consent" to work longer than the eight-hour daily maximum. The General Court passed the measure in 1909 and again in 1910, and Governor Draper vetoed it both times.[35]

Eben Draper's defiance of labor agitation marked him for destruction by the organized labor groups throughout the state. "Counting up their blessings," remarked one news reporter after the 1909 legislative session, "will not make the labor men tired this year. What will they do about it?" [36] The defeat of Governor John L. Bates in 1904 had already demonstrated what the labor groups might do about it. Although Draper won re-election over James Vahey in 1909, the narrow margin of his victory might have served as a warning. Most leading Republicans, however, including Draper himself, chose to attribute the sharp reduction of his plurality to the public's "misunderstanding" of the Payne-Aldrich Tariff Act. ("The tariff was the heaviest load I had to carry because of its being so misrepresented to the people," Draper complained.)[37] Election figures for 1909 showed (1) that Republican losses were confined almost entirely to the gubernatorial race, (2) that normally Republican cities like New Bedford, Lynn, Fall River, and Brockton turned against Draper, while they returned the same number of Republican legislators as in 1908, and (3) that the Democrats made only nominal gains in the House and no gains at all in the Senate, where party disunity had reduced

[35] In 1910, the House gave it a 128 to 85 majority, and the Senate, 22 to 15. *MHRJ,* April 20, 1910, pp. 988–990; see also pp. 1355–1357 (June 1, 1910) for the effort to override the veto. The Senate vote is in *MSJ,* May 10, 1910, p. 898.

[36] *Springfield Republican,* June 17, 1909.

[37] Draper to George Meyer, November 4, 1909; see also a memorandum of a statement by Draper dated November 10, 1909 (both in Meyer MSS). Meyer had already concluded that Republican losses derived from "the prevailing high cost of living, which had increased so materially and which the Democrats have made the masses believe is due to the tariff," while Senator Lodge concurred that "we did not discuss the tariff as we should have done," adding: "I have no doubt how the manufacturing towns will vote [next year] when they understand." Meyer to Lodge, November 3, 1909 (Lodge MSS); Lodge to Meyer, November 7, 1909 (Meyer MSS); Lodge to Crane, November 4, 1909 (Lodge MSS). See also Lodge to Roosevelt, November 30, 1909, in *Correspondence,* II, 353–354.

their ranks to an unusual low the previous year. But the figures
failed to impress upon the governor that his opposition to labor
measures had at least as much to do with his losses as the
"misunderstood" tariff.

When the coalition of labor legislators and Democrats threw
the eight-hour bill at Draper again in 1910, Senator Lodge
— now "meddling" increasingly often in legislative matters —
urged Draper to consider the consequences of a second veto
and to try to have an acceptable bill written. "Is there any
possibility," the Senator wrote early in January, "of coming
to some agreement on the Eight Hour bill? . . . If some bill
could be arranged which you could approve it would take an
awkward element out of the campaign and simplify it to that
extent." [38] But Draper refused to budge. He fought the bill,
lost again, and again issued his veto. The action portended
trouble for that November.

III

Even before the second struggle over the eight-hour bill
there was evidence of serious demoralization within the G.O.P.
ranks. If the dissidents within the party had ever found a vital
common cause beyond their discontent with particular features of old guard leadership, Massachusetts might have developed an insurgent movement comparable to movements elsewhere in the country.

Draper helped to undermine his own position by petulantly
labeling the Republican labor representatives "insurgents,"
thereby identifying them with the Congressional reformers who
were enjoying an excellent press. Most of the labor men had
had no intention of breaking with party regularity on other
issues — as their steadfast support of the Draper holding company bill in June 1909 had indicated — but party leaders
could not continue to count on their loyalty if the labor legislators believed they were to be read out of the party for supporting measures essential to their re-election. Labor legislators

[38] Lodge to Draper, January 4, 1910 (Lodge MSS).

from Essex and Middlesex counties in particular soon became leading advocates of "anti-organization" measures such as direct primaries and popular election of United States senators.

The outstanding individual insurgent in the General Court was Arthur L. Nason of Haverhill. Nason was one of the few Republican insurgents in the state who could legitimately claim the label "progressive." As a legislator since 1906, Nason consistently had supported not only the labor measures which his militant constituents demanded, but, unlike New Bedford's Samuel Ross and Andrew P. Doyle, for example, he also had attacked the gas and electric companies, had taken the steam out of the Haverhill socialist parties by fighting for municipal ownership of public utilities, and had denounced the New Haven merger. In addition, he had demanded direct election of United States senators, direct primaries, the initiative and referendum, woman suffrage, and state and federal income and inheritance taxes. Finally, he had gratified the vigorous temperance groups of the Haverhill area by supporting every measure they presented in the General Court.

Nason's bid for control of the G.O.P. organization of Essex County in 1909 marked the first of several sporadic challenges to old guard leadership in the Bay State which culminated finally in the schism of 1912. At the close of the 1909 legislative session, in which the Draper administration had pushed through the New Haven–Boston & Maine merger, Nason formally announced his intention of overthrowing "Boss" J. Otis Wardwell as state committeeman from Essex.[39] Wardwell was a top lieutenant for Congressman A. P. Gardner and Senator Lodge. In the party caucuses that September, Nason achieved his objective, and in addition won the G.O.P. nomination for state senator.

Nason's triumph, however, was not a simple victory for progressivism over "the machine." In Nason's corner were many men who opposed Wardwell, Gardner, and (or) Lodge for special reasons of their own, none of which had more than

[39] *Boston Herald,* June 24, 1909.

a remote relationship to progressivism. Nason had the interested support of Congressman Butler Ames, who in January
1907 had already intimated he would seek Senator Lodge's
seat in 1911.[40] The grandson of Benjamin F. Butler (Brahmin
Republicans' pet horror), and the son of Adelbert Ames (the
carpetbagger governor of Mississippi), Butler Ames had always been an ugly duckling of the party. His "distinctiveness,"
however, had never affected his regularity on party issues.
While at every opportunity he took swipes at Cabot Lodge,
his family's bitter enemy, he remained a Republican in good
standing with the orthodox followers of Murray Crane. (In
1908 he set out to establish himself as a "progressive" by pro-
posing a non-Taft national ticket with Albert Beveridge of
Indiana or "any westerner" for President, and Murray Crane
in the second place.)[41] His record in Congress was distinguished for little more than the number of private petitions he
introduced, and an occasional speech in favor of tariff revision
which he made chiefly to heckle Senator Lodge. (He voted
"regular" on the provisions of the Payne-Aldrich tariff.) Nason
and Ames enjoyed the support of many Frothingham followers
who apparently resented Wardwell's neutrality in the lieutenant-governor nomination fight of 1908.[42] Finally, state senator
James F. Shaw, an independent railway promoter whose father
had lost a bitter campaign against Gardner for the Congressional nomination in 1902 and had himself unsuccessfully
sought Lodge's support for president of the state senate in
1908, also lent aid to the Haverhill anti-organization forces
which promoted Nason.[43]

[40] *Ibid.*, January 8, 1907. Ames repeated his intentions "to friends" in
January 1908 (*Springfield Republican,* January 17, 1908).

[41] *Springfield Republican,* January 7, 1908.

[42] See J. O. Wardwell to Lodge, September 23 and December 20, 1909
(Lodge MSS).

[43] Lodge to Gardner, October 8, 1908, Gardner to Lodge, October 9, 1908,
and Lodge to Gardner, October 12, 1908 (Lodge MSS). Lodge and Wardwell worked actively in the spring and summer of 1909 to defeat Shaw for
re-election, calling on President Lucius Tuttle of the Boston & Maine Railroad, among others, for assistance. Lodge to Wardwell, May 19, 1909
(Lodge MSS); P. M. Longan to George Meyer, July 21, 1909 (Meyer

In addition to the loosely associated Nason-Ames-Shaw group, another trio made up of Robert Luce, Norman White of Brookline, and Robert Washburn of Worcester constituted another source of Republican insurgency, based primarily on their vehement opposition to the administration's New Haven policy. Luce had not stood for re-election to the legislature in 1908 after his defeat for the lieutenant-governor nomination, but he continued to work actively with the Public Franchise League against Draper's railroad program, and lobbied for his direct primary and "public opinion" measures. White was a man given to quick indignation and violent language. Like Luce he opposed the trend toward collectivization of business and tended to ascribe "evil" intentions to corporate managers; he was equally opposed to the collectivization of labor and, on at least one occasion, described union action as "un-American." Unlike Luce, White opposed direct primaries, the initiative and referendum in all forms, and popular election of United States senators, though he favored woman suffrage. Washburn's "insurgency" was even more limited to the New Haven issue; he frequently voted against Luce and White on other corporation issues, and, even more consistently than they, opposed labor and popular government measures, though he too endorsed woman suffrage after 1908. In addition, he was as steadfast an opponent of tariff reductions as Eben Draper and usually led assaults upon the revisionist elements in the party.

Thus, although there were several figures of leadership caliber within the G.O.P. who by 1909 were establishing strong positions in opposition to the old guard, they formed no cohesive faction, had no common program, and frequently fought one another as hotly as they fought the incumbent leadership. Except on a limited number of issues, most of them had little in common with progressivism. With the exception of Nason

---

MSS). They were successful. Shaw was the Senate sponsor of the bill for direct election of United States senators in 1909 (*Boston Herald,* January 21, 1909).

and (perhaps) Ames and their personal followers, none of these men would even have admitted to being an insurgent. Because of Ames's peculiar familial connections, and Nason's unusual progressivism on social issues, neither man ever commanded a significant following among anti-organization Republicans. Nevertheless, all together they helped to break down the long-standing harmony of their party.

Signs of intraparty conflict multiplied throughout the winter of 1909–10. That the troubles had only a vague relationship to the recognized issues of insurgency lent little comfort to G.O.P. leaders. In December 1909, a Democrat captured the mayoralty in Lynn, once Senator Lodge's own bailiwick. Local resentment against an effort by the party organization to discipline certain nonconforming members sent the city into the Democratic column for the first time in at least a generation. In January 1910, John F. Fitzgerald recaptured Boston's mayoralty from the Republicans. The Good Government Association and the leading state Republicans had supported James J. Storrow, a partner in Lee, Higginson & Company. Under the new city charter the election was technically nonpartisan, but that did not conceal the fact that only the defection of certain dissident Republicans, including the incumbent mayor, made possible "Honey Fitz's" narrow margin in a record total vote.[44] Then in March, Eugene Foss, the erstwhile Lodge-baiting Republican, critically wounded G.O.P. prestige when he won a special election for Congress on the Democratic ticket in a district which had consistently gone Republican by pluralities up to 15,000 for the previous ten years or more. Although Democrats and some insurgents, especially from outside the state, attempted to interpret Foss's victory as a rebuke to the old guard Republicans for their responsibility

[44] See *Springfield Republican* and any Boston paper for December 15, 1909, through January 10, 1910. For the efforts of the Republican leaders to heal the breach in the Boston ranks, see Curtis Guild to Lodge, December 28, 1909, Lodge to Guild, December 30, 1909, and various letters in December and January from R. A. Southworth and H. L. Higginson to Lodge (all in Lodge MSS).

for the Aldrich tariff, and Norman White saw it as evidence "that the people of the United States will no longer submit to the dictation of the vested interests," [45] Foss actually won only because of a factional fight among Republicans in the district. Having pledged during his campaign that he would be a nonpartisan Congressman and would not run for re-election in November, Foss had given the local Republicans an opportunity to punish their party's nominee, who had won the nomination only after a bitterly fought caucus contest.[46]

The Republican party had always been noted for the way in which it settled internal disputes without the scandalous crises which wracked the Democratic party. But by 1910 even old-line Republicans aired their grievances in the headlines. At the beginning of the year, a small group of conservative state committeemen issued a public denunciation of the party leadership for selecting the officers of the committee without calling a general meeting of committeemen and legislators. None of the discontented committeemen was or ever would be an insurgent; the dissidents' grievance, like many of the irritations which led to insurgency in the state and nation, originated simply in wounded pride. But the style of their objections signified the deterioration of party manners, and lent additional encouragement to those Republicans, seriously bent on insurgency, who accused the party leaders of "bossism."

Having diverse reasons for opposing the party leadership, the dissidents within the Massachusetts G.O.P. recognized no leader. The circumstances were ripe, however, for an able man

[45] *Boston Herald*, April 20, 1910.

[46] In addition to fomenting bad feelings during his fight for the Republican nomination, Foss's opponent had had the bad taste to desert the Republicans in 1904 when he served as William Douglas' private secretary. See Baker, p. 119; Hennessy, *Twenty-five Years*, pp. 223–226; and L. Ethan Ellis, *Reciprocity, 1911 — A Study in Canadian-American Relations* (New Haven, 1939), p. 15. Cf. *Fitchburg Sentinel*, March 5, 1910, and *Springfield Republican* and *Boston Herald*, March 23, 1910. The Republicans retook the Congressional seat from the Democrats in November 1910. Richard B. Sherman, in "Foss of Massachusetts — Demagogue or Progressive?" *Mid-America*, 43:75–94 (April 1961), disagrees with the view that Foss's election had little if any significance as a "progressive" triumph.

to harness the energies of public and party discontents for his own political ambitions. In 1910, Joseph Walker, the Speaker of the House, emerged to assume that role.

Walker's father, Joseph H. Walker of Worcester, had been a wealthy leather-goods manufacturer and an independent Republican who in 1884 had repudiated Blaine and three years later won election to Congress, where he went his way adamantly resisting party discipline. One Congressional colleague later referred to him as among "the most stubborn, the most obdurate, the most perverse men" he had ever known.[47] His son was a chip off the old block — with a difference. Joseph Walker the younger was upright to the point of self-righteousness, independent to the point of aloofness, conservative to the point of reaction — but ambitious enough to equivocate when necessary.[48] In the General Court since 1904, representing the upper-class Boston suburb of Brookline, Walker until 1910 voted "wrong" on almost every measure associated with progressivism. He consistently opposed every measure to reduce the laboring hours of women and children, or of public employees; he opposed measures to facilitate labor organization or make strikes effective; he opposed a state pension plan. In 1906, he voted against a preferential primary for United States senators. He helped kill Robert Luce's public opinion bill in 1907. In 1909 as Speaker he refused to break a tie vote on a bill which would have required labeling convict-made goods as such. He supported the New Haven merger program from the beginning, including the absorption of street railways. He never withdrew his opposition to a federal income tax.

He took each position in turn out of seriously considered principle; he was a conservative Republican by conviction. His orthodoxy and obvious integrity won him election as president of the Republican Club in August 1907. By January 1908 he already had enough pledges from fellow legislators to assure

---

[47] James E. Watson, *As I Knew Them* (Indianapolis 1936), p. 35.
[48] Cf. sketch by Robert M. Washburn in the *Boston Evening Transcript,* September 16, 1929.

him of election to the speakership of the House in 1909.[49]
He was, in a word, very much of the stuff of which Republican
governors were made — except for that independent streak
which made him reject regularity for its own sake and led him
to seek the governorship without the usual second place apprenticeship. To achieve his objective he needed more than righteous independence.

Walker joined the ranks of the insurgents almost immediately after the 1909 elections with an announcement that
he would henceforth support direct primary proposals. The
following February he took charge of the cause of the dis-
gruntled party members against the officers of the state committee. At a "grievance meeting" of Republican legislators and
state committeemen, Walker warned the party leadership that
the public was losing confidence in the G.O.P. "Mr. Chairman," he declared, "we cannot afford to have the party candidates chosen and the party policies outlined by a few men in
private consultation." He asserted that he was referring "not
to individuals but to methods," but he denounced in strong
terms the arbitrary selection of state committee officers.

Walker's efforts to take the lead in a "progressive Republican" movement did not go smoothly. His own proposal for
direct primaries legislation, for which he dramatically left the
Speaker's chair to join the debate, met with opposition as a
"halfway measure" from insurgent Arthur Nason as well as
from the Democrats because, they argued, it required 10 per
cent of the voters in each county to petition the General Court
before the system could be set up.[50] The bill passed the House,
but without Nason's support in the Senate its failure was inevitable. (A milder bill establishing primaries by "local option"
in each legislative district did pass.) In March, Walker joined
Robert Washburn's and Norman White's anti-New Haven
forces for the first time and again left the Speaker's chair to
oppose Governor Draper's proposal to permit savings banks to

[49] *Boston Herald,* January 22, 1908.
[50] *Boston Herald,* April 17, 1910.

purchase the bonds of the Boston Railroad Holding Company.[51] He deserted them again, with many of the labor representatives, to vote for the administration's bill to allow the Holding Company to issue nontaxable preferred stock, and he remained silent while the legislature passed a bill, with almost unanimous labor support, to legalize the merger of the New Haven with the Berkshire Street Railway Company against the recommendation of the Railroad Commission. In April, the House passed a resolution calling for popular election of United States senators; reversing his earlier stand, Walker gave his support to the measure, and this time drew denunciations from many labor representatives loyal to Lodge and Crane, as well as from Washburn and White.[52] Later in the year, that sometimes insurgent pair joined Lodge in rebuking Walker for designating himself a "progressive Republican"; they charged him with disrupting the party.[53]

Walker also sabotaged the party's campaign to "educate" the public on the tariff question in order to ease the agitation over the Payne-Aldrich Act. Most insurgents had at least agreed on that much of party policy. In January, Robert Luce, an unswerving protectionist despite his "irregular" tendencies, accepted the chairmanship of a special commission to investigate the high cost of living. The agency's purpose, like its counterpart in the United States Senate headed by Senator Lodge, was to establish that the tariff had nothing significant to do with rising prices. In February, however, in the same speech in which he chided the party for "bossism," Walker voiced his doubts about the Payne-Aldrich tariff; he demanded that the Massachusetts Republicans support Taft's tariff board and press for a commission. "It seems to me," he said, "that our statesmen are not dealing quite frankly with the people when they assume to give out statistics to prove that the present tariff is just and fair and at the same time oppose establish-

[51] *Boston Herald*, March 17, 1910; see also *Springfield Repulican*, May 11, 1910.

[52] *Springfield Republican*, April 26, 1910.

[53] *Boston Herald*, August 18, 1910.

ing an unprejudiced commission to tell us the simple truth." [54] In May, after three months' cursory "investigation," the Luce commission reported that neither tariffs nor trusts significantly raised prices, and added that there was very little the government could do to restrain prices.[55] The conclusions of the Luce report were endorsed by cosigners Henry Abrahams, a Boston labor leader, and Democrat Edward F. McSweeney, William Gaston's right-hand man, but they did not deter Walker from keeping the tariff issue alive.

While insurgency underwent growing pains within the Grand Old Party, Massachusetts farmers, the old reliables of Republicanism, suddenly became rambunctious too. In many ways, their disaffection would have presented a more serious danger to Republican power than all the various insurgent challenges put together. Discontented over recent enforcement of an old law which made it a crime to sell milk below a fixed standard, and also determined to fight Boston milk contractors who obtained preferential treatment from railroads because they could ship milk by the carload, the smaller dairy farmers of Middlesex and Worcester counties organized for political action the Massachusetts Farmers' Association.[56] In their case, the Draper administration decided on mollification. From the General Court in 1910 the farmers obtained virtual nullification of the penalties for selling substandard milk. They also secured an act requiring equal treatment for less-than-carload milk shipments. But the second law backfired. The Boston & Maine and the Boston & Albany railroads equalized rates by simply raising the carload price; meanwhile, they maintained lower long-haul rates which the law did not cover because the rates applied to shipments from outside the state.

The farmers declared war, and deftly struck at the state's most vulnerable points. For thirty days in July and August, the small milk producers refused to release milk for shipment to

[54] *Boston Herald,* February 15, 1910.
[55] Robert Luce, *et al., Report of the Commission on the Cost of Living* (Boston, 1910), esp. pp. 529–533.
[56] See especially *Springfield Republican,* March 15, 19, 26, 1910.

Boston, and their spokesman declared they would hold the already beleaguered governor responsible if they failed in their objectives. "What our program is," the head of the Farmers' Association said, "we are not ready at this time to publicly announce, but . . . in our own way, at the right time, we shall hold Mr. Draper responsible for his failure to see we had the relief to which we were entitled." [57] Charging "discrimination," "railroad arrogance," and "corporate cabal," the farmers called for and received an investigation by the Interstate Commerce Commission. But the Commission's conclusion gave them no comfort: "The effect of the carload system is inevitably to create a monopoly," Chairman Charles A. Prouty conceded; "but," he added, mindful of the high cost of living, "that may be better for the Boston people." The same day, the chief of the milk marketing section of the United States Department of Agriculture called the contractor-carload system of Boston suppliers the best marketing system in the country.[58]

Although the farmers certainly did not have the strongest possible case, they had nonetheless successfully adopted the familiar language of their insurgent midwestern cousins. The administration had to act dramatically or risk the spread of anti-railroad, anti-monopoly, and inevitably anti-administration sentiment throughout the rural districts. Once more Senator Lodge intervened:

It is no doubt perfectly true [he wrote to Draper] that it is unjust and unreasonable to hold the Republican party responsible for [the railroads' action] but when men are hurt in this way and see milk coming in and displacing their own they are no longer reasonable. They . . . want to punish somebody, and the party in power is the only thing they can punish . . . If we cannot get the railroad to suspend the new rates . . . the only thing will be to call the Legislature . . . We must get relief in some way.

When Draper procrastinated, Lodge wrote again: "I think that there is more feeling among the farmers . . . than you sup-

[57] *Boston Herald*, August 3, 1910.
[58] *Springfield Republican, Boston Herald*, August 17, 18, 1910.

pose . . . It seems to me that the railroads which have put on those high rates desire an extra session of the Legislature still less [than we] . . . We ought to get them to restore the old rates for the present at least." [59]

With his re-election evidently at stake, Draper finally swung into action. Asserting that he had dealt fairly with the railroads (*too* fairly, Norman White might have observed), he attacked their officers for stupidity and bad faith. Their treatment of the farmers seemed "very shortsighted policy for any railroads of this state to pursue," he said.[60] Within a month, President Mellen of the New Haven and Boston Railroad Holding companies eased President Tuttle of the Boston & Maine out of office. On September 14, Mellen, as the new president, announced the restoration of the old milk rates — in time for the approaching state elections.[61] It was the only positive step which the G.O.P. leadership took to avert defeat that fall.

IV

Republican leaders looked forward to the elections of 1910 with great trepidation. Intraparty conflicts everywhere had overshadowed the traditional rivalry between the two major parties. Throughout the summer the news from other states had told of disaster for regular party organizations. President Taft had endorsed the old guard's declaration of war on insurgency and had thrown the full weight of his patronage into the purge. He succeeded only in confirming insurgent opposition within his party. June primaries in Iowa produced a complete victory for anti-administration Republicans. The same news came from Kansas at the beginning of August. In California, the insurgent Roosevelt-Lincoln League swept the Republican ticket. And in September, the roof fell in: insurgents triumphed in Wisconsin, Michigan, and Washington, while in

[59] Lodge to Draper, August 6 and 13, 1910; see also Lodge to Draper, August 11, 1910, and Draper to Lodge, August 15 and September 5, 1910 (all in Lodge MSS).
[60] *Boston Herald,* August 17, 1910.
[61] *Ibid.,* September 14, 1910.

the early Maine elections the Democrats elected a senator for the first time in forty years. Robert Bass's victory in New Hampshire further warned Massachusetts Republicans of the appeal insurgency had in the East.

Many Republicans had held out hope that Theodore Roosevelt, the returned lion hunter, would reunite the party. But the ex-President had his own reasons for disliking Taft, a good many of them quite unrelated to reform issues. He did not ally himself with the insurgents, but neither did he repudiate their use of him as their champion against Taft. In fear of a Democratic victory, he made a half-hearted effort at rebuilding support for the administration. But, for whatever he could or would do about it, he became the principal focus of insurgency within the Republican party. He did even more. He gave heart and publicity to that minority of reformers in the country who had visions of a great new nation inspired by the Golden Rule and reorganized along "scientific" lines to make the most efficient as well as the most humane use of the nation's resources. In a midsummer tour through the West, Roosevelt expounded his "New Nationalism." His program probably had considerably less support than he did personally as an alternative to Taft. When he spoke of restraints upon the judiciary and of submitting the use of private property to the test of the national interest, he sent shivers up and down the spines of insurgents back East; when he spoke of consolidating industry under the regulation of powerful federal commissions he gave pause to the individualist-minded westerners. But at all times he excited bright expectations. He made a reconstructed society seem an imminent reality. And he made the insurgents appear the heralds of the new order to come.

Against this backdrop, Massachusetts insurgency appeared pale and myopic. While reformers elsewhere earnestly debated plans for the fulfillment of the promise of American life, chewed epigrams like "concentration, cooperation, and control," whipped up a semi-revivalist spirit and called on the

American people to harken to "the new day of spiritual awakening" when the voice of the people would indeed be the voice of God,[62] Joseph Walker labored, in the name of "progressive Republicanism" in Massachusetts, to include a proposal for a tariff commission in the Republican platform of 1910. The state committee had sought to squelch every man who had "any insurgency virus in his veins,"[63] but under the circumstances Lodge and Crane were happy to bow to Walker's wishes. Walker himself wrote the entire tariff plank.[64]

When the state convention met, the party presented a picture of perfect harmony. With a tactful genuflection to the party's restive element, the state committee gave the chairmanship to Robert Luce, who began his address to the convention: "The peculiarity of this campaign is that there are no vital issues." Luce crooned over Republican progressivism and party unity. There are no standpatters and no insurgents in Massachusetts, he said; just Republicans. "There is no insurgency in Massachusetts worth the name," he went on, "because there is no reason for insurgency." "Most of the measures that divide our brothers in other states," he remarked, "are already part of Massachusetts law." He then read off the long list of progressive measures which other states were fighting for but

[62] From Herbert Croly's *The Promise of American Life* (New York, 1909), Charles R. Van Hise's *Concentration and Control* (New York, 1912), and William A. White's *The Old Order Changeth* (New York, 1910), p. 253, and *A Certain Rich Man* (New York, 1909), p. 326.

[63] H. P. Field to Lodge, September 26, 1910 (Lodge MSS). Field was chairman of the executive committee.

[64] The plank called for "a permanent, independent, expert tariff commission . . . to discover and report to Congress from time to time such facts and statistics as will enable Congress to amend the tariff law intelligently and scientifically according to the principle of protection"; it recommended in addition a change in Congressional rules "to make practicable the amendment of the tariff, one schedule at a time." There is information on Walker's bid for support from party leaders in letters and clippings held by Walker's son, Mr. George Walker of Concord, Massachusetts (Walker MSS). In addition see John Candler Cobb of the National Tariff Commission Association to Taft, October 7 and 11, 1910, Cobb to Crane, October 4, 1910, and Taft to Cobb, October 8, 1910 (Taft MSS); and Lodge to Brooks Adams, October 13, 1910 (Lodge MSS).

which Massachusetts had achieved "without blare of trumpets." In an ecstatic conclusion, Luce exclaimed, "We have the best governed state in the land." [65]

Luce may well have stated the condition of Massachusetts government correctly, but he missed the point of much of the intraparty rebellion, to say nothing of the general disquietude. In the first place, insurgency filled a popular need for *action* to keep pace with the rapid metamorphosis of the society; yet, except for the tariff commission — a dubious offering for a state platform — Luce's party offered absolutely nothing new. Secondly, even granting Massachusetts' advanced position on matters which concerned progressives, it was exceedingly impolitic (if nothing else) to suggest that the state had gone far enough. The proliferation of "voluntary associations" (that is, holding companies in transparent disguise) which evaded existing state controls — to mention only one growing problem that Luce ignored — had already suggested to many that the state had to overhaul its public service commissions to meet the transformation in the character of modern business. Even Luce had to acknowledge — his only concession — that the state income tax was inadequately drawn (though he justifiably boasted that at least the state *had* an income tax which progressives elsewhere still fought for); he might have noted in addition the need for a thorough tax reform. Luce had *nothing* to say about labor.

Finally, Luce and the Republicans failed to recognize that insurgency, at large as well as within the party, began and continued very much as an *ad hominem* assault on the old guard. When the convention officially endorsed Senators Lodge and Crane, and then renominated Eben Draper and Louis Frothingham to head the state ticket a third time, it made irrelevant all that Luce had said about the general agreement between the aims of the progressives and the achievements of Massachusetts. Consequently, the Republicans in Massachusetts went into November 1910 leading with their chins.

[65] *Springfield Republican,* October 7, 1910.

CHAPTER TEN

FOSS—AND MUCH FUSS

I need hardly say how earnestly I hope for Frothingham's success. It seems to me that when the Progressives select Foss as a champion they secure the very embodiment in politics of everything that they profess to be most against in the abstract.

Theodore Roosevelt*

$\mathbf{F}$ROM 1910 to 1913, the progressive movement swept toward a climax with the election of Woodrow Wilson and the inauguration of a program that went far to meet the demands of bipartisan reform elements throughout the country. Wilson's course had been prepared before he entered the Presidency. More than a decade of state reform programs, four years of Congressional insurgency, a series of investigations and prosecutions of "trusts," continued high prices, outbreaks of labor violence, and the "respectability" that Theodore Roosevelt gave to reform, had all helped set the mood. The public had been further conditioned by a profusion of reform literature which heralded the dawn of a New Era and beckoned Americans to respond to the New Competition and the New Immigration with a New Nationalism, a New Democracy, and a New Freedom. Those were the pinnacle years of the Progressive Era.

During those years Massachusetts, too, experienced a quickening of the reform tempo. Reform, however, followed an old vein; it represented no such striking departure from old political habits as the progressive movement signified in other states. To protect child and female labor, to provide in addition minimal protection for male workers, to regulate public service corporations, to safeguard democratic procedures — such acts in Massachusetts meant only the extension of activities long accepted there as normal governmental functions. This is not

* To Charles G. Washburn, October 27, 1911 (C. G. Washburn MSS).

to say that the reforms were not themselves "progressive," as the word was customarily applied at the time. But it is to say that in Massachusetts they derived from no purposeful, insurgent movement, as such reforms generally did elsewhere.

Republican insurgency meanwhile continued in sporadic fashion, culminating in the organization of the Massachusetts Progressive party in August 1912. But for the most part, the insurgent factions failed to rise above the level of court rebels seeking to displace the old guard. Certainly they took no direct note of the social forces which remained essentially outside the political arena, namely, immigrants and wage earners. Indeed, few of those who joined the third party in 1912 had had anything to do with even the more conventional reform or social justice causes. Until Theodore Roosevelt announced his candidacy for the Presidency as a Progressive, Republican rebels had found no issue or objective to unite any significant number of them. The new party attracted a wide range of dissidents, from Irish-American Republicans, who resented the snubs they customarily received in their chosen party, to militant nativists reminiscent of the American Protective Association. Some felt a simple loyalty to Roosevelt, while others had personal feuds to settle with particular party leaders. There were several, of course, who, like Roosevelt, had reform as well as political or personal reasons for "going Progressive," but this contingent was inconsequential. The Progressives conspicuously failed to lure veteran reformers like Louis Brandeis and Joseph Eastman into the party. The leading Republican reformers — Luce, Walker, Washburn, Ross — remained with the G.O.P. throughout the Battle of the Bull Moose at Armageddon, 1912.[1]

---

[1] In 1912, Ross did accept the Progressive party's endorsement in addition to his Republican nomination. Walker bolted to the Progressives in 1913 in protest against the G.O.P. caucus selection of Congressman John W. Weeks to succeed Murray Crane in the Senate. In 1912, however, Walker supported Taft for the Republican nomination against Roosevelt, and later that year suffered defeat as standard bearer for the regular Republican state ticket.

In sum, between 1910 and 1913 Massachusetts continued to enjoy progressive reform while experiencing no new departure in politics. Progressive Republican insurgency proved a sterile codling. The socially insurgent labor and immigrant groups remained essentially subordinated as before. And the Democratic party continued to serve primarily as a vehicle for the personal ambitions of wealthy men: specifically, in these years, Eugene Foss.

I

Republican schisms coupled with the inadequacies of insurgency in 1910 combined to give the Democrats their opportunity to exploit the public's restive mood. With victory a strong possibility, Democratic politicians elbowed ferociously for position. John F. Fitzgerald's return to office had made the Boston Democracy once more a power to be considered. Rumors flew early in the year that James Vahey, who had never been popular with the Bostonians, was to be dumped. ("No matter what you hear from other sources," confided one of Lodge's lieutenants, "you may rest assured that Vahey is not to be the [Democratic] candidate.")[2] Vahey himself had begun muttering that if the party refused him a third try after his fine run in 1909, his friends would cut the ticket.[3] Meanwhile, the state committee, from Chairman Fred J. MacLeod down, had made it clear by summer that it favored the nomination of Eugene Foss.

Eugene Noble Foss, manufacturer, speculator, and tariff crusader, had given up his struggle to win prominence in the Republican party and in 1909 had bought his way onto the Democratic state ticket as a candidate for lieutenant governor. His candidacy had provided Vahey's second campaign with almost $40,000, or more than 95 per cent of all Democratic

---

[2] A. E. Cox to Lodge, April 30, 1910 (Lodge MSS).
[3] See C. S. Groves (Executive Secretary of the Republican State Committee) to Lodge, May 24, 1910 (Lodge MSS).

campaign expenditures reported that year.[4] But if Foss had been an asset to the Democrats otherwise, it could only have been because his single-minded campaigns for tariff revision had made him a symbol of reform — even in the face of his opposition to most of the major reforms then agitated by the Democracy. Foss did not even renounce his Republicanism during the 1909 campaign. "I still insist," he had told his campaign audience, "that in view of the pledges of the Republican party in behalf of reciprocity and tariff reform, and of the manner in which these pledges have been persistently betrayed . . . the true situation is not that I and the men who think as I do have abandoned the party, but that our party has deserted us." (Foss took with him into the Democratic party no active political following.) Failing to foresee that when his pet reform, reciprocity, came up for Senate approval in late 1910 the western insurgents would oppose it, Foss had hailed them as "the greatest leaders of the Republican party" who had taken the course of "consistency and progress." "In the West," he had said, "we reform Republicans would have some place in the party." But in Massachusetts, "there is no place for us. And we must go where we can." [5]

The tariff aside, Foss was a poor measure of a reformer. To be sure, like most political "outs" at the time, he had long stood for popular election of senators and some other popular government measures. But like Henry Whitney, he was himself a conspicuous example of the kind of financial manipulators who had done so much to incite criticism of the economic system. Although he harbored a personal hostility to Eben Draper (with whom he appears to have had business dealings in the 1890's)[6] and would not support the Governor's Railroad Holding Company bill, he had called the New Haven–Boston &

[4] Foss personally signed checks made out to the Democratic State Committee totaling $21,000, and the "Foss Campaign Committee" reported a contribution to the state committee of $18,757, which presumably constituted aggregate contributions from Foss supporters as well as Foss's own money. *Springfield Republican*, December 3, 1909.

[5] Quoted in Hennessy, *Twenty-five Years*, pp. 216–217.

[6] See Lodge to Albert Clarke, December 4, 1910 (Lodge MSS).

Maine merger "the greatest step that has been taken for a generation toward the advancement of the commercial and business interests of Boston and New England." [7] During the Payne-Aldrich debate he had joined with the Boston Chamber of Commerce in denouncing Taft's proposal for a 2 per cent corporation tax.[8] But, most pertinent to the campaign of 1909, candidate Foss had signed a petition to Governor Draper which urged him to veto the new eight-hour bill, and he had also gone on record against the 54-hour bill. He thus had undermined the Democrats' strongest reform argument against the Republican administration.[9]

Whatever his shortcomings as a reformer in the reform-conscious year of 1910, Foss became an "obvious" candidate for the Democratic nomination by virtue of his wealth and his striking victory in the special Congressional election in March that year. Although he continued to assert that he would "not lift a finger" to take the nomination away from Vahey, he spent a large part of his brief Congressional term making speeches throughout New England, and his statement that he was not a candidate for re-election to Congress that fall reinforced the suspicions of his gubernatorial ambitions; consequently, his following grew. In addition to the state committee, before the end of the summer Foss obtained the support of Mayor Fitzgerald of Boston and even of the "radical" leaders George Fred Williams and E. Gerry Brown.

Meanwhile, a "Stop Foss" movement developed. Labor leaders lined up behind Vahey. They denounced Foss for his op-

[7] *Boston Herald,* June 15, 1907.

[8] See signed petition enclosed in J. S. Lawrence to George Meyer, June 25, 1909 (Meyer MSS).

[9] For all his money, his supposed interparty popularity, and the ostensible appeal of the tariff issue, Foss had run behind Vahey by more than 2000 votes in 1909, and he had lost to his colorless Republican opponent, Louis Frothingham, by about the same margin as Vahey had trailed Draper. Although it was not unusual for the second-place candidate to poll fewer votes than the gubernatorial candidate, in 1905 — when the tariff was more clearly the central issue of the campaign — Henry Whitney ran several thousand votes ahead of his ticket as Democratic candidate for lieutenant governor.

position to the eight-hour bill, and for his votes in Congress against all labor measures. They pointed out, quite accurately, that Foss had behaved in Congress on almost all issues like an orthodox Republican. At the same time, self-designated "good government" forces headed by ex-Governor William Douglas rallied behind Charles S. Hamlin, who finally announced his "willingness to accept" the nomination if offered. Douglas and others attempted to "buy off" Vahey for Hamlin. Lucius Tuttle, ousted president of the Boston & Maine, was among those approached to contribute to a fund of $10,000 to compensate Vahey for the costs of his two campaigns. Hamlin, however, typically refused to make any deals; he urged Vahey to withdraw "naturally" and earn his good will.[10]

Although throughout the summer Foss's nomination appeared certain, just before the convention met, Fitzgerald withdrew his support, claiming that Foss could not win without the support of labor. Foss countered that "Honey Fitz" was piqued because he had refused to let the Boston mayor direct the use of campaign funds in the city. Fitzgerald's move set off a series of countermoves by rival city leaders, like Martin Lomasney, who hoped to hold the balance of power in the nomination while staying on whatever side was opposed to Fitzgerald. The situation was thus highly fluid when party leaders converged on Boston "to name a governor."

The state convention met at Faneuil Hall on the hottest October 6 on record. Nearly 1000 delegates and about as many spectators and police jostled each other in the ancient little convention hall. Tempers ran with the weather, and proceedings frequently approximated a brawl. Fists flew; chairs and heads were smashed. Several members of the state committee were seen hurtling from the platform at various intervals in the program.

Hamlin and Vahey each claimed at the outset about 200 pledged delegates; Foss backers claimed most of the unpledged winners of the district caucuses. To win, a candidate needed

[10] Hamlin Diary entries for August 15, 17, and 29, 1910 (Hamlin MSS).

a majority of the votes cast. On the first ballot, with 496 needed, Foss led Vahey and Hamlin with 382 to 302 and 295, in that order. By prearrangement, Hamlin attempted to swing his support to Vahey, but about 50 deserted to Foss, about another 125 appeared to evaporate, and 20 stuck fast to Hamlin. That left Foss 6 short of a majority of the votes cast, and Vahey 13 behind Foss. A free-for-all broke out when the results were announced. A deadlock followed.

Since the party managers believed the nominations had to be registered with the Secretary of State by the next afternoon — actually they erred by forty-eight hours — the convention adjourned after it had accepted a dummy nomination and set up a Committee of Five (which was to pick its own fifth member) to select a gubernatorial candidate. Both Foss and Vahey withdrew their candidacy, but the committee apparently recognized only Vahey's declination. The four-man group stalled over the choice of a fifth, and then remained evenly divided between Eugene Foss and Charles Hamlin. The Hamlin-Vahey men charged Foss with Republicanism and unwillingness to foster a program of genuine social reform. Foss men accused Hamlin of apostasy for supporting James Storrow against Fitzgerald in the Boston mayoralty, and (of all things) serving as legal advisor to the Boston & Maine Railroad. (The latter charge came from George Fred Williams, who somehow managed to overlook Foss's membership on the Boston & Maine's board of directors.)

After a week of this nonsense, Foss announced he would run anyway under his own name. "I am not seeking to be Governor of Massachusetts," he said, "but I do stand for a principle . . . I want all tariff barriers between the United States and Canada removed." He concluded by demanding the Democratic nomination. Chairman MacLeod then called the state committee into emergency session and over the vehement protests of the Hamlin men ordered a poll of the party delegates. The committee mailed special delivery letters with ballots and return-addressed special delivery envelopes enclosed. A few days later, the committee announced that Foss had won a bare majority of one, and a plurality over Hamlin of eleven. Though his supporters protested that the whole proceeding was illegal, Hamlin secured Foss's nomination by withdrawing his own name.[11]

Through the genius of State Chairman Fred MacLeod and the magic of Foss's money, the Democrats closed ranks behind their nominee. The state committee gave the second-place nomination to a noncontroversial politician named Cassidy who had not appeared on the state scene before, so that Foss had the stage to himself. Every major figure in the party, including William Douglas, took to the stump.

Leaving the labor interests to take care of Draper, Foss himself turned his guns on Senator Lodge. It was an especially deft stroke because Lodge symbolized "standpattism" exactly as Foss symbolized reform. He charged the elder senator with using money to control the state legislature, and with being the principal obstacle in the Senate to Canadian reciprocity. He promised a conservative alternative to the "boss-dominated" Republican party. He appealed to the anti-Lodge followers of Butler Ames by rehashing the campaigns of Greenbacker Ben Butler and the more recent Shaw-Gardner feud. He virtually turned the gubernatorial contest into one between himself and Lodge, at a time when Lodge had hit the nadir of his popularity in the state.

The Republicans brought Theodore Roosevelt into the campaign to take the standpat stigma off Draper. Roosevelt attempted to make Draper out to be a "progressive" for recommending that the legislature substitute a "commission of experts" on state lands and harbors for the traditional legislative logrolling on the appropriation and allocation of funds. (Roosevelt called this achievement "a first class instance of progressive legislation.")[12] But for the most part, Roosevelt

---

[11] This account of the proceedings is taken from the Boston daily newspapers.
[12] *Boston Herald*, September 4, 1910.

concentrated on depicting 'Gene Foss as a man who hoped to win office "by sheer effrontery and the power of Money" which he had earned through speculation,[13] while Lodge and Congressman Gardner similarly assailed the renegade for corrupting politics with his money.

In the end, Foss won a tremendous personal triumph. He ran ahead of his adopted party on the Democratic ticket alone, and compiled 21,000 more votes under his own name. (Many of those votes must have come from Republicans like one E. Peabody Gerry, who wrote to Lodge: "I . . . will gladly support you, but Mr. Foss' name is synonymous with Canadian Reciprocity.")[14] Foss beat Draper by 34,000 votes, with 52 per cent of the total vote, 5 per cent of which "belonged" to him but not his party. He captured cities like Taunton, Northampton, and Worcester which had not gone for a Democratic gubernatorial candidate in more than twenty years. Meanwhile, the Democracy failed to win any other state offices; Frothingham was re-elected lieutenant governor by the same margin (8,000) as in 1909. And the party failed to increase its representation in Congress, although Democratic candidates did come within a thousand votes of taking four additional seats.

Republican losses in Massachusetts were nevertheless quite substantial, as they were in many states throughout the country in 1910. In the General Court, the G.O.P. gave up 44 seats in the House and 8 in the Senate. Although the Democrats remained 15 seats short of control of the legislature, it was clear that a coalition of "irregular" Republicans and Democrats could prevail on any issue. In particular, the increased Democratic minority meant the certainty of reform legislation which had teetered on the brink of passage for several years.

II

In Eugene Foss, reformers found a governor whose opportunism served their cause well. His first inaugural address read

---

[13] *Ibid.*, October 22, 1910.
[14] Gerry to Lodge, November 6, 1910 (Lodge MSS).

like a progressive manifesto — though it was remarkable at least as much because it represented an about-face for him on several important issues. For example, his denunciation of Draper's Railroad Holding Company Act as legalizing "some of the most objectionable corporate methods" thoroughly exasperated those like Representative Washburn who recalled Foss's earlier endorsement of the New Haven's methods. ("Oh, I guess I won't discuss it," Washburn told reporters, "say anything you like.") Foss was perhaps consistent in his demand that the state investigate the "financial subterfuge" of all holding companies and voluntary associations, though it was surprising that an attack on modern business techniques should come from one whose own business methods had notoriously deviated from the traditional. His reference to excessive campaign expenses brought down the house, and he did not even seem to catch the joke on himself. He hinted at minimum wage legislation, limitations on court injunctions in labor disputes, workmen's compensation, and further statutory limitation of working hours for women and children, again in contradiction to his earlier attitude toward labor. Much more in his style was his pledge to run the state "along well established business lines, such as prevail in any great corporation." [15]

When ultimately faced with the necessity for action, Foss resisted many of the labor legislators' demands and accepted others reluctantly; twice he vetoed a bill to permit strikers to picket and to persuade "peacefully" other workers to join them, and he opposed as too radical several other labor measures including the 54-hour bill which he ultimately signed. Nor did he entirely please the Public Franchise League with his proposals to rehabilitate the dying New Haven–Boston & Maine merger. In addition, his vetoes of a bill to give tenure to public school teachers and of another to raise teachers' salaries did not fit the progressive category; nor did his promotion of a bill which helped enhance the value of his own

[15] *Boston Herald,* January 6, 1911.

real estate investments. His interests as a businessman and employer frequently prevailed over his political opportunism.

Yet Foss always understood that his political fortunes depended on his catering to the public's mood for action. With his usual flamboyance, he fed, just as he fed upon, that mood. In the process, he trod upon Republican and Democratic toes with about equal frequency — a maverick trait which helped re-elect him twice, even while his adopted party suffered reverses in its still premature surge toward ascendancy.

During Foss's three-year administration, considerable reform legislation passed which, in quantity and quality, compared favorably with anything achieved elsewhere in the country. To that extent, Massachusetts may be said to have caught the spirit of change which was sweeping the country. Robert Luce's direct primary bill for all state legislators finally became law, as did his public opinion bill. Another primary law gave voters an opportunity to instruct delegates to the national party conventions on their choice for presidential nomination. The state also established a Public Service Commission with greater power over railroad rates than the superseded Railroad Commission had had.[16] Thomas Hisgen's antimonopoly bill, which prohibited discriminatory pricing tactics by producers and distributors, was at last approved. In addition, the legislature passed an elaborate law to regulate the construction of multiple-resident housing in towns (subject to approval by a referendum in each town). By far the greater number of reform bills made labor the chief beneficiary. The 54-hour and eight-hour bills, which had failed during the Draper administration, readily passed in 1911.[17] The General Court also refashioned the employers' liability laws and set up a workmen's

---

[16] See J. B. Eastman, "The Public Service Commission of Massachusetts," *Quarterly Journal of Economics,* 27:699–707 (August 1913).

[17] A major clause of the Eight-Hour Act to which Draper had objected in his veto messages was declared unconstitutional in an advisory opinion by the state supreme court before passage in 1911, and was omitted; the language of the law, however, was changed so that employers were forbidden to *permit* workers more than eight hours labor. See MBSL, *Labor Bulletin,* No. 84 (Boston, October 1911), pp. 103–104.

compensation system such as other states already had, while it pioneered in setting a minimum wage standard for women and minors by founding a minimum wage commission. Labor union leaders won their long struggle for jury trials for alleged violations of strike injunctions, as well as the right to impose fines on members for disciplinary purposes.[18]

As during Curtis Guild's administration, the Foss years were good ones for reform within an old tradition. They represented as yet no significant shift in the power structure of the state. No radical or quasi-radical group took control to force social or moral reconstruction on the Commonwealth; no dominating vested interests, either economic or political, were reduced; no interests-on-the-make, ethnic or political, gained ascendancy. Some of the labor legislation, in conceding recognition of the legitimate role of unions, foretold organized labor's rise to the councils of policy making in future years. But, as yet, the old order in Massachusetts remained intact.

III

The Democrats' election victory in 1910 provided Republican insurgents with ammunition for use against the incumbent leadership. Their best opportunity to strike at the old guard came almost at once. Henry Cabot Lodge's Senate term had expired, and the new legislature which would meet in January 1911 would determine his fate. The Republican margin was so narrow, it would require less than a dozen Republican defectors to unseat Lodge. ("A number of persons of moderate size have discovered that a narrow margin gives them importance," Lodge complained to his colleague, Elihu Root.)[19] Since many of the Republicans elected to the General Court had declared their "independence" of Lodge during their campaign, Lodge knew that there was great danger of defections (though he wrote bravely to Roosevelt: "unless they go in and deliberately

---

[18] See MBSL, "Labor Legislation in Massachusetts, 1911," *Labor Bulletin,* No. 84, and "Labor Legislation in Massachusetts, 1912," *Labor Bulletin,* No. 92 (Boston, June 1912).

[19] Lodge to Root, November 29, 1910, quoted in Garraty, p. 279.

buy members of the Legislature — which is difficult and dangerous in this State . . . I shall be re-elected").[20] Butler Ames alone might tie up enough votes from Essex County to cause a deadlock. That would encourage all those who hoped to dump Lodge — a contingent not at all confined to reformers. The staunchly standpat *Worcester Evening Gazette,* for example, smitten by the defeat of its favorite son, Congressman Charles G. Washburn, exclaimed: "Lodge is a millstone on the neck of the party and should be allowed to retire as gracefully as may be. The party cannot carry him longer." [21]

At first Lodge could not even be sure of Murray Crane's support. Their relationship, never more than polite, had not been made warmer by their conflict over the Taft nomination in 1908. After the first few months of Taft's administration, moreover, it was Crane, not Lodge, who became Taft's confidant,[22] and it is possible there were bad feelings between them because of it. Lodge did not conceal his bitterness toward Taft, at least from his own friends, and as early as March 1910 expressed his enthusiasm over the possibility that Roosevelt might be a candidate for President again in 1912.[23] Although no existing Lodge letter directly indicates hostility toward Crane, some letters to him by his own confidants are suggestive. ("By the way, when is the Junior Senator going to publish

---

[20] Lodge to Roosevelt, November 13, 1910, in *Correspondence,* II, 394–398.

[21] *Worcester Evening Gazette,* November 9, 1910. Washburn, the elder brother of state legislator Robert M. Washburn, was somewhat to the right of Lodge in political philosophy. The *Gazette* tried to boom Washburn for Lodge's seat.

[22] Before his inauguration, Taft privately referred to Crane as "a mole," but by July 1910 he was thanking the Senator for standing by him as his chief aide during the 61st Congress, and soon after was writing to him as "My dear old Murray." See typescript of a paragraph from a Taft letter, probably to Roosevelt and forwarded to Lodge for his private enjoyment, dated January 4, 1909 (Lodge MSS); and Taft to Crane, July 14, 1910, and August 30, 1911 (Crane MSS).

[23] Lodge wrote in March 1910: "The feeling that is arising in the country in regard to Theodore is indescribable . . . As it looks today, his nomination for the Presidency in 1912 is inevitable — nothing can prevent it — and if he is nominated, nothing can defeat him." To W. S. Bigelow, March 25, 1910 (Lodge MSS). See also Garraty, pp. 274–276.

his public speeches?" wrote J. Otis Wardwell, in a wry allusion to Crane's taciturnity. "Now I have told you I would be good for a year and a half and not mention his name to anyone. I haven't even to you. Please note that.")[24] Lodge must have become just a bit apprehensive when Congressman John W. Weeks stated he would be a candidate if it appeared Lodge could not make it. Weeks, a wealthy banker from Newton who had been brought into politics by State Chairman Fred Hatfield, an ex-mayor of Newton, was generally regarded as aligned with the Crane section of the party. It must have been with some jubilation, therefore, that Lodge welcomed Crane to Boston in the second week of November to keep Republicans in line. "My good colleague has come on here and taken hold of things," Lodge wrote to Henry Lee Higginson, "and I believe I am going to be re-elected again." [25]

Lodge won his re-election with little to spare. He doubted the outcome "up to the last minute." [26] He failed of a majority on the first ballot, and won on the second by only five votes (including two Democrats).

Yet, from the viewpoint of those who looked for a reform movement or even a limited political challenge to the old-line leaders of the Republican party, what was most significant about the election was not Lodge's close call but the failure of most of the outspokenly rebellious elements in the party to stand against the senior senator. Robert Washburn and Norman White became Lodge's chief aides within the General Court. Most of the labor representatives outside of Essex County followed the lead of Samuel Ross whose loyalty Lodge had been assured of more than a year in advance,[27] despite a resolution by the New Bedford Central Labor Union which called on Ross, Andrew Doyle, and other Bristol County

[24] Wardwell to Lodge, December 20, 1909 (Lodge MSS). See also W. S. Bigelow to Lodge, June 20, 1916, in which he called Crane "that little, burrowing, bat-eared demagogue" (also Lodge MSS).

[25] Lodge to Higginson, November 11, 1910 (ibid.).

[26] Lodge to Brooks Adams, January 21, 1911 (ibid.).

[27] J. O. Wardwell to Lodge, September 23, 1909 (ibid.).

Republicans to oppose Lodge.[28] Robert Luce, no longer in the General Court but getting ready to announce his candidacy for lieutenant governor, also supported Lodge (though it may have required a minor *quid pro quo*).[29]

One difficulty was the inability of anti-Lodge men to find a suitable candidate of their own. Arthur Nason spearheaded the campaign for Butler Ames, but, in paying his debt to the Lowell congressman, the most consistently progressive man in the General Court helped destroy any possibility of presenting a reform candidate against Lodge. When they had to choose between Lodge and Ames, most Massachusetts reformers, especially those of the genteel set, preferred Lodge. At the same time, a second anti-Lodge Republican in the field could hardly have a chance of winning.

Aside from ex-Governor Curtis Guild, whose obligations to Lodge removed him from contention, the one man who might have united reformers and others disinclined to line up behind Lodge was Speaker Joseph Walker. Walker, however, announced immediately after the November elections that he sought only re-election as Speaker, and that his ultimate ambition lay in the gubernatorial nomination the next fall.[30] His hold on the speakership, meanwhile, was as tenuous as Lodge's on his Senate seat. Many Republicans resented Walker's apparent opportunism during the past year, while the Democrats displayed an extraordinary degree of unity in backing Martin Lomasney for the position. In order to defeat Lomasney, Walker, with Norman White acting as floor leader, pushed

[28] F. C. Dumaine, a railroad man and financier actively working for Lodge, told Lodge after his election that Ross had had to impress his constituents that he was "uncommitted," but had let the "right" people know he intended to vote for Lodge all along. Dumaine to Lodge, February 21, 1911 (Lodge MSS).

[29] In the A. P. Gardner file of the Lodge MSS, which is given over to the 1910–11 Senate campaign, there is an undated note from Murray Crane to Lodge urging Lodge to place an order with Luce's news clipping company — very likely to help persuade Luce to use his influence with friends in the legislature. "Please telephone Capt. Gardner at once, that Norman White should order the clippings from Mr. Luce, assume all the responsibility, and be prepared to so state in case of any criticism," Crane wrote.

[30] *Springfield Republican*, November 8, 1910.

through a new rule requiring open balloting so that anti-Walker Republicans would have to answer to charges of irregularity if they voted against him.[31] Throughout the Lodge fight, Walker cooperated fully with White and Congressman Gardner in arranging choice committee appointments for shilly-shallying legislators, to "compensate" them for the possible bad effect a vote for Lodge might have with their constituents. Walker ultimately made the nominating speech for Lodge in the Republican caucus.[32]

In addition to White, Walker, and his Senate colleague, Lodge received aid from unexpected quarters. Probably no one damaged the cause of the anti-Lodge Republicans quite so much as Eugene Foss. The Governor-elect responded to his triumph like the man in the fable who "killed seven with one blow" and sought his townsmen's awe and acclaim as a giant killer. Asserting that his election represented a repudiation of Lodge, Foss set out by automobile on a wild barnstorming tour in which he all but suggested that he be allowed to choose Lodge's successor. If Foss hoped to build a great swell to buoy up anti-Lodge Republicans who feared acting alone, he achieved exactly the opposite effect.

"The man is clean daft," expostulated Charles Francis Adams. "As you very well know," the old Mugwump wrote to his long-standing enemy, "there has for a long time been very little political sympathy between you and me. Our antagonism has been nearly complete. I am, however, already so tired, not to say disgusted with the Gyrations, Pronunciamentoes [sic] and Proclamations of our extraordinary Governor-elect that I wish to say, if it is in any way in my power . . . to forward

[31] *Boston Herald,* January 4, 1911.

[32] The Gardner file in the Lodge MSS contains several letters which discuss appointments Walker should, and did, make to mollify troubled legislators. After his election, Lodge wrote to Walker, "I am overwhelmed with telegrams and letters but I cannot let the day pass without writing to you to thank you most warmly for all you have done for me and for your support which has been of such great value to me" (January 19, 1911).

your re-election to the Senate, you have but to command me." [33] Adams was not alone among the old Mugwumps who found Foss harder to take than their traditional antagonist. "It is a rather curious fact," wrote Democrat Godfrey Cabot, "that among the many personal friends I have, who have in times past, made it rather a fad to criticize you, there is only one who has expressed his wish that you should lose this fight and there are a great many who . . . hope that you will win." [34] If there were many Republican legislators who feared unpopularity if they voted for Lodge, but who wished they could avoid embarrassing their position with the party leaders, Foss gave them their opportunity. "Foss is the reason they can assign for voting for you," former Senator William E. Chandler wrote to Lodge; and Senator Elihu Root observed, "No Republican can persist in voting against you . . . without advertising himself as submitting to that . . . blatant renegade." ("A bumptious ass Foss is! Bounder . . . A disgusting bounder!") [35]

In addition to demoralizing the anti-Lodge cause in the Republican party, Foss discouraged every Democrat who might have had a chance to draw the necessary Republican votes for election. ("We got a gold brick," James Vahey wearily confided to Joseph Walker.) [36] William Gaston was the leading candidate, but on December 21 he withdrew, charging that Foss had ruined the chances of anyone winning *except*

[33] Adams to Lodge, November 25, 1910. This was one of two letters from Adams written on the same date and the same theme. See also another dated November 30, 1910 (Lodge MSS).

[34] Cabot to Lodge, December 21, 1910 (*ibid.*). Lodge let Cabot persuade himself that Lodge had had nothing to do with the Boston Railroad Holding Company bill in 1909, and even permitted him to publish a letter in the *Boston Common* in which he asked rhetorically, "Did Senator Lodge directly or indirectly assist in passing this measure?" — although Cabot had first asked Lodge if the letter contained anything inaccurate. See Cabot to Lodge, November 26, 1910.

[35] Chandler to Lodge, November 28, 1910 and Root to Lodge, November 27, 1910 (Lodge MSS). Lodge agreed that things were "looking much better owing to Foss's attacks." Lodge to Chandler, November 29, 1910.

[36] Related in A. E. Cox to Lodge, December 27, 1910 (Lodge MSS).

Lodge.[37] Foss gave no encouragement to Vahey, Hamlin, Whitney, or other well-known Democrats who were available though undeclared candidates. By January Whitney went over to Lodge, arguing that no one would be able to aid reciprocity in the Senate more than he.[38] In the end, the Democrats accepted as their candidate one Sherman L. Whipple, a friend of Foss's and a corporation lawyer who had frequently appeared in court against labor, and whose most conspicuous recent appearance had been as chief lawyer for the Boston milk contractors in their unpopular fight against the dairy farmers. ("Verily," observed the *Boston Herald*, "the Democracy . . . must have been at some pains to pick out so valorous a champion of the 'peepul' as Mr. Whipple.")[39]

Throughout most of his motorized circus, Foss enjoyed the company of four or five dissident Republicans who also sought Lodge's defeat. They included a former labor legislator from Boston who had run poorly in the 1910 open caucuses for nomination to Congress, a former mayor of Cambridge, at least one other defeated and officeless politician of little renown, and Arthur Nason himself. That was about the measure of Republican insurgency. Beyond them there were some, like Representative Russell A. Wood of Cambridge, who sought to rally anti-Lodge sentiment away from the Nason-Ames axis. Wood persuaded few others besides his colleague and townsman, Russell Crane. Significantly, except for Wood's support of some "popular government" measures like woman suffrage, neither Wood nor Crane had revealed any conspicuously insurgent tendencies before the Lodge fight. They were both militantly antilabor, had supported each detail of the New

[37] *Boston Herald*, December 22, 1910. See also G. H. Doty to Lodge, December 7, 1910: "I had the good fortune to sit next to Mr. Gaston last night at dinner, and may say to you confidentially that Mr. Foss's campaign against you is doing more to seat you . . . than anything that could possibly have been done." Cf. A. E. Cox to Lodge, December 21, 1910, in which it is suggested that a fight between Gaston and Fred MacLeod precipitated Gaston's withdrawal. (Both in Lodge MSS.)

[38] *Boston Evening Transcript*, January 2, 1911.

[39] *Boston Herald*, January 17, 1911.

Haven Railroad's demands (though in 1910 Wood came out against the New Haven's merger with Berkshire street railways), had opposed the Hisgen antimonopoly bill, had fought direct primaries bills, and voted against an investigation of holding companies. Crane had even opposed the House resolution in 1910 for direct election of United States senators. It is possible that their hostility to Lodge may be traceable to Congressman Samuel McCall, whose Harvard constituency savored his coolness toward the senior senator apparently as much as it did his aggressively standpat record in Congress. Wood ultimately threw his vote to President Lowell of Harvard. Put together, these men represent a fair cross section of Massachusetts insurgency.

IV

On January 21, 1911, two days after Senator Lodge's successful fight against retirement, about thirty-five leading Republican insurgents and nonpartisan reformers across the nation announced the organization of the National Progressive Republican League. They dedicated the League to the nomination of a progressive Republican for President in 1912 and to the promotion of progressive principles. The organization purported to confirm insurgency's identification with progressivism on the national scene. Throughout the year, reformers girded themselves for the coming showdown with the forces of the old order. An English visitor in the United States, sensing the approaching crisis of the American polity, remarked: "Never has there been such an example of a nation sitting in judgment on itself as America of this year 1911." [40]

Meanwhile, Massachusetts insurgency remained impotent. Joseph Walker's efforts to rally "progressive Republican" sentiment behind him in his bid for the gubernatorial nomination failed dismally. Both Walker and Norman White entered the race against the escalator candidate, Lieutenant Governor Louis Frothingham. White campaigned with the slogan, "Any-

[40] Quoted in Sullivan, *Our Times,* IV, 124.

thing to defeat the machine and save the party." "If you don't vote for me," he urged, "vote for Joseph Walker." [41] Walker made a virtue of the state committee's opposition to him, charged it up to his endorsement of direct election of United States senators, and said he aimed to reduce the power of money in politics. Neither Walker nor White was in a position to criticize Frothingham for his labor record, which was worse than average for even conservative Republicans in the state. Frothingham presented himself simply as a quiet, sober, able man; he offered no program, took no stand on any issue. The nomination contest was the first conducted under the direct primary law passed that spring. Their power presumably enhanced, "the people" gave Frothingham a landslide victory — a 10,000 vote majority over the combined opposition. In addition, Russell Wood, running for the nomination for Secretary of State against a septuagenarian who had held the office for twenty years, lost by more than a three to one margin.[42]

Frothingham failed to unseat Governor Foss in the November election, but his defeat did not represent Democratic strength. Foss's victory was a personal one. Almost 42,000 or 10 per cent of all voters voted for him on non-Democratic tickets. Frothingham, moreover, was a poor match for the ebullient Governor; his laconic Cranean qualities which made him a party paragon in the secure years before 1909 served him poorly against Foss. Nevertheless, he raised the Republican share of the total vote from 44 to 47 per cent, and cut Foss's majority from 34,000 to a bare 8,500. New Bedford, Haverhill, and Fall River, among other cities, returned to the Republican column, and the Republicans made great gains in Lowell. Curiously, the farm vote gave Foss his victory; the Governor had won the support of the farmers by vetoing a bill which would have tightened milk inspection requirements. Foss's party, meanwhile, elected no other state officer and lost seventeen seats in the legislature. Robert Luce, whom the

[41] *Boston Herald,* September 20, 1911.
[42] *Ibid.,* September 27, 1911.

Republicans rewarded for his stalwart services with the lieutenant-governor nomination, won a narrow victory over a rising young Irishman from Worcester County named David I.
Walsh, but ran slightly behind Frothingham's poll of the previous year; Luce's vaunted identification with reform apparently helped him very little.[43] In sum, regular Republicanism
emerged essentially as strong as ever; insurgency was a flop in
Massachusetts.

There were two uncomplicated reasons for insurgency's failure. First, it had no vital *raison d'être*. The Bay State G.O.P.
proved itself considerably more responsive to dissidence than
its national counterpart. As in the past, Republicans fell over
each other in adopting positions on issues which Democratic
gains had proved popular. Even before the 1911 legislative
session had begun, for example, President Allen Treadway of
the Senate declared his conversion to both the Luce direct
primaries and the 54-hour bill which he himself had killed in
1910.[44] Dozens of Republicans in the General Court reversed
their previous opposition to labor and popular government
measures to help them pass in 1911.[45] Moreover, if the insurgents' objective was to rid the party of leaders who compromised the party's appeal to the public, Walker's charge that
"the machine" opposed him because he advocated popular election of United States senators must have struck the electorate
as singularly meaningless in view of his support of Lodge in
the recent Senate contest. As one "regular" Republican put it
in a direct assault on Walker: "Within the party in power are
the ins, who boast of the 'party and its leaders', and the outs,
who decry 'the machine and its bosses' . . . The ins want to
stay in and the outs want to get in — that is all there is to
it." [46] Insurgents like Walker and White gave the public little
reason to disagree with that analysis.

[43] *Boston Herald, Springfield Republican,* November 8, 1911.
[44] Speech before the Essex County Republican Club, December 31, 1910,
in *Boston Herald,* January 1, 1911.
[45] Based on my own calculations from roll calls in the General Court
journals for 1911.
[46] *Boston Herald,* March 9, 1911.

In the second place, since Massachusetts insurgency owed much to the national agitation over reform issues and old guard politics, the failure of Bay State insurgents to link up with the cause of the National Progressive Republicans seriously impaired their efforts to persuade the public of the need for a change in their favor. The League had listed five reforms as the basis of its program: (1) direct election of United States senators; (2) popular election of delegates to national party conventions; (3) a corrupt practices act; (4) initiative and referendum; and (5) recall of elected state officials. Of these, Massachusetts already had had the third since the early 1890's (the special baby of standpatter Congressman Samuel McCall) and had frequently improved it; the leading insurgents in the state remained opposed to the initiative and referendum in the forms suggested by the National Progressives; and the last reform had little urgency in a state with annual elections. But even more important, the League was too obviously a "nominating machine" for the benefit of Senator Robert LaFollette's candidacy against the renomination of President Taft.[47] In the Bay State, especially in 1911, it was difficult to convince the most important reform interests that Taft was undesirable, much less that LaFollette should be his successor.

Louis Brandeis was unique among political and semi-political figures of any renown in the Commonwealth in his endorsement of the Progressive Republican movement. By 1911 Brandeis had for the most part shifted his view to national affairs. He had served as an attorney for Louis Glavis and Gifford Pinchot in the Ballinger investigation, and was working closely with LaFollette in the drafting of antimonopoly legislation. From that perspective, he regarded the Progressive Republican movement as the great hope for enlightenment in the country.[48]

[47] Mowry, *Roosevelt and the Progressive Movement,* pp. 172–173.

[48] It should be kept in mind that Brandeis was chafing under the rather sordid personal attacks made upon him by the New Haven Railroad leaders, with whom many Massachusetts insurgents had cordially cooperated.

For reform interests in Massachusetts, meanwhile, nothing made an alliance with the Progressive Republicans seem more incongruous than the fight for ratification of the reciprocity treaty which the Taft administration had concluded with the Canadian government in January 1911. No issue had been dearer to Massachusetts Republican insurgents for more than a decade; it had been the most important single cause of intra-party hostility to Senator Lodge in particular, and to the party's overly rigid protectionist policy generally. On the other hand, by admitting Canadian agricultural products, pa-per, and wood pulp into the United States free of duty, reci-procity gravely jeopardized the economic interests of the con-stituents of the most militant Congressional insurgents behind the Progressive League. It was their turn now to stand for the principle of protectionism, painfully embarrassing as it was to those especially who had made the fight against Payne-Aldrich a fight for "the consumer versus the interests." [49] Unavoidably, they pointed up the sectional origin of much of the insurgent movement. The *Boston Herald,* which was prepared to agree with the midwestern insurgents that Payne-Aldrich gave too much to the "special interests" and even that it did too much for New England, undoubtedly spoke for great numbers of reform-inclined Bay Staters when it denounced the apparent hypocrisy of the Progressive Republicans. ("Among the shal-low pieces of pretense with which a serious people have ever been treated, the present attitude of the Middle West insur-gents toward the tariff deserves high rank. It is really an anti-New England movement. It gained headway by its opposition to the Payne-Aldrich bill . . . But that the insurgents were

[49] Taft delighted in the predicament in which he had placed his Congres-sional foes. "I hope I am above advocating a policy so fraught with impor-tant consequences to my country on the mere ground that it puts some of my unscrupulous opponents in the hole," he wrote to Senator Aldrich, "but it would be contrary to human nature not to smile at the plight of Clapp, Cummins, LaFollette, and the insurgent delegations . . . after the bitter at-tacks they made on you and me in what they called the interest of the 'ulti-mate consumer'" (January 29, 1911). "It may break the Republican party for a while," he wrote to Roosevelt; ". . . at least it will show the hypocrisy of some people" (January 10, 1911). (Both in Taft MSS.)

not moved by any righteous principles is shown by the prompt-
ness with which they have become stand-patters as Canadian
reciprocity arrived on the scene.")[50] Massachusetts insurgents
meanwhile kept the pressure on Senator Lodge (whose favorite fishing village, Gloucester, flew the flag at half-mast when
the treaty was signed) to prevent him from backtracking on
his promise to support Taft's treaty; and Speaker Walker went
so far as to force through the House a resolution "instructing"
Lodge and Crane to oppose an amendment which might have
complicated the treaty's passage.[51]

In sum, the pattern of politics in Massachusetts at the end of
1911 seemed the reverse of that in most other states. While
Taft had his detractors in the Bay State, by now they probably
numbered more among the old guard than among insurgents. In
the reciprocity fight Senator Crane had loyally supported Taft,
and Lodge had dutifully followed Crane; but Crane probably,
and Lodge and others certainly, opposed the treaty not only because it divided the party but also because it undermined
venerated protectionist principles. ("The policy of protection
may be wrong," wrote Congressman Charles G. Washburn,
who with A. P. Gardner had defied party regularity and voted
against the treaty, "but it is the policy of the Republican party
and when protection ceases to exist the party will cease to
exist.")[52] Taft's vigorous prosecution of corporations for violations of the antitrust laws, meanwhile, further alienated conservative Republicans. Lodge went so far as to hold it respon-

[50] *Boston Herald,* April 27, 1911. Cf. *ibid.,* August 5, 1910.

[51] In question was the Root amendment, which was designed to prevent
free importation of paper and wood pulp until all the Canadian provinces
ended export restrictions on those products. See Ellis, *Reciprocity,* p. 126;
Boston Herald, June 9, 26, 1911; and, in Lodge MSS: Robert M. Washburn
to Lodge, June 9, 1911 (commending Lodge for supporting the Root
amendment), Lodge to Washburn, June 12, 1911 (expressing indignation at
Walker's suggestion that he had broken faith with Taft by working to
"cripple" reciprocity), and Henry M. Whitney to Lodge, June 11, 1911. The
Senate rejected the Root amendment; but in the end the Canadian Parliament refused to ratify the treaty, and the efforts of the reciprocitarians
proved in vain.

[52] Quoted in George H. Haynes, *The Life of Charles G. Washburn* (Boston, 1931), p. 114.

sible for Frothingham's defeat,[53] while Crane dropped not too subtle hints to Taft to ease up a little.[54] Consequently, Lodge, Gardner, Frothingham and their supporters looked to dump Taft in 1912, preferably in favor of Roosevelt, while at the same time insurgents such as Joseph Walker assured Taft of "cordial and active support." "As you know," Walker wrote to Taft, "I am in entire accord with you and your policies . . . I know that you have the respect and confidence of the people of Massachusetts." [55]

V

Two separate developments in the early months of 1912 gave renewed life to Republican insurgency in the Bay State. One was the greatest series of labor upheavals in the state since 1881 when the Labor Bureau first began tabulating statistics on labor disputes. The other was the candidacy of Theodore Roosevelt for the Presidency, first for the Republican nomination and then as a Progressive. Labor strife vividly recalled the anxieties of 1910, while Roosevelt's candidacy seemed to offer many down-and-out political irregulars an opportunity at last to vault over the old-liners into the top ranks.

Beginning with the violent, terrifying strike in Lawrence which broke out in January, labor flare-ups made idle a total of nearly 100,000 workers before election time, 1912. In addition to Lawrence, almost every manufacturing town in the state experienced some unpleasantnesses, though Lowell, New Bedford, and Boston were hardest hit. Though the most serious conflicts occurred before midsummer, the early imprisonment and autumn trial of three Lawrence strike leaders (for the "murder" of two strikers killed by the militia during demonstrations) kept the Commonwealth in a state of constant

[53] Lodge to Roosevelt, November 13, 1911, in Roosevelt MSS (LC); cf. Mowry, *Roosevelt and the Progressive Movement*, p. 185.

[54] See A. F. Esterbrook to W. M. Crane, September 26, 1911, and Crane to C. D. Hilles (Taft's secretary), September 23, 1911 (Taft MSS).

[55] Walker to Taft, November 27, 1911 (Walker MSS).

tension. On September 30, in Lawrence and several other cities, workers staged protest strikes to demand the release of the prisoners.

The Lawrence strike was easily the worst of the upheavals. Ironically, it was indirectly the consequence of the labor-sponsored 54-Hour Act, which went into effect on January 1, 1912. Two years earlier, when the 56-Hour Act had taken effect, the companies had adjusted the wage rates so as to maintain approximately the same weekly wages. But this time, with a spectacular display of class arrogance, the company managers refused to repeat the practice, while also refusing to discuss the matter with — or even notify — the employees in advance. When the first pay envelopes of the year, with the reduced wages, were distributed on January 11, some 14,000 workers left the mills.

The strike lasted until March 18, directly involved up to 23,000 strikers or about 40 per cent of the city's working population, left a maximum of 62 per cent of the population without any source of income, and resulted in two fatalities and the arrest of 296 persons, 54 of whom went to jail. On the second day of the strike, thousands of operatives stormed the factories and caused serious damage to buildings and machinery. The companies and the government responded with equal disregard for New England decencies by calling out the militia and dispatching "special police" who bullied the foreign-speaking strikers, their women, and their children.

For many of the comfortable classes, perhaps the most disturbing element was the fact that the strike was the first in New England led by the radical International Workers of the World, whose avowed and much advertised objectives included the destruction of the wage system and the expropriation of the profits of labor for the laborers. "It became, therefore," as the Labor Bureau put it, "more than an industrial strike, and . . . took on some of the aspects of . . . a social revolution." What was more, the Bureau reported, "The textile strike in Lawrence and the conditions which followed were not primarily due to any condition peculiar to Lawrence. The general conditions of the industry in Lawrence are more or less typical . . . The strike . . . and the conditions attending it might just as easily have occurred in any of [the textile] towns." [56]

The I.W.W. had moved into a vacuum in Massachusetts. The old-line craft unions, led almost entirely by men of British origin (English, Welsh, Scottish, and Irish), had essentially the same social outlook as their employers toward the great mass of unskilled, foreign-speaking workers. They appeared impervious even to developments which progressively undermined the effectiveness of their own organizations. The fact that inventions had steadily reduced the proportion of skilled jobs in the factories evoked few efforts to organize the less skilled workers. That the factory owners steadily replaced the British workers with Italians, Poles, Syrians, Greeks, and others similarly failed to impress on the union leaders the need for expanding union activity into the ranks of the newcomers. (In Lawrence, only 2500 workers belonged to ten craft unions affiliated with the United Textile Workers of America.) Instead, union leaders tended to regard the newcomers with little more than contempt.[57] Consequently, as the Labor Bureau reported, the mass of workers had "no ready means of formulating any protest against the conditions under which they felt themselves to be suffering.[58]

The conditions at Lawrence were sufficiently appalling. As the state Labor Bureau put it, in its traditional mode of understatement: "The actual condition of the families of the workers in the textile mills in Lawrence cannot be easily pictured by a mere statement of individual earnings. It is obvious from the figures . . . that the full-time earnings of a large number of adult employees are entirely inadequate to maintain a family." The report pointed out that such wages were not at all peculiar

[56] MBSL, *43d Annual Report* (Boston, 1913), pp. 191, 182.
[57] See Rowland T. Berthoff, *British Immigrants in Industrial America, 1790–1950* (Cambridge, Mass., 1953), esp. pp. 36, 97, 100, 133.
[58] MBSL, *43d Annual Report*, pp. 194–195.

to Lawrence but were as low in other textile cities. "The plain fact is," it said, "that the textile industry . . . is in large part a 'family industry'. It gives employment to men, women, and children." What that meant was that "the normal family of five . . . [was] compelled to supply two wage earners in order to secure the necessaries of life." [59]

There was no easy answer to the problem of what to do about conditions such as those at Lawrence. In the absence of national labor laws, substantially higher wages — enough to make possible only a single breadwinner per family or to make available amenities somewhat greater than merely "the necessaries of life" — would have driven the industry out of the state. But what was clear was that driving wages down still further was *not* the answer. Enough people in the state opposed the companies' policy of wage reductions to force the manufacturers to concede the workers' major demands by the middle of March. An equivalent rise in wages ensued in all the major textile centers in New England. A strike in Lowell in April over the same issue, and another in New Bedford in July on a different issue but again led by men from the I.W.W., sent more chills through the Commonwealth. Meanwhile, a Congressional investigation of the Lawrence situation highlighted the possibilities of "revolution," while it exposed the arrogant stupidity of the manufacturers.

Even had there been no Roosevelt in 1912, fear and disorder would have been sufficient to stir up once more the moribund political insurgency in Massachusetts. As in 1910, social turbulence jeopardized Republican majorities and exposed Republican leadership to charges of inadequacy. Roosevelt's availability in 1912 appeared for a time to offer insurgents first-rate leadership, which their disunity on issues had deprived them of two years earlier.

[59] *Ibid.;* this account of the Lawrence strike is taken also from the United States Department of Labor, "Report on the Strike of Textile Workers in Lawrence, Massachusetts, in 1912," printed as Senate Document 870, 62 Cong., 2 Sess.; Marc Karson, *American Labor Unions and Politics, 1900–1918* (Carbondale, Ill., 1958), pp. 182–186; and from several Massachusetts daily newspapers and the *New York Times.*

VI

As Roosevelt moved toward entering the presidential race near the end of 1911, it seemed at first that he might be the principal ally of the old guard rather than the instrument of its demise. Until the day (February 21, 1912, in Columbus, Ohio) that Roosevelt first formally announced his long-obvious candidacy for the Republican nomination, he enjoyed major support within the Bay State old guard. While insurgent leaders like Walker, Luce, and Washburn declared for Taft all the way, Senator Lodge, Congressman A. P. Gardner, and defeated gubernatorial candidate Louis Frothingham, among others, looked to Roosevelt to raise the national party from its broken, dispirited condition. Roosevelt's attack (in November 1911) on Taft's corporation policies as "archaic" and on the antitrust progressives as "rural tories" had heightened his appeal to anti-Taft conservatives in Massachusetts.[60] In advocating industrial consolidation with government regulation, he had in fact struck a theme which appealed not only to advanced progressives like Herbert Croly but to big businessmen like George W. Perkins and Frank Munsey and to old-line Hamiltonians like Henry Cabot Lodge.[61] Meanwhile, although they cared little for Roosevelt's views on corporations, most of the leaders of the National Progressive Republican League rallied to Roosevelt as soon as he began hinting in the fall that he might be available as a candidate against Taft. (The League had formally endorsed Wisconsin's Robert LaFollette in October 1911 but few members believed he could win; when they failed to persuade him to withdraw in Roosevelt's favor, most of them simply deserted the Senator early in February.) For a short time, Roosevelt thus seemed to many old guard leaders in Massachusetts to be the one man to unite insurgents and

[60] Theodore Roosevelt, "The Trusts, the People, and the Square Deal," *Outlook,* 99:649–656 (November 8, 1911); Mowry, *Roosevelt and the Progressive Movement,* pp. 192ff.

[61] Cf. Mowry, *Roosevelt and the Progressive Movement,* pp. 202ff, and Garraty, pp. 284–285.

conservatives who for different reasons were dismayed or antagonized by the Taft administration. In other words, whatever
a Roosevelt nomination might have meant to old guard leadership in other states, in Massachusetts it promised to fortify
the most vulnerable segment of the old guard leadership —
the Lodge faction — against a divisive insurgency.

Roosevelt's Columbus speech abruptly altered the situation.
By advocating popular recall of state judicial decisions which
bore upon constitutional questions, Roosevelt appalled his
Brahmin friends. To most of them his proposal suggested the
doom of an independent judiciary and the beginning of a
plebiscitary democracy. Actually Roosevelt was suggesting
nothing of the sort, and many of them knew it; but knowing
it did not reduce their dismay. As one of them put it:

. . . [Roosevelt] was not in favor of the recall of judges, but of judicial
decisions, and . . . what he had in mind were not civil and criminal
cases, but cases where the several States had declared humanitarian
Acts passed by the Legislature to be unconstitutional. Of course in
England, there is no Constitution; Parliament can pass what laws it
sees fit without check . . . The doctrine had less terrors for me than
for most people . . . But the effect produced on me was that it was
still an "indigestaque moles", — an ethical social idea not yet properly
worked out. After all, although our constitutions may be too sacred
white elephants . . . [recall of judicial decisions] is a little vague and
has served incidentally to throw the property owning classes and all
reverers of our institutions into pink fits.[62]

Roosevelt's friends among the old guard glumly withdrew their
support and gathered behind the safe and sound figure of
President Taft. No crisis could make them accept an "indigestaque moles," particularly one which gave the comfortable
classes "pink fits." "Roosevelt's Columbus speech," Senator
Lodge wrote ruefully to Brooks Adams, "has turned Taft from
a man into a principle." [63]

The desertion of the old guard left Roosevelt's candidacy in

[62] Robert Grant to James Ford Rhodes, March 22, 1912 (C. G. Washburn
MSS).
[63] Lodge to Adams, March 5, 1912 (Lodge MSS).

the hands of the political insurgents, or at least those insurgents who had not already announced for Taft. At the time Roosevelt formally threw his hat in the ring, there were two groups of anti-organization Republicans in the state. One was led by a thirty-year-old Boston alderman named Matthew Hale, who only a few years earlier had worked in the Roosevelt household as a tutor. Hale's group called itself the Massachusetts Progressive Republican League, and indeed had been assisted in its organization by several members of the National Progressive Republican League who had never given up the hope of inducing T.R. to become a candidate. It soon became a poorly disguised campaign committee for Roosevelt's nomination, though at the time of its founding in December 1911 the League declared it intended only "to advance generally progressive plans, chiefly in the State Legislature," and "to straighten out the general [Republican party] machinery so the people can express themselves more easily." Most of the members of the League were young, like Hale, and were almost entirely without political experience.[64]

About the same time, Senator Arthur Nason and Representative Russell Wood founded a rival group that they called the "Militant Progressive Republican League." Made up of several anti-Lodge legislators, the Militants announced a four-point program: direct election of United States senators, the initiative and referendum, abolition of the electoral college, and direct primaries for national convention delegates. With evident derision, they referred to Hale's League as "the intellectuals." Although they functioned initially as a legislative bloc for political reform measures, the Militants declared for Roosevelt on February 10.[65]

[64] *Boston Journal,* December 11, 1911; Morison, VII, 455n–456n.
[65] *Boston Journal,* December 30, 1911, January 25, 1912; *Springfield Republican,* February 11, 1912. There are two unpublished papers which adequately present the chief events of the rise of the Massachusetts Progressive party and the election contests of 1912. See Norman M. Goldberg, "The Progressive Party in Massachusetts and the Election of 1912," Harvard College senior thesis, 1952; and Gloria J. Barron, "A Study of Massachusetts in the Election of 1912, with Concentration upon the Progressives,"

Roosevelt first tried to persuade old guard leaders to take charge of his campaign;[66] when he failed he turned, not to the seasoned politicians among the Militants, but to Matt Hale's amateurs. There were probably three reasons for Roosevelt's choice. In the first place, Roosevelt's closest acquaintance among his supporters in Massachusetts was Arthur D. Hill, a conservative lawyer and Senator Lodge's personal attorney. Since Hill was Roosevelt's most prominent supporter in the Bay State after the Columbus speech, Roosevelt evidently found it desirable to work through him in determining campaign assignments; although T.R. apparently already had a preference for Hale among those available, he put Hale's selection to Hill in the form of a request.[67] Hill could hardly have thought well of the Militants' fight to oust Lodge from the Senate; moreover, he had always opposed most of the legislative measures to which the Militants as a group were dedicated, including the public opinion bill, the initiative and referendum, recall of judges and judicial decisions, and most particularly the Militants' efforts to overthrow the party "machine." [68] Secondly, it is not clear that before the debacle at

Columbia University Master's essay, 1956. There is also a Harvard dissertation on the Progressive party in Massachusetts by Richard B. Sherman, c. 1959; however, Dr. Sherman has declined to make his study available. His paper "Charles Sumner Bird and the Progressive Party in Massachusetts," *New England Quarterly*, 33:325–340 (September 1960), is not very helpful.

[66] His first choice was Charles S. Baxter, who had managed Louis Frothingham's gubernatorial campaign in 1911. Like many conservatives, Baxter remained behind Roosevelt until after the Republican National Convention, which he attended as the chairman of the Roosevelt delegation; but he rejected any major role in the Roosevelt campaign.

[67] "I have written to [Hill] that I hope he will let you . . . manage the campaign," Roosevelt wrote to Hale, adding without an attempt to conceal his disappointment that bigger men were not available: "You and the other progressives are evidently the people upon whom I must lean in Massachusetts." Roosevelt to Hale, March 5, 1912; see also Roosevelt to Arthur D. Hill, March 5, 1912 (both in Morison, VII, 517–519).

[68] There is no general account of Arthur D. Hill except for some guesswork, in various studies of the Progressives, based on his 1912 correspondence in the Roosevelt MSS. I have traced Hill's position through the newspapers and in several manuscript collections. See, e.g., *Boston Herald*, February 19, 1908, February 18, 1909, February 15, 1911, and Hill to Henry Cabot Lodge, January 11, 1912 (Lodge MSS). Like the position of

the Republican National Convention Roosevelt saw himself in the role of anything more than a conservative deliverer of both his party and his country — to avert "a general smash up of our civilization," as he put it.[69] He was not prepared to endorse either the position on labor for which the more radical insurgents like Nason stood, or the single-minded fight to overthrow the state party leadership in which Representative Wood was engaged.[70] Finally, Roosevelt may have believed that those who had no political career of their own to foster might more devotedly promote his.

In any case, Roosevelt's choice of Hale had a lasting effect upon insurgency in Massachusetts. It made it clear that at least in the Bay State Roosevelt was unwilling to permit his national ambitions to serve as a springboard for any "Young Turk" movement.[71] As a consequence, anti-organization Republicans in Massachusetts still lacked a unifying leader against the state "machine" even while most of them joined in supporting Roosevelt's bid for the Presidency. Although Republican insurgency's ultimate failure in Massachusetts had many causes, the clash of personal loyalties which inhibited Roosevelt (and Arthur Hill as well) put it in a hopeless position from the start.

Excitement over political developments in Massachusetts

many conservatives, Hill's support of Roosevelt was based on the belief that some kind of reform was necessary, and that Roosevelt could be counted on to save as much of the old order as was possible. Senator Lodge's son stated this sentiment in its extreme, though not too uncommon, form when he wrote to his father: "We are going to have the initiative, recall, and general chaos anyway, and under those circumstances T.R. happens to be my choice for dictator." John Ellerton Lodge to Henry Cabot Lodge, n.d. (1912), in Lodge MSS, quoted in Garraty, p. 292.

[69] Roosevelt to R. Haggard, June 28, 1912, in Roosevelt MSS (LC); also quoted in Mowry, *Roosevelt and the Progressive Movement,* p. 255.

[70] Nason and Wood both gave their support to Roosevelt, but, though experienced politicians, they never took leading positions in Roosevelt's campaign.

[71] Roosevelt's friendship with Lodge probably influenced him on this. Roosevelt also respected Lodge's wishes that he refrain from attacking Murray Crane at any time in Massachusetts. Roosevelt to Lodge, May 2, 1912, in Morison, VII, 539–540 and footnotes. See also W. Sturgis Bigelow to Lodge, May 4, 1912, and Lodge to Bigelow, May 2, 1912 (Lodge MSS).

reached a high pitch as spring arrived. Roosevelt believed he would have a chance to win a majority of delegates from Massachusetts to the national convention only if he could obtain a state-wide popular vote on his candidacy.[72] When the General Court made such a vote possible in March with the presidential-preference primary bill, T.R. boosters were ecstatic and predicted a Roosevelt landslide.[73] Although personally pessimistic about his chances against the full weight of the Republican organization,[74] Roosevelt toured the state in a vigorous campaign and drew enormous crowds. The Roosevelt National Committee poured in $52,000 of its total funds of $144,000 to carry the state.[75] When the voters went to the polls at the end of April, Roosevelt had already won primaries in Illinois and Pennsylvania. A victory in traditionally conservative Massachusetts, it was predicted, would practically clinch his nomination over Taft.[76]

But as T.R. had anticipated, his drive in Massachusetts fell short. Taft won the straight-out presidential preference vote 86,722 to 83,099; due to a mix-up in the balloting for delegates, however, Roosevelt was awarded the eight delegates at large. Taft won the two delegates from each of nine of the fourteen districts, though in two of the nine the voters paradoxically indicated a "preference" for T.R. In the end, although Taft forces claimed the eight delegates at large on the basis of the "preference" vote, and Roosevelt men countered with demands for four district delegates on the same basis, the Massachusetts delegation went into the national convention split down the middle, 18 to 18. Taft's nominal victory in Massachusetts served to stop the Roosevelt snowball in other states.

[72] Robert Grant to James Ford Rhodes, March 22, 1912 (C. G. Washburn MSS).

[73] *Boston Journal,* March 16, 1912.

[74] Robert Grant to James Ford Rhodes, March 22, 1912 (C. G. Washburn MSS); also Roosevelt to Francis Heney, April 30, 1912 (RMA MSS).

[75] *Boston Evening Transcript,* October 1, 1912.

[76] Lodge to Curtis Guild, April 26, 1912 (Lodge MSS); *Fitchburg Sentinel,* April 30, 1912.

When Taft emerged the victor from the tumultuous national convention that June, a large segment of Roosevelt's supporters from Massachusetts, including the chairman of the Roosevelt delegation, abandoned its defeated champion and pledged to campaign for Taft in an "Association of Progressive Republicans." Roosevelt was left primarily with those who had already cut themselves off from the mainstream of Republican politics, or who had never become a part of that stream. They included a handful of liberal-minded men, like Matt Hale, whose social outlook closely resembled that of Louis Brandeis (who supported Woodrow Wilson); fundamentally conservative, they nevertheless recognized the urgency of the fight for social justice. There was also a small group of Irish-Americans who had long been at odds with Republican leaders because they had been excluded from the rewards they believed they deserved for giving their support to the party. As early as 1906 they had organized the "Roosevelt Republican Club," which, according to its founders, was "formed upon the basic idea that the immigrant and son of the immigrant who believed in the protective policy and an honest financial system properly belonged in the Republican party." [77] Their fortunes unimproved by five years of organized efforts within the G.O.P., these men moved easily into the Roosevelt party in 1912.[78] In addition, there were a few of the more radically inclined Republicans like Arthur Nason (whose benefactor, Butler Ames, supported Taft all the way). But at the same time, the Roosevelt candidacy attracted a wide variety of political misfits and has-beens with whom in other circumstances Roosevelt would have been appalled to be associated. They included one of John B. Moran's campaign managers in 1906, the Hearst-Independence League gubernatorial candidate in 1908, and a garrulous, once powerful Boston customs officer who had been ousted from his place in 1909 by Senator

[77] *Boston Globe,* October 21, 1906; *Boston Journal,* February 27, 1912.
[78] See the plaintive letters of Thomas F. Doherty and William E. Elton to Henry Cabot Lodge, January 1910 and July 14, 1910 (Lodge MSS).

Lodge and had subsequently been counted among John F. Fitzgerald's leading supporters. Each of these men and others like them held leading positions in the Roosevelt campaign.

When Roosevelt failed to persuade former Congressman John A. Sullivan, the Back Bay Democrat who had defeated Eugene Foss for Congress in 1902 and 1904, to accept the Progressive gubernatorial nomination, he turned reluctantly to Charles Sumner Bird, a wealthy paper manufacturer and the father-in-law of insurgent Governor Robert P. Bass of New Hampshire.[79] Bird had become a Democrat in 1884, but after 1896 had taken only occasional interest in party affairs and in 1908 had voted for Taft.[80] Descended from Francis W. Bird, a leading Bostonian who had participated prominently with Charles Sumner in the antislavery cause, Charles Bird was in fact an old Mugwump of the very type that Theodore Roosevelt had always heartily detested. Either unaware of Roosevelt's sentiments or unwilling to reciprocate, Bird contributed his name, his energy, and (most important) his money to the Bull Moose fight with the belief that only Roosevelt could save what appeared to him to be a crumbling civilization. Actually, Bird was a kindly autocrat whose views on labor, industry, and all kinds of social problems more closely mirrored Cabot Lodge's than Theodore Roosevelt's in 1912, but the man was acutely fearful of a social cataclysm and convinced that the Grand Old Party was no longer capable of dealing with the problems of the day.[81]

The three-cornered elections that fall were anticlimactic. On

[79] See Roosevelt to Arthur D. Hill, July 23, 1910, to James P. Magenis (President of the Roosevelt Republican Club), July 23, 1912, to Richard W. Child, July 30, 1912, and to Robert P. Bass, August 20, 1912 — all in Roosevelt MSS (LC). Roosevelt had wanted Sullivan particularly "in view of the Catholic feeling against me" (Roosevelt to Child, *supra*), and also because he hoped to attract Democratic voters.

[80] Charles Sumner Bird to Charles Sumner Hamlin, April 6, 1904, and November 23, 1907 (Hamlin MSS); and *Springfield Republican,* August 6, 1913.

[81] Interview with Charles Sumner Bird, Jr., in June 1956. Cf. Sherman, "Charles Sumner Bird." Bird's campaign speeches suggest that the old man liked to imagine himself fighting a cause similar to that which his father had fought in the 1850's.

the national level, Roosevelt's bolt from the G.O.P. assured the victory of the Democratic ticket led by Woodrow Wilson; President Taft barely troubled to campaign. As for Massachusetts, it is hard to see that the dramatic political shuffling of the day had more than a superficial impact on the state's politics. Although the Republican schism guaranteed Governor Foss's second re-election, this time he won only 40 per cent of the vote. The Republican candidates for President, Governor, and Lieutenant Governor each won the greater portion of the Republican-Progressive vote. In addition, G.O.P. regulars secured majority control in the General Court. The old guard demonstrated its continued mastery when the new legislature met in January by forcing the election of ultraconservative Congressman John W. Weeks to replace Murray Crane in the Senate. Significantly, Weeks's only important rivals were Eben Draper and the equally conservative though "independent" Congressman Samuel McCall.

Subsequent events confirm the view that Republican insurgency and the Progressive party were little more than abortive episodes in Massachusetts politics, episodes which received disproportionate notoriety in the state due to their superficial resemblance to progressive insurgency elsewhere in the country. The Progressive party itself quickly crumbled and died. It reached a "high point" in 1913 when Charles Bird polled more votes than A. P. Gardner, who had captured the Republican gubernatorial nomination after a typically bitter primary campaign. But Bird's success in running second that year indicated only Bird's personal popularity and Gardner's very considerable unpopularity, while it suggested nothing about insurgency in Massachusetts except perhaps its complete dependence on personalities. After the 1913 contest Bird retired to his paper mills. Theodore Roosevelt had already long indicated his lack of further interest in the organization. Without Roosevelt's glamor and Bird's money, the party had nothing at all to sustain it.

The Progressives' greatest shortcoming was their utter failure to develop any important issues. The party had nothing to say about corporate problems; its remedy for poor labor conditions was merely an even-handed application of the "Golden Rule"; and Bird's own endorsement of the New Haven–B. & M. merger effectively removed that subject from Progressive campaigns. The Progressives were reduced to echoing the Democrats on the initiative and referendum, which was nothing more than a placebo, and to complaining about child labor conditions — in a state with some of the country's best laws, and the smallest percentage of child labor among all industrial states in the country. In 1913, they took to predicting disaster from the newly passed Underwood tariff, and in 1914, the party turned "dry." In the end, it forsook its Irish-American comrades and became — in Theodore Roosevelt's words — "practically an A.P.A. side-show." [82]

EPILOGUE

At the same time, other forces were indeed reshaping Massachusetts politics. The election of David I. Walsh in 1913 as Massachusetts' first Roman Catholic governor marked the initial break-through by the Irish-Americans toward conclusive control of the Democratic party and a leading role in state policy making. Probably only Woodrow Wilson's patronage policies prevented immediate Irish ascendancy in the party. Depending for guidance on patronage in the Bay State upon Dudley Field Malone (a New Yorker) and Louis Brandeis, President Wilson systematically disregarded the demands of the state committee, and almost entirely excluded Irish-Americans from important offices. His selection of Edmund Billings, the Good Government Association's executive secretary, as Collector of the Port of Boston ignored the strenuous protests of almost every important party official in the state. Although it was true that most organization Democrats had supported Champ Clark for the Democratic nomination in 1912, there had been no open hostility to Wilson after the Baltimore con-

---

[82] Roosevelt to Dwight B. Heard, July 3, 1916, in Morison, VIII, 1085.

vention; moreover, George Fred Williams, who had been a leading Clark supporter, received an ambassadorship from Wilson, while on the other hand John F. Fitzgerald, who was most directly offended by the Billings appointment, had actively supported Wilson from the beginning.[83] In short, Wilson's patronage policy was specially designed to revitalize the strength of the old-line Democrats, and to thwart the ascendancy of the Irish, in the state organization.[84] It had only temporary effect.

From David Walsh's governorship on, the story of Massachusetts politics takes a distinctive turn. The struggle continued for the maintenance of traditional standards, but it was a struggle already essentially lost. Only the coming of World War I averted the concurrent doom of the state's economic eminence as well. Meanwhile, the war brought to a head deep-seated ethnic rivalries, and effectively mobilized the subordinated ethnic groups for political battle. The story of Massachusetts politics thereafter focuses perforce on a different theme — a theme perhaps symbolized by the senatorial campaign of 1916. In the past, the subordinated labor and immigrant groups had had little to choose from in contests such as those between Crane and Quincy, between Douglas and Bates, and even between Foss and Frothingham. Now, however, it was the traditionalist reformer who had no place. What, after all, did the Brandeises have to choose from in a contest between Cabot Lodge and "Honey" Fitzgerald?

[83] See Chapter Six for some reasons for Fitzgerald's enmity toward Billings. Aside from Billings, the biggest patronage plums went to Charles S. Hamlin (Assistant Secretary of the Treasury), George W. Anderson (successively United States District Attorney for Massachusetts, Interstate Commerce Commissioner, and Judge of the United States Circuit Court of Appeals), Joseph B. Eastman (Interstate Commerce Commissioner), and, of course, Louis Brandeis. President Wilson also offered a cabinet position and then the ambassadorship to Great Britain to Richard Olney, but Olney preferred retirement.

[84] Wilson apparently pursued the same policy in New Hampshire. See Senator Jacob H. Gallinger to James O. Lyford, April 21, 1913 (Gallinger MSS).

CONCLUSION

In an appraisal of Massachusetts politics almost half a century after the Progressive Era, a *New York Times* correspondent was struck by what he called "an extraordinary parochialism" among the interest groups which contended for power in the state. Labor unions and business leaders alike, the reporter found, agreed in "their rejection of any larger community view," and "clung wholly to bread and butter objectives." The *Times'* correspondent noted, moreover, "an overdeveloped racial consciousness" which further divided the Massachusetts polity. "The immigrant era," he wrote, "seems closer here than in other states, and voters much more consciously think of themselves as members of a racial bloc that must watch out for its own." [1]

It is not within the purview of this study to assess the accuracy of the *Times'* analysis of mid-twentieth-century politics in Massachusetts. But the study of Massachusetts politics during the Progressive Era does suggest that the trend of developments was clearly toward the mid-century condition described. The trend was evidence that the overarching cause to which the progressive movement was dedicated — the effort to maintain standards of social behavior which focused on a "larger community view" and which transcended "bread and butter objectives" — had failed in Massachusetts.

When the century opened, the native New Englander was made aware that what he regarded as the principal standards of his old Commonwealth were in jeopardy. They were conservative standards, but Massachusetts conservatism had much in common with the spirit of innovation that was characteristic of the era. Massachusetts conservatism had held corporations

[1] Anthony Lewis, in the last of a series of articles on corruption in Massachusetts, *New York Times,* June 21, 1961.

accountable to public authority in a manner which some of the most progressive states in the country failed to achieve even in the hey-day of progressivism. It included a view of the state's responsibilities to its wage-earning citizens that produced the most advanced labor legislation in the country. It included a respect for democratic procedures that made the state relatively free of the political crimes which had inspired much of the reform agitation throughout the country at the time. Above all, Massachusetts conservatism included a sense of community and an assumption of a solidarity of interest among the diverse classes and interests in the community that placed real restraints upon the force of self-preference in business and public affairs.

Typically, the native New Englander viewed as the greatest threat to the old values the massive immigration which had begun in the 1880's (especially) and continued until 1914. It may have been that the more he felt hemmed in by the strangers in his land, the more the native tended to *insist* on the old standards. From this viewpoint, immigrants may even have had a leavening effect upon actual social behavior in the old Puritan Commonwealth. Surely it was not the Slavs, the Celts, the Latins, or the Semites who introduced graft, blackmail, or parochialism into American politics. Indeed, in 1869, when the immigrant "menace" still seemed reasonably remote, Charles Francis Adams, Jr., expressed his doubts that government regulation could ever work in America because, he asserted, "government supervision among Anglo-Saxons is apt to degenerate into jobbery." [2]

Whatever the case, the erosion of social standards in Massachusetts was very real. The chief troubles, however, at least for the first decade of the new century, arose from entirely native sources. The dominant theme of Massachusetts politics during those years was the effort to maintain the state's standards despite economic innovations that threatened the condi-

[2] Quoted in Leonard D. White, *The Republican Era: 1869–1901* (New York, 1958), p. 3.

tions on which those standards thrived. The effort was in some ways doomed from the start by a failure of character among the state's own traditional leaders.

Massachusetts had always been a commercial, business-minded province, which had been able to enjoy the luxury of noncommercial ideals at least in part because of its great commercial success; one need not be preoccupied with money when one has more than almost anyone else. Its advanced position on progressive issues at the beginning of the era undoubtedly derived from many "bread and butter" efforts by various "parochial" interests over a period of time; and the early maturity of the Massachusetts polity unquestionably brought into play earlier than in the western and southern states the forces responsible for progressive measures. But it cannot be denied that the noncommercial, public-spirited ideals, the sense of Commonwealth, also contributed substantially to those achievements. It was not "inevitable," for example, that an industrial community should pass laws relatively early in its development to regulate employers' treatment of wage earners; nor was it "inevitable" that an industrial community should place private enterprises under government supervision. What effective control required was that regulators and regulated share a large community view. Charles Francis Adams was able to make the Massachusetts Railroad Commission an enviable success, despite his pessimism about government supervision by "Anglo-Saxons," primarily because he possessed that view and for the most part was able to impart a similar view to the railroad managers as well.

Rather special circumstances favored the cultivation of social responsibility in Massachusetts. The fact that Massachusetts enterprises had been largely financed and controlled locally went a long way toward subduing illicit temptations in the business community; the managers of a Boston investment house, for example, were not likely to attempt in Boston the things they did in Seattle, when they could expect to meet at their social club the business leaders whom they had injured by their clever coups. Massachusetts law, meanwhile, helped to maintain conditions that tended to preclude the kinds of social tensions which had gripped many other states in the last decades of the nineteenth century. The effective regulation of public and private corporations, for instance, helped to avert fraud and the hostilities which inevitably followed upon its revelation. When supported by public approval, state authority could hold business practices to particular standards even when it applied sanctions no stronger than exposure. Each of these forces — the law, the prestige of the government, the social pressures which enforced conformity to "understood" standards — contributed vitally to the community of interest which underlay much of Massachusetts' advanced position on the matters which stirred the American public during the Progressive Era.

The transformation of the American economy soon swept much of this away. The "large view" was less possible when in the short run the state's economic prosperity lay in jeopardy. The invasion of Massachusetts businesses by "foreign" investors tended to divorce the control of the Commonwealth's properties from what Governor Curtis Guild called "the inspiration of its ideals." It had been the distant ownership of local enterprise which had produced much of the frightening social tensions in western and southern states during the Populist era. At the same time, Massachusetts businesses sought "foreign" corporate charters of their own to escape the restrictions of Massachusetts standards and in order to meet the strong competition of out-of-state businesses which had thrived with liberal charters. With the corporation acts of 1903 and 1908, Massachusetts began to resign its responsibility to maintain standards, a policy to which it gave final effect in the 1920's. Finally, southern and western competition, particularly in shoes, leather, and textile goods, made it increasingly difficult for Massachusetts manufacturers to pose as paternalistic benefactors to their employees. The community of interest among employers and operatives, which politically had focused on the protective tariff, now began to break down; the tariff could not help Bay State manufacturers against domestic competition; and, when the workers demanded higher wages to cope with the cost of living, it was every man for himself.

For the immigrant, meanwhile, the condition of "every man for himself" did not wait upon the erosion of Commonwealth traditions; it had always been an everyday fact of life. The business of mere survival left little space for the niceties of civilization. In his own life he understood the principle of the *quid pro quo* in politics and in business, and he was provoked to raw irony by the efforts of the dominant classes to assert that the guidelines of business and political intercourse under their aegis were marked instead by integrity, honesty, and ability. From his viewpoint, the leaders of his adopted land too often served up such principles as substitutes for enlightened social policy. This seemed as true for the reformers as for the old guard conservatives; the difference between them lay principally in the old guard's certainty that everything that could be done to solve social problems had been done, and in the reformers' charge that social problems derived primarily from corruption. Under the circumstances, perhaps it *required* shortsighted, parochial, "bread and butter" efforts to obtain relief from oppressive conditions for which no particular malfeasance could be blamed.

In 1912 Massachusetts simulated the conditions of progressive insurgency elsewhere by fielding a Progressive party of its own; but the event, like the national progressive movement as a whole, had only shallow meaning for the Bay State. The national movement, which was the chief stimulus for the local party, simply did not serve the interests of the Massachusetts electorate. The sectional characteristics of progressive insurgency especially militated against Massachusetts' participation in the national movement; the fight to redress the inequitable balance of political and economic advantages which had favored the East over the West held no charms for Bay Staters. In addition, the political or institutional reforms which dominated the platforms of insurgents elsewhere failed to produce the same sense of urgency in Massachusetts. For one thing, the effectiveness of Massachusetts' democratic institutions had long served as the standard for other states. But more important, much of the insurgent spirit that existed in Massachusetts derived from apprehension about the ascendancy of so-called undesirable social elements, in particular the non-Yankee wage-earning classes; to broaden popular participation in public affairs through political innovations meant only to facilitate that ascendancy. The dominant elements of the Massachusetts electorate could hardly have become enthusiastic about such supposed palliatives.

It was the more general character of the national progressive movement — the effort to lift the moral standards of American political and commercial life — which could have had meaning for Massachusetts. Yet, the Progressive party in Massachusetts was not organized around and did not generally attract the men who stood above all else for that cause. For the most part, the leaders of the Massachusetts Progressive party, like the leaders of Republican insurgency earlier, had failed to respond as progressives to the crucial tests that came before 1912; afterward, as well, they seemed to miss the point.

The point was most clearly evident in the New Haven merger scandal. In that sordid affair, the principles of the old Commonwealth gave way before the claims of commercial need and in-group loyalty. The state's easy capitulation to the Morgan empire highlighted the chief flaws in the social fabric, and signaled the decline of an ethic which had once held even the most exalted to the limits of the law and to the test of social responsibility. Neither the old guardsmen of the Commonwealth, who declared themselves the stalwarts of traditional standards, nor those who promoted the state's Progressive party, ostensibly to reaffirm those standards and restore their relevance to modern conditions, showed themselves capable of living up to the virtues they proclaimed. It could hardly be expected that either the law or the venerated principles on which the law had rested could ever regain their old influence in the old Commonwealth. The state was ready for Jim Curley.

BIBLIOGRAPHY

INDEX

SELECTED BIBLIOGRAPHY

MANUSCRIPT AND SCRAPBOOK COLLECTIONS

Atkinson, Edward A. Massachusetts Historical Society, Boston, Massachusetts.

Brandeis, Louis D. Law Library, University of Louisville, Louisville, Kentucky.

Bridgman, Raymond L. Massachusetts State Library, Boston, Massachusetts.

Crane, Winthrop Murray. Private collection, held by Mr. Winthrop M. Crane, Dalton, Massachusetts.

Democratic Club of Massachusetts, Young Men's. Department of Rare Books, Boston Public Library.

Eastman, Joseph B. Converse Memorial Library, Amherst College, Amherst, Massachusetts.

Gallinger, Jacob H. New Hampshire Historical Society, Concord, New Hampshire.

Gettemy, Charles. Massachusetts State Library, Boston, Massachusetts.

Good Government Association of Boston. Massachusetts Historical Society, Boston, Massachusetts.

Hamlin, Charles Sumner. Manuscripts Division, Library of Congress, Washington, D. C.

Higginson, Thomas Wentworth. Houghton Library, Harvard University, Cambridge, Massachusetts.

Lodge, Henry Cabot. Massachusetts Historical Society, Boston, Massachusetts.

Lyman, George H. Massachusetts Historical Society, Boston, Massachusetts.

Mellen, Charles S. New Hampshire Historical Society, Concord, New Hampshire.

Meyer, George von L. Massachusetts Historical Society, Boston, Massachusetts.

Moody, William H. Manuscripts Division, Library of Congress, Washington, D. C.

Olney, Richard. Manuscripts Division, Library of Congress, Washington, D. C.

O'Meara, Stephen P. Department of Rare Books, Boston Public Library, Boston, Massachusetts.

Roosevelt, Theodore. Roosevelt Memorial Association Collection, Widener Library, Harvard University, Cambridge, Massachusetts.

—— Manuscripts Division, Library of Congress, Washington, D. C.

Taft, William Howard. Manuscripts Division, Library of Congress, Washington, D. C.

Walker, Joseph. Private collection, held by Mr. George Walker, Concord, Massachusetts.

Walsh, David I. The College of the Holy Cross, Worcester, Massachusetts.

Washburn, Charles G. American Antiquarian Society, Worcester, Massachusetts.

Washburn, Robert M. Massachusetts State Library, Boston, Massachusetts.

Wilson, Woodrow. Manuscripts Division, Library of Congress, Washington, D. C.

NEWSPAPERS

Boston American

Boston Evening Transcript*

Boston Globe

Boston Herald *

Boston Post

Brockton Enterprise

Fitchburg Sentinel

Haverhill Evening Gazette

New Bedford Times-Standard

Springfield Republican*

Springfield Union

Worcester Evening Gazette

SELECTED PUBLIC DOCUMENTS

Boston Chamber of Commerce. *Annual Reports,* 1895 to 1910.

Boston Finance Commission. *Final Report.* Boston: Wright & Potter Printing Company, 1909.

Massachusetts Board of Gas and Electric Light Commissioners. *Annual Reports,* 1890 to 1915.

Massachusetts Board of Railroad Commissioners. *Annual Reports,* 1890 to 1913.

Massachusetts Bureau of the Statistics of Labor. *Annual Reports,* 1890 to 1915.

Massachusetts Bureau of the Statistics of Labor. *Labor Bulletins,* 1898 to 1915.

Massachusetts Commission on Commerce and Industry. *Report.* Boston: Wright & Potter Printing Company, 1908.

Massachusetts Commission on Immigration. *The Problem of Immigration in Massachusetts.* Boston: Wright and Potter Printing Company, 1914.

* Every issue searched for the period 1898 to 1918.

Massachusetts, General Court. *Journal of the House of Representatives.*

Massachusetts, General Court. *Journal of the Senate.*

Massachusetts, General Court. *Manual,* 1890 to 1920.

Massachusetts Reform Club. *Annual Reports,* 1895 to 1905.

U. S. Congress. House Subcommittee on Trusts. *Majority Report on a Bill to Amend the Sherman Anti-trust Act.* House Report 3375, 57 Congress, 2 Session. Washington, D. C.: Government Printing Office, 1903.

U. S. Congress. Senate Committee on Interstate Commerce. *Hearings on Proposed Amendment of the Interstate Commerce Act.* Senate Document 243, 58 Congress, 3 Session. Washington, D. C.: Government Printing Office, 1905.

U. S. Congress. "Evidence taken before the Interstate Commerce Commission relative to the financial transactions of the New York, New Haven & Hartford Railroad Company, together with a report of the Commission thereon." Senate Document 543, 63 Congress, 2 Session. Washington, D. C.: Government Printing Office, 1914.

U. S. Bureau of Corporations. *Annual Reports,* 1904 and later.

U. S. Department of Commerce. *Historical Statistics of the United States, 1789–1945.* Washington, D. C.: Government Printing Office, 1949.

U. S. Department of Labor. *Report on the Strike of Textile Workers in Lawrence, Massachusetts, in 1912.* Senate Document 870, 62 Congress, 2 Session. Washington, D. C.: Government Printing Office, 1912.

U. S. Industrial Commission. *Report on Transportation,* vol. IX. House Document 178, 57 Congress, 1 Session. Washington, D. C.: Government Printing Office, 1901.

BOOKS AND ARTICLES

Abbott, Leonard D. "The Socialist Movement in Massachusetts," *Outlook,* 64: 410–412 (February 17, 1900).

Ainsley, Leslie G. *Boston Mahatma: Martin Lomasney.* Boston: Bruce Humphreys, 1949.

Allen, Walter S. "Street Railway Franchises in Massachusetts," *Annals of the American Academy of Political and Social Science,* XXVII (January 1906) 91–110.

Allen, William R. "Issues in Congressional Tariff Debates, 1890–1930," *Southern Journal of Economics,* 20: 340–351 (April 1954).

Baker, Richard C. *The Tariff Under Roosevelt and Taft.* Hastings, Neb.: Democratic Printing Company, 1941.

Barnes, Irston R. *Public Utility Control in Massachusetts.* New Haven: Yale University Press, 1930.

"The Battle Between The Plutocracy and The Democracy in The Democratic Party of Massachusetts,"*Arena,* 36: 418–419 (October 1906).

Bemis, Edward. "Control of the Capitalization of Public Service Corporations in Massachusetts," *American Economic Association Quarterly,* 10: 415–430 (1909).

Berthoff, Rowland T. *British Immigrants in Industrial America, 1790–1950.* Cambridge: Harvard University Press, 1953.

Black, John D. *The Rural Economy of New England: A Regional Study.* Cambridge: Harvard University Press, 1950.

Blicksilver, Jack. *Cotton Manufacturing in the Southeast: An Historical Analysis.* Atlanta, Ga.: Bureau of Economic Research, Georgia State College of Business Administration, Bulletin No. 5, 1959.

Blum, John M. *The Republican Roosevelt.* Cambridge: Harvard University Press, 1954.

————— "Theodore Roosevelt and the Hepburn Act: Toward an Orderly System of Control," in Elting E. Morison, ed., *The Letters of Theodore Roosevelt,* VI, 1558–1571. Cambridge: Harvard University Press, 1953.

————— "Theodore Roosevelt and the Legislative Process: Tariff Revision and Railroad Regulation, 1904–1906," in Elting E. Morison, ed., *The Letters of Theodore Roosevelt,* IV, 1333–1342. Cambridge: Harvard University Press, 1952.

Bonbright, James C. *Railroad Capitalization: A Study of the Principles of Regulation of Railroad Securities.* New York: Columbia University Press, 1920.

Bradlee, Francis B. C. *The Boston and Maine Railroad: A History of the Main Road with its Tributary Lines.* Salem, Mass.: The Essex Institute, 1921.

Brandeis, Louis D. "How Boston Solved the Gas Problem," *Review of Reviews,* 36: 594–598 (November 1907).

————— "Massachusetts' Substitute for Old Age Pensions," *Independent,* 65: 125–128 (July 16, 1908).

————— *Other People's Money and How the Bankers Use It.* New edition. New York: Frederick A. Stokes Company, 1932.

————— "Savings Banks' Life Insurance," *American Federationist,* 14: 776–780 (October 1907).

————— "Wage Earners Life Insurance: A Great Wrong and a Remedy," *Collier's,* September 15, 1906.

Bridgman, Raymond L. "Legislative Efficiency and Morals," *New England Magazine,* 32: 337–343 (May 1905).

Brown, H. La Rue. "Massachusetts and the Minimum Wage," *Annals of the American Academy of Political and Social Science*, XLVIII (July 1913) 13–21.

Brunner, Edmund de S. *Immigrant Farmers and Their Children*. Garden City: Doubleday, Doran & Company, 1929.

Bryce, James. *The American Commonwealth*. 2 vols. London and New York: The Macmillan Company, 1888.

Bullock, Charles J. "Control of the Capitalization of Public Service Corporations in Massachusetts," *American Economic Association Quarterly*, 10: 384–414 (1909).

Burgess, Thomas. *Greeks in America: An Account of Their Coming, Progress, Customs, Living and Aspirations*. Boston: Sherman, French & Company, 1913.

Bussing, Irvin. *Public Utility Regulation and the So-Called Sliding Scale*. New York: Columbia University Press, 1936.

Calkins, Grosvenor. "The Massachusetts Anti-Stock Watering Law," *Quarterly Journal of Economics*, 22: 640–645 (1908).

—— "The Massachusetts Business Corporation Law," *Quarterly Journal of Economics*, 18: 269–280 (1904).

Chandler, Alfred D., Jr. "The Origins of Progressive Leadership," in Elting E. Morison, ed., *The Letters of Theodore Roosevelt*, VIII, 1462–1465. Cambridge: Harvard University Press, 1954.

—— "Patterns of American Railroad Finance, 1830–1850," *Business History Review*, 28: 248–263 (September 1954).

Clapp, Edwin J. *The Port of Boston: A Study and a Solution of the Traffic and Operating Problems of Boston, and Its Place in the Competition of the North Atlantic Seaports*. New Haven: Yale University Press, 1916.

Cole, Arthur H. *The American Wool Manufacture*. 2 vols. Cambridge: Harvard University Press, 1926.

"Contrasting Records of Pennsylvania and Massachusetts," *Independent*, 53: 1568–1570 (July 4, 1901).

Crafts, William A. "The Second Decade of the Massachusetts Railroad Commission," *Railroad Gazette*, 25: 551–552, 581, 625 (July 21, 1893).

Croly, Herbert. *The Promise of American Life*. New York: The Macmillan Company, 1909.

Davis, Horace B. *Shoes: The Workers and the Industry*. New York: International Publishers, 1940.

Dennett, Tyler. *John Hay: From Poetry to Politics*. New York: Dodd, Mead & Company, 1933.

Depew, Chauncey. *My Memories of Eighty Years*. New York: Charles Scribner's Sons, 1922.

Dineen, Joseph F. *The Purple Shamrock*. Boston: W. W. Norton, 1949.

Dodd, E. Merrick, Jr. "The Evolution of Limited Liability in American Industry: Massachusetts," *Harvard Law Review*, 61: 1351–1379 (September 1948).

———— "The First Half Century of Statutory Regulation of Business Corporations in Massachusetts," in Roscoe Pound, ed., *Harvard Legal Essays*. Cambridge: Harvard University Press, 1934.

Dodd, Walter F. *State Government*. Second edition. New York: The Century Company, 1928.

Dorgan, Maurice B. *Lawrence, Yesterday and Today (1845–1918)*. Lawrence: Press of Dick & Trumpold, 1918.

Eastman, Joseph B. "The Public Service Commission of Massachusetts," *Quarterly Journal of Economics*, 27: 699–707 (August 1913).

Ellis, L. Ethan. *Newsprint: Producers, Publishers, Political Pressures*. New Brunswick: Rutgers University Press, 1960.

———— *Reciprocity, 1911 — A Study in Canadian-American Relations*. New Haven: Yale University Press, 1939.

Faulkner, Harold U. *The Quest for Social Justice, 1898–1914*. New York: The Macmillan Company, 1931.

Fine, Sidney. *Laissez Faire and the General-Welfare State; A Study of Conflict in American Thought, 1865–1901*. Ann Arbor: University of Michigan Press, 1956.

Flint, Winston A. *The Progressive Movement in Vermont*. Washington, D. C.: American Council on Public Affairs, 1941.

Flynt, Josiah. "Boston, A Plain-Clothes Man's Town," *McClure's*, 17: 115–121 (June 1901).

Friedman, Harry G. *The Taxation of Corporations in Massachusetts*. New York: Columbia University Press, 1907.

Fuess, Claude M. *Calvin Coolidge: The Man from Vermont*. Boston: Little, Brown and Company, 1940.

———— *Joseph B. Eastman: Servant of the People*. New York: Columbia University Press, 1952.

Garraty, John A. *Henry Cabot Lodge: A Biography*. New York: Alfred A. Knopf, 1953.

Gates, William B., Jr. *Michigan Copper and Boston Dollars*. Cambridge: Harvard University Press, 1951.

Gras, N. S. B. *The Massachusetts First National Bank of Boston, 1784–1934*. Cambridge: Harvard University Press, 1937.

Green, Constance M. *Holyoke, Massachusetts: A Case History of the Industrial Revolution in America*. New Haven: Yale University Press, 1939.

Griffin, Solomon B. *People and Politics Observed by a Massachusetts Editor*. Boston: Little, Brown and Company, 1923.

———— *W. Murray Crane, A Man and Brother*. Boston: Little, Brown and Company, 1926.

Gulick, Luther H. *The Evolution of the Budget in Massachusetts*. New York: The Macmillan Company, 1920.

Handlin, Oscar. *Boston's Immigrants, 1790–1865: A Study in Acculturation*. Cambridge: Harvard University Press, 1941.

———— *The Uprooted*. Boston: Little, Brown and Company, 1951.

Handlin, Oscar and Mary Flug Handlin. *Commonwealth: A Study of the Role of Government in the American Economy, 1774–1861*. New York: New York University Press, 1947.

———— "Origins of the American Business Corporation," *Journal of Economic History*, 5: 1–23 (May 1945).

Hansen, Marcus L. *The Immigrant in American History*. Cambridge: Harvard University Press, 1940.

Hapgood, Norman. *The Advancing Hour*. New York: Boni & Liveright, 1920.

Hartmann, Edward G. *The Movement to Americanize the Immigrant*. New York: Columbia University Press, 1948.

Haynes, George H. *The Life of Charles G. Washburn*. Boston: Houghton Mifflin Company, 1931.

Hays, Samuel P. *Conservation and the Gospel of Efficiency: The Progressive Conservation Movement, 1890–1920*. Cambridge: Harvard University Press, 1959.

Hechler, Kenneth W. *"Insurgency: Personalities and Politics of the Taft Era*. New York: Columbia University Press, 1940.

Hennessy, Michael E. *Four Decades of Massachusetts Politics, 1890–1935*. Norwood, Mass.: The Norwood Press, 1935.

———— *Twenty-five Years of Massachusetts Politics, 1890–1915*. Boston: Practical Politics, Inc., 1917.

Herlihy, Elisabeth M., ed. *Fifty Years of Boston*. Boston, 1932.

Higginson, Henry Lee. "Justice to the Corporations," *Atlantic Monthly*, 101: 9–16 (January 1908).

Higham, John. *Strangers in the Land*. New Brunswick: Rutgers University Press, 1955.

Hofstadter, Richard. *The Age of Reform*. New York: Alfred A. Knopf, 1956.

Howe, Frederic C. *The City: The Hope of Democracy*. Madison: University of Wisconsin Press, 1905.

Howe, Mark A. de Wolfe. *Boston, The Place and the People*. New York: The Macmillan Company, 1903.

———— *Portrait of an Independent: Moorfield Storey.* Boston: Houghton Mifflin Company, 1932.

Hoxie, R. F. "The Rising Tide of Socialism," *Journal of Political Economy,* 19: 609–631 (October 1911).

Jessup, Philip C. *Elihu Root.* 2 vols. New York: Dodd, Mead & Company, 1938.

Johnson, Arthur M. "Theodore Roosevelt and the Bureau of Corporations," *Mississippi Valley Historical Review,* 45: 571–590 (March
1959).

Johnson, Gerald W. *A Liberal's Progress.* New York: Coward-McCann,
1948.

Josephson, Matthew. *The President Makers: The Culture of Politics
and Leadership in the Age of Enlightenment, 1896–1919.* New
York: Harcourt, Brace and Company, 1940.

Kallen, Horace M. *Zionism and World Politics.* Garden City: Doubleday, Page & Company, 1921.

Karson, Marc. *American Labor Unions and Politics, 1900–1918.* Carbondale, Ill.: Southern Illinois University Press, 1958.

Kirkland, Edward C. *Men, Cities, and Transportation: A Study in New
England History, 1820–1900,* vol. II. Cambridge: Harvard University Press, 1948.

Latané, John H. *America as a World Power, 1897–1907.* Vol. XXV
of *The American Nation: A History,* ed. A. B. Hart. 28 vols. New
York: Harper, 1904–1918.

Lawrence, Bishop William. "The Relation of Wealth to Morals,"
World's Work, 1: 286–292 (January 1901).

Leuchtenburg, William E. "Progressivism and Imperialism: The Progressive Movement and American Foreign Policy, 1898–1916,"
Mississippi Valley Historical Review, 39: 483–504 (1953).

Link, Arthur S. "What Happened to the Progressive Movement in the
1920's?" *American Historical Review,* 64: 833–851 (July 1959).

Lippmann, Walter. *Drift and Mastery: An Attempt to Diagnose the
Current Unrest.* New York: M. Kennerly, 1914.

———— *The Phantom Public.* New York: Harcourt, Brace and Company, 1925.

Lockard, Duane. *New England State Politics.* Princeton: Princeton University Press, 1959.

Lodge, Henry Cabot, ed. *Selections from the Correspondence of Theodore Roosevelt and Henry Cabot Lodge, 1884–1918.* 2 vols. New
York: Charles Scribner's Sons, 1925.

Lord, Everett W. "Child Labor in the Textile Industries and Canneries
of New England," in "The Child Workers of the Nation," pp.

73–78, March 1909 Supplement to *The Annals of the American Academy of Political and Social Science* (Philadelphia, 1909), vol. XXXIII.

Lower, R. R. M. "The New France in New England," *New England Quarterly,* 2: 278–295 (1929).

Luce, Robert. *Legislative Assemblies.* Boston: Houghton, Mifflin Company, 1924.

———— *Legislative Principles.* Boston: Houghton, Mifflin Company, 1930.

———— *Legislative Procedure.* Boston: Houghton, Mifflin Company, 1922.

Luce, Robert, et al. *Report of the Commission on the Cost of Living.* Boston: Wright & Potter Printing Company, 1910.

Mann, Arthur. *Yankee Reformers in an Urban Age.* Cambridge: Harvard University Press, 1954.

Mason, Alpheus T. *Brandeis: A Free Man's Life.* New York: The Viking Press, 1946.

———— *Brandeis: Lawyer and Judge in the Modern State.* Princeton: Princeton University Press, 1933.

———— *The Brandeis Way: A Case Study in the Workings of Democracy.* Princeton: Princeton University Press, 1938.

Mason, Edward S. *The Street Railway in Massachusetts: The Rise and Decline of an Industry.* Cambridge: Harvard University Press, 1932.

"Massachusetts and the Foreigner," *New England Magazine,* 33: 726–727 (February 1906).

Masson, Robert L. *New Shares for Old: The Boston & Maine Stock Modification.* Boston: Harvard Graduate School of Business Administration, 1958.

Maxwell, Robert S. *LaFollette and the Rise of the Progressives in Wisconsin.* Madison: State Historical Society of Wisconsin, 1956.

May, Henry F. *The End of American Innocence: A Study of the First Years of Our Own Time.* New York: Alfred A. Knopf, 1959.

McNeill, George E. *The Labor Movement: The Problem of Today.* Boston: A. M. Bridgman & Company, 1887.

McQuade, Vincent A. *The American Catholic Attitude on Child Labor Since 1891.* Washington, D. C.: Catholic University Press, 1938.

Merriam, Charles E., and Louise Overacker. *Primary Elections.* Chicago: The University of Chicago Press, 1928.

Morison, Elting E., ed. *The Letters of Theodore Roosevelt.* 8 vols. Cambridge: Harvard University Press, 1951–1954.

Mowry, George E. *The California Progressives*. Berkeley: University of California Press, 1951.

———— *The Era of Theodore Roosevelt, 1900–1912*. New York: Harper & Brothers, 1958.

———— *Theodore Roosevelt and the Progressive Movement*. American Century Series edition. New York: Hill and Wang, 1960.

Munro, William B. *The Government of American Cities*. New York: The Macmillan Company, 1912.

Navin, Thomas R., and Marian V. Sears. "The Rise of a Market for Industrial Securities, 1887–1902," *Business History Review*, 29: 105–138 (June 1955).

Noble, Ransom E. *New Jersey Progressivism Before Wilson*. Princeton: Princeton University Press, 1946.

Norton, Thomas L. *Trade Union Policies in the Massachusetts Shoe Industry, 1919–1929*. New York: Columbia University Press, 1932.

Olney, Richard, II. "The Laboring Man of Today as Compared with 50 Years Ago," *New England Magazine*, 42: 81–85 (March 1910).

Parker, Margaret T. *Lowell, A Study of Industrial Development*. New York: The Macmillan Company, 1940.

Parsons, Frank. *The City for the People*. Revised edition. Philadelphia: C. F. Taylor, 1901.

Passer, Harold C. *The Electrical Manufacturers, 1875–1900*. Cambridge: Harvard University Press, 1953.

———— "Frank Julian Sprague, Father of Electric Traction, 1857–1934," in William Miller, ed., *Men in Business*. Cambridge: Harvard University Press, 1952.

Pierson, George Wilson. "The Obstinate Concept of New England: A Study in Denudation," *New England Quarterly*, 28: 3–17 (March 1955).

Plaisted, John W. *Legislative Procedure in the General Court of Massachusetts*. Boston: Wright & Potter Printing Company, 1948.

Pringle, Henry F. *The Life and Times of William Howard Taft*. New York: Farrar and Rinehart, Inc., 1939.

———— *Theodore Roosevelt, A Biography*. New York: Harcourt, Brace & Company, 1931.

Pusey, Merlo J. *Charles Evans Hughes*. 2 vols. New York: The Macmillan Company, 1952.

Putnam, Frank. "Massachusetts in an Era of Industrial Prosperity and Political Buncombe," *New England Magazine*, 37: 395–418 (December 1907).

Quincy, Josiah. "Municipal Progress in Boston," *Independent,* 52: 424–426 (February 1900).

Read, Burton Lester. *The Public, the Investor and the Railroads of New England.* Boston: The Financial Publishing Company, 1913.

Rees, Albert. *Real Wages in Manufacturing, 1890–1914.* Princeton: Princeton University Press, 1961.

Reeves, Edith, and Caroline Manning. "The Standing of Massachusetts in the Administration of Labor Legislation," in Susan M. Kingsley, ed., *Labor Laws and Their Enforcement, With Special Reference to Massachusetts.* New York: Longmans, Green & Company, 1911.

Reinsch, Paul S. *American Legislatures and Legislative Methods.* New York: The Century Company, 1907.

Richards, James L. "The Boston Consolidated Gas Company: Its Relation to the Public, Its Employees, and Investors," *Annals of the American Academy of Political and Social Science,* XXXI (January-June 1908) 593–599.

Richardson, Leon B. *William E. Chandler: Republican.* New York: Dodd, Mead & Company, 1940.

Ripley, William Z. *Railroads: Rates and Regulation.* New York: Longmans, Green & Company, 1912.

——— *Trusts, Pools and Corporations.* Boston: Ginn & Company, 1905.

Roosevelt, Theodore. "The Trusts, the People, and the Square Deal," *Outlook,* 99: 649–656 (November 8, 1911).

Rowe, L. S. "Relation of Cities and Towns to Street Railway Companies," *Annals of the American Academy of Political and Social Science,* XII (July-December 1898) 103–108.

Saveth, Edward N. *American Historians and European Immigrants, 1875–1925.* New York: Columbia University Press, 1948.

Schlesinger, Arthur M. *New Viewpoints in American History.* New York: The Macmillan Company, 1922.

——— *The Rise of the City, 1878–1898.* New York: The Macmillan Company, 1933.

Schriftgiesser, Karl. *The Gentleman From Massachusetts: Henry Cabot Lodge.* Boston: Little, Brown & Company, 1944.

Seager, Henry R., and Charles A. Gulick, Jr. *Trust and Corporation Problems.* New York and London: Harper & Brothers, 1929.

Shepard, Harvey N. "The Boston Finance Commission," *Cincinnati Conference on Good Government, Proceedings.* Cincinnati, 1909.

Sherman, Richard B. "Charles Sumner Bird and the Progressive Party in Massachusetts," *New England Quarterly,* 33: 325–340 (September 1960).

——— "Foss of Massachusetts — Demagogue or Progressive?" *Mid-America,* 43: 75–94 (April 1961).

Shlakman, Vera. *A Study of Chicopee, Massachusetts: Economic History of a Factory Town.* New Haven: Yale University Press, 1935.

Smith, Thomas Russell. *Cotton Textile Industry of Fall River, Massachusetts: A Study of Industrial Localization.* New York: Columbia University Press, 1944.

Solomon, Barbara M. *Immigrants and Ancestors: A Changing New England Tradition.* Cambridge: Harvard University Press, 1956.

——— "The Intellectual Background of the Immigration Restriction Movement in New England," *New England Quarterly,* 25: 47–59 (March 1952).

Staples, Henry L., and Alpheus T. Mason. *The Fall of a Railroad Empire: Brandeis and the New Haven Merger Battle.* Syracuse: Syracuse University Press 1947.

Steffens, Lincoln. *The Autobiography of Lincoln Steffens.* New York: Harcourt, Brace & Company, 1931.

Stewart, Frank Mann. *A Half Century of Municipal Reform: The History of the National Municipal League.* Berkeley: University of California Press, 1950.

Stimson, Frederick J., and Charles G. Washburn. *Report of the Committee on Corporation Laws.* Boston: Wright & Potter Printing Company, 1903.

Sullivan, Mark. *Our Times. The United States, 1900–1925.* 6 vols. New York: Scribner's Sons, 1926–1935.

Summers, Festus P. *William L. Wilson and Tariff Reform.* New Brunswick: Rutgers University Press, 1953.

Tansill, Charles C. *Canadian-American Relations, 1875–1911.* New Haven: Yale University Press, 1943.

Taussig, Frank W. *The Tariff History of the United States.* New York: G. P. Putnam's Sons, 1923.

Thorelli, Hans. *The Federal Anti-Trust Policy: Origination of an American Tradition.* Baltimore: Johns Hopkins Press, 1955.

Turner, Frederick Jackson. *The Frontier in American History.* New York: Henry Holt & Company, 1920.

Underwood, Kenneth W. *Protestant and Catholic: Religion and Social Interaction in an Industrial Community.* Boston: Beacon Press, 1957.

Van Hise, Charles R. *Concentration and Control: A Solution of the Trust Problem.* New York: The Macmillan Company, 1912.

Van Nostrand, A. D. "The Lomasney Legend," *New England Quarterly,* 21: 435–458 (December 1948).

Watson, James E. *As I Knew Them.* Indianapolis: The Bobbs-Merrill Company, 1936.

White, Leonard D. "The Origin of Utility Commissions in Massachusetts," *Journal of Political Economy,* 29: 177–197 (March 1921).

—— *The Republican Era: 1869–1901.* New York: The Macmillan Company, 1958.

White, William A. *A Certain Rich Man.* New York: The Macmillan Company, 1909.

—— *The Old Order Changeth.* New York: The Macmillan Company, 1910.

Whittelsey, Sarah S. *Massachusetts Labor Legislation: An Historical and Critical Study.* Philadelphia: American Academy of Political and Social Science, 1901.

—— "Massachusetts Labor Legislation," in John R. Commons, ed., *Trade Unionism and Labor Problems.* New York: Ginn & Company, 1905.

Whitten, Robert H. "Trend of Legislation in the United States," [*New York*] *State Library Bulletin,* No. 12 (Albany, 1902).

Wiebe, Robert H. "The House of Morgan and the Executive, 1905–1913," *American Historical Review,* 65: 49–60 (October 1959).

Wittke, Carl. *The Irish in America.* Baton Rouge: University of Louisiana Press, 1956.

Wolfbein, Seymour L. *The Decline of a Cotton Textile City: A Study of New Bedford.* New York: Columbia University Press, 1944.

Wood, Gordon S. "The Massachusetts Mugwumps," *New England Quarterly,* 33: 435–451 (December 1960).

Woods, Robert A., ed. *Americans in Process.* Boston: Houghton, Mifflin and Company, 1902.

Woods, Robert A., and Joseph B. Eastman. "The Boston Franchise Contest," *Outlook,* 82: 835–841 (April 14, 1906).

UNPUBLISHED MATERIAL

Barron, Gloria J. "A Study of Massachusetts in the Election of 1912, with Concentration upon the Progressives." Unpublished Master's essay, Columbia University, 1956.

Blodgett, Geoffrey T. "Massachusetts Democrats in the Cleveland Era." Unpublished Ph.D. dissertation, Harvard University, 1960.

Cole, Donald Barnard. "Lawrence, Massachusetts: Immigrant City, 1845–1912." Unpublished Ph.D. dissertation, Harvard University, 1956.

Goldberg, Norman M. "The Progressive Party in Massachusetts and the Election of 1912." Unpublished senior thesis, Harvard College, 1952.

Lane, Roger. "Municipal Reform in Boston, 1902–1910." Unpublished honors thesis, Yale College, 1955.

McCaffrey, George Herbert. "The Political Disintegration and Reintegration of Metropolitan Boston." Unpublished Ph.D. dissertation, Harvard University, 1937.

O'Brien, Robert Lincoln. "Reminiscences of Robert Lincoln O'Brien." Columbia University Oral History Project, Butler Library.

Rosenthal, Herbert. "The Progressive Movement in New York State, 1906–1914." Unpublished Ph.D. dissertation, Harvard University, 1955.

Wood, Thomas J. "Distinctive Legislative Practices of the Massachusetts General Court." Unpublished Ph.D. dissertation, Harvard University, 1947.

INDEX

Abrahams, Henry, labor leader, 243
Adams, Brooks, 278
Adams, Charles Francis, Jr.: railroad commissioner, 5–6; on Bryanites, 48; on New Haven merger, 211; and Lodge, 264–265; on regulation, 289, 290
Adams, Henry C., on Massachusetts' corporation law, 9n
Alabama, insurgency in, 131
Aldrich, Nelson, vii, 98, 221, 222, 271n. See also Payne-Aldrich tariff
American Express Company, 212ff
American Protective Association, 120, 143, 250, 286
Ames, Butler: as "insurgent," 219, 238; and Lodge, 236, 256, 261, 263; on Payne-Aldrich, 236; supports Taft, 283
Anderson, George W.: against "foreigners," 49; Wilson appointee, 287n
Anti-Merger party, 170, 171
Anti-Stock Watering Law: of Massachusetts (1894), 8n, 16, 70, 79, 88, 212n; federal, 184
Arena, on Moran, 153
Associated Board of Trade, 66ff, 72, 148n
Australian Ballot, 4, 134

Baer, George F., 162
Ballinger, Richard A., *see* Pinchot-Ballinger affair
Bank deposit guarantees, 184
Barnes, Irston, on utilities regulation, 8n
Bartlett, Charles W.: Democratic candidate, 121, 123; Anti-Merger candidate, 169, 171, 172
Bass, Robert, N. H. insurgent, 223–224, 246
Bates, John L., 118, 151, 180, 287; sketch, 95–96; victim of class sentiment, 96, 162, 179; Republican governor, 96–97, 100–105; and labor, 104, 105; personal scandal,

102n; defeated, 107, 123, 233; and Crane, 174, 176. *See also* Elections
Baxter, Charles S., chairman of T.R. delegation, 280n, 283
Berkshire Street Railway Company, 242, 267
Beveridge, Albert, 220n, 236
Bigelow, W. Sturgis, on Gardner and Lodge, 32n
Billard, John A., New Haven Railroad dummy, 205, 209, 213
Billings, Edmund: and Fitzgerald, 147; Wilson appointee, 286–287
Bird, Charles Sumner: on New Haven merger, 210, 286; Progressive, 284ff
Blaine, James G., 31, 32, 33, 46, 58, 240
Blodgett, Geoffrey, cited, 50
Blum, John M.: treatment of Hepburn Act, 125n; quoted, 128; disputed, 202n
Bond, Sir Robert, 112–114. *See also* Reciprocity, Newfoundland
Boot and shoe industry, 20, 55, 74, 90n, 114, 185, 229, 231, 291
Borah, William E., 220n
Boston: Democratic party in, 44ff, 84–85, 86, 99, 120, 144ff, 251 (*see also* Democratic party); Republican reformers, 42ff; reform in, 134–138, 149; blue laws, 100, 102, 103, 135; referendum, 64 (*see also* Initiative and Referendum); direct primary law, 82; conservative financial mode, 17n (*see also* Massachusetts: business conservatism); export center, 20, 75–77, 126, 202, 210, 211n; Harbor, 52, 82, 86; railroad terminus, 21, 195; and reciprocity, 81, 122, 123; Back Bay, 92, 96, 177, 179, 284; "Old Boston" dies, 146, 146n; labor troubles, 81, 273; milk distribution (*see* Milk shipment controversy)